CONSIDER the SOURCE

A Critical Guide to 100 Prominent News and Information Sites on the Web

James F. Broderick
and
Darren W. Miller

CyberAge Books

Information Today, Inc.
Medford, New Jersey

First printing, 2007

Consider the Source: A Critical Guide to 100
Prominent News and Information Sites on the Web

Library of Congress Cataloging-in-Publication Data

Broderick, James F., 1963-
   Consider the source : a critical guide to 100 prominent news and information sites on the Web / James F. Broderick and Darren W. Miller
     p. cm.
   Includes bibliographical references and index.
   ISBN 978-0-910965-77-4
1. Electronic journals--Directories. 2. News Web sites--Directories. 3. Web sites--Directories.
I. Miller, Darren W., 1979- II. Title.
   PN4833.B76 2007
   070.5'7973--dc22

2007012463

President and CEO: Thomas H. Hogan, Sr.
Editor-in-Chief and Publisher: John B. Bryans
Managing Editor: Amy M. Reeve
VP Graphics and Production: M. Heide Dengler
Book Designer: Kara Mia Jalkowski
Cover Designer: Shelley Szajner
Copy Editor: Barbara Brynko
Proofreader: Phaedra Trethan
Indexer: Wendy Catalano

To find out about other CyberAge Books from Information Today, Inc. or to request a free catalog, visit books.infotoday.com.

Contents

Acknowledgments

Jim Broderick wishes to thank the following people: professor Bruce Chadwick of New Jersey City University, for his guidance and advice regarding all book-related matters, from proposal preparation to manuscript submission. His considerable body of work remains an invaluable source of inspiration; the staff of the Glen Ridge (NJ) Public Library for their tireless pursuit of arcane yet essential research materials; my parents, for their interest and support of all my professional endeavors; and my writing partner Darren Miller, whose insights, enthusiasm, and immense talent made this potentially arduous project a pleasure from start to finish (and I haven't even mentioned his gift for finding just the right wine to suit any occasion). Finally, I wish to thank my family for all their help, accommodation, and support: my wife Miri, whose editorial acumen far exceeds my own (thankfully), and whose love and counsel made this book—and so many other things—possible, and my daughters Olivia and Maddy, for their helpful suggestions and even more helpful distractions.

Darren Miller wishes to thank the following people: Malcolm Power, for his unconditional generosity, without which my pursuit of this project would have been all but impossible; the publisher and staff of *The Mountaineer* for their willingness to take a chance on an unseasoned reporter and for allowing me the space to grow as a writer and journalist; and Ben Hicks, a talented photographer and dear friend whose encouragement and advice have been irreplaceable. I am forever indebted to my mother, who, aside from doing all the things that great mothers do, opened my world to the immense power of books, and to my father, who taught me about life, determination, and courage in way no book could. I will always be grateful to Jim Broderick, a great writer and better friend, for his unwavering confidence in my abilities, for inspiring me to write as well as I can, and for making this challenging project enjoyable. And, most importantly, I wish to thank my wife Heather, for her constant support and immeasurable patience throughout this adventure. Her role as sounding board and editor makes me a better writer; as best friend and loving wife, she makes me a better man.

Both of us wish to thank our editor John Bryans for his unswerving support and invaluable advice. Managing editor Amy Reeve saved us countless hours and lots of worry with her resourcefulness and guidance. And William Zinnser for his wisdom, warmth, and commitment to raising the standards for writers—and the people who rely on them.

About the Web Site
www.TheReportersWell.com

The authors have created a Web site to update and critique any changes in the news and information sites discussed in this book. In addition, readers of this book are encouraged to share their comments, criticisms, or questions about *Consider the Source* through the Web site at www.TheReportersWell.com. Look for the *Consider the Source* link for more information about this book.

The Reporters' Well, in addition to offering detailed information of interest to writers and readers, provides a user-friendly portal that allows visitors to quickly connect to prominent news and information sites on the Web. Links are available to sites ranging from Agence France-Presse to Yahoo! News. These sites, which are discussed and critiqued fully in this book, are only one of many features available to those who log on to TheReportersWell.com. You'll also find a regularly updated media-watch column (click on "Taking Notes"), which addresses everything from trends in the newspaper industry to the latest journalistic controversies.

The Reporters' Well also features extensive coverage of the world of nonfiction writing, including lists of significant books and authors, as well as detailed bibliographical information about the authors of this book. Comments, criticism, and general thoughts from readers of this book are certainly welcome. Please e-mail us at news@thereporters well.com.

Disclaimer
Neither the publisher nor the authors make any claim as to the results that may be obtained through the use of this Web page or of any of the Internet resources it references or links to. Neither publisher nor authors will be held liable for any results, or lack thereof, obtained by the use of this page or any of its links; for any third-party changes; or for any hardware, software, or other problems that may occur as the result of using it. This Web page is subject to change or discontinuation without notice at the discretion of the publisher and authors

Introduction

The digital revolution has changed the world in innumerable ways, but one idea has remained constant from the time of Gutenberg to *our* time: Knowledge is power.

In the information age, that knowledge comes, frequently, from the Internet. The better that source of knowledge—its credibility, its clarity, its utility—the greater the power. With almost incalculable speed, new Web sites, new sources of knowledge, are becoming available to anyone with access to a computer. But is all this information a good thing? Can there be too many places on the Web to seek information?

Even if you had unlimited time to spend on the Web (when, in fact, the opposite is increasingly true for most people), it would be difficult to assess which Web sites offer the "best" information. More and more, Web sites are tailoring their content to meet some demographic, political, or social agenda. Which sites are ideologically driven? Conversely, which sites pride themselves on their "neutrality"? What kind of "news" does each cover well: domestic, world, entertainment, sports, even weather? Where are the best places to go when you need to find breaking news or insightful commentary? And what else will you find when you get there?

Let us help you out. *Consider the Source* takes you to 100 prominent news and information Web sites on the Internet and offers a candid, comprehensive analysis of the good, the bad, and the unusual. We help you get to those places that give you what you need most—whatever your information needs. What's the difference between traditional printed newspapers and their Web sites? How about magazines online: Do they differ at all from their newsstand counterparts? Can political Web sites be objective in discussing the news of the day? Should they be? Must "hard news" be dull? Can pop culture be treated in a serious way? Are most of the high-profile news sites on the Web filled with great writing—or is the prose banal and eye glazing?

We've got the answers—and a slough of opinions and suggestions about many sites you've probably never thought about visiting. *Consider the Source* gives you a glimpse behind the screens of the most important news and information Web sites—from those connected to global news services to those connected only to the modems of independent journalists and idiosyncratic culture watchers. We offer a clear and detailed discussion of each site's strengths and weaknesses, what it lacks, and where it links. And for those who want a quick and easy way of telling the best from the worst, we offer an overall rating system (from one to five newspapers) that provides what you need at a glance.

A word about our criteria for evaluating each Web site: As unique as each news and information site might seem, we believe some qualities are—or ought to be—indispensable to information providers on the Web. These qualities include balance, thoroughness, compelling writing, and a sensible use of available technology. These time-honored components of well-wrought journalism haven't changed since the age of movable type.

These qualities were the basis for our rating system, which readers can find at the end of each review. These are offered in both words and newspaper icons (which we chose to represent both our backgrounds in the newspaper industry and journalism's continuing debt to the printing press regardless of new mediums). With that in mind, our rating system—which we hope and expect will generate debate and discussion among active Internet users—can be broken down in the following way:

Five newspapers – Superior sites worth checking in with every day

Four newspapers – Very good information, so log on regularly

Three newspapers – Keep these on your radar

Two newspapers – Some value but not a great return on your time

One newspaper – Disappointing, definitely look elsewhere

Though these evaluations are intended to help readers gain quick insight into each site, they are far from the whole story. Each review includes an "Overview," focusing on a site's origins and development; "What You'll Find There," which assesses a site's main features; "Why You Should Visit," offering reasons to (or not to) check in with the site; "Keep This In Mind," which highlights lesser-known aspects of the site's history or ideological leanings; and "Off the Record," featuring factoids off the beaten path of the information superhighway.

Obviously, with thousands of news and information sites to choose from and more coming online every day, it would be impossible to critique them all. So we decided to focus on those sites that had achieved a certain prominence or reputation. Motivated by the belief that information on the World Wide Web belongs to the worldwide community of Web users, we decided to limit our reviews to sites with content that remains largely free. As news agencies continue to grapple with new business models to provide information on the Web, this might not always be the case. For now, however, most news and information is readily available to any computer user without charge. And that's why we focused on those sites.

Knowledge *is* power—so arm yourself with the knowledge of where to get the best of every type of news on the Web. You'll save countless hours and discover a new source of power to plug into: the power of the information age.

1

Agence France-Presse (AFP)
www.afp.com

Overview

Even if you're only a sporadic consumer of news, chances are you have spotted the acronym AFP before, probably in the dateline at the beginning of an article or in a credit beneath a photo. AFP (Agence France-Presse), which is most noticeably seen in newspapers but also now online, is indeed a pervasive purveyor of news—and has been for a very long time.

Founded in 1835 by Charles-Louis Havas, referred to as "the father of global journalism" on the organization's Web site, AFP is considered to be the oldest news agency in the world, although it did not operate under its current name until 1944.

Despite its strong stature as the third-largest news agency in the world (behind the Associated Press and Reuters), AFP's Web site is weak, functioning more as a product catalog for existing and potential clients than as a service for the masses.

What You'll Find There

AFP, which is headquartered in Paris but operates four other regional centers and bureaus in more than 100 countries, generates about 500,000 words and 1,000 photos daily; very little of that production can be read or viewed at AFP.com.

The blue banner that spans the top of its home page (and all other pages of the site) displays a continuous vertical scroll of items from AFP's news ticker, each with a subject line (for example, "Mideast-unrest-Palestinian-Nablus"), a dateline, and a one-sentence blurb. Don't be fooled into thinking you can click on one to access a full story—you can't. Instead, click on the link to the site's "Photo Gallery"

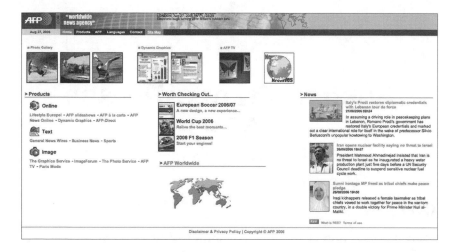

in the top left corner of the home page, just below the banner. You will be directed to a slideshow that features a dozen of the agency's latest still images, which are often astounding examples of AFP's renowned photography department. While on this page, you can use the menu in the left column to access AFP.com's "Stories" page to read a selection from a list of its top 10 articles—the nuts-and-bolts sort—by clicking on one of the blue headlines that are each accompanied by a photo and lead paragraph. (Note to American users: Don't make a mistake reading the European date stamps beneath the headlines—05/07/2007 is July 5, 2007, not May 7, 2007.)

That is about all you'll find here, unless of course you're interested in buying a wire, photo, or online service from AFP—products that dominate the content on the home page and much of the site. You do have the ability to change the language of the site (to Arabic, French, German, Portuguese, Russian, and Spanish); the content changes depending on the language—slideshows and news stories usually vary (sometimes only slightly) based on the language choice.

Why You Should Visit

AFP is, as it promotes at the top of each page on the site, a "worldwide news agency." Much of what you read in newspapers and on Internet news sites is likely to have originated from an AFP journalist. By visiting the agency's Web site, you may not get an abundance of news, but you will gain an understanding of this major producer and distributor of news. And surfing this site lasts as long as riding the smallest of waves—so no real valuable time, which could be spent immersed in a site with deeper coverage, is wiped out.

Keep This in Mind

It's not that AFP is averse to Web content or lacks the ability to create it; it just doesn't want to give it away for free. For example, the Online News Association bestowed the agency with an Online Journalism Award for its Tour de France coverage in a category that "honors achievement in the combined use of audio and/or visual techniques, design, navigation, multimedia, interactivity." The AFP-produced content was available through the Web sites of the *New York Times* and *USA Today*, which paid for the service, but not to visitors of AFP.com. So if you want news from AFP on the Web, use a site that subscribes to products of the news agency, especially Yahoo! News. Don't expect AFP content to grace the pages of Google News. In March 2005, AFP sued Google for copyright infringement, seeking $17.5 million in damages for including AFP stories and photos on the

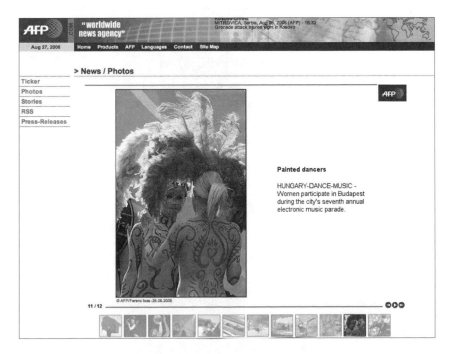

Google News site without permission. Google responded by removing AFP from its news site.

Off the Record

AFP has had its share of significant scoops, boosting its reputation as a force to reckon with in the global media arena. In March 1953, the news agency broke the news of Joseph Stalin's death and gained international fame.[1] Nineteen years later, AFP reported the deaths of the Israeli hostages at the Munich Olympic Games an hour before any other news outlets, prompting the *Washington Post* and the *Los Angeles Times* to subscribe to its service the following month.[2]

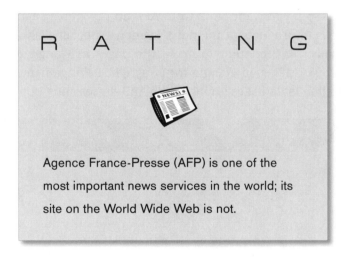

R A T I N G

Agence France-Presse (AFP) is one of the most important news services in the world; its site on the World Wide Web is not.

Endnotes

1. From "Some Key Dates" on AFP's history page (www.afp.com/english/afp/?pid=history)
2. Ibid.

2

Al Jazeera

www.aljazeera.net

Overview

On the crowded battlefront of online news sites, Al Jazeera is a mine-field. The site seems to make as much news as it reports. It has been condemned by the U.S. government as an instrument of Arab propaganda. Its reporters have been thrown off the floor of the New York Stock Exchange. Its offices in Kabul were damaged in a U.S. air strike. And it has been the subject of countless op-ed articles arguing its worth (inestimable or invidious, depending on the writer). In a time of perpetual Mideast tension, the Al Jazeera site—the cyber companion for the better-known television network of the same name—has become a must-read.

What You'll Find There

Sign on to the site and you'll quickly discover the source of much of the controversy surrounding Al Jazeera's reputation in the Western World: a plethora of uncensored Arab voices. No other prominent news sites carry as many Arab-centered perspectives on the world's events. (Al Jazeera incurred the wrath of U.S. officials when it aired an unedited tape from Al Qaeda leader Osama bin Laden.)

The site is not unlike its Western counterparts in organization and design. A lead story, tied to some breaking news in the Middle East (usually related to the war in Iraq), is featured prominently, with a picture and links to several related stories. The content appears to be mostly written by Al Jazeera correspondents, though there are occasional links to stories from outside news agencies.

The site offers almost as much opinion as news. There are generous doses of editorial opinion (even within the news stories), regular Al Jazeera columnists, and "guest" columnists, drawn from the Arab street as well as the power centers of Middle East politics.

Most of the stories have a political content. The site covers lots of political news about Israel as well as the U.S., and also features dispatches from correspondents in places such as Bahrain, Tehran, and Baghdad.

Readers will also find a handful of lighter, less-political news and feature stories, such as a profile of a British artist who crawled for two weeks on his hands and knees from London to Canterbury Cathedral to raise awareness of "the plight of people spending Christmas alone."[1]

Why You Should Visit

For those who value a different perspective on the news from the Middle East, Al Jazeera comes through—loud and clear. The stories on the Web site feature points of view that don't often filter through the sieve of more mainstream news sites. Its coverage of the Iraq War has featured graphic images of civilians wounded in attacks, first-person accounts of battles on the ground, videos of coalition POWs, and searing commentary about American aggression. Much of the site is inflammatory. Yet Al Jazeera provides a window into the Arab world that has an undeniable ring of authenticity to it. Officials with Al Jazeera say they stir up as much anger among the Arab community for their reporting of rights abuses and criminal acts in the Arab world as they do among Westerners (and they proudly trumpet the fact that they regularly showcase Israeli journalists as well as Arab journalists).

Keep This in Mind

Almost no one is neutral on Al Jazeera. Its detractors claim the organization is nothing more than a propaganda tool for extremist elements in the Middle East. (It has even been reported that U.S. President George W. Bush and British Prime Minister Tony Blair discussed the prospect of bombing the network's headquarters in Qatar.[2]) Former U.S. Secretary of State Colin Powell told National Public Radio that Al Jazeera portrays "our efforts in a negative light," but the *New York Times* defended the news agency, saying "Al Jazeera is feisty and frequently controversial, but it does real journalism, and it is the only uncensored TV network in the Arab world."[3]

Off the Record

Al Jazeera was launched after 250 journalists who were working for BBC Arabic television lost their jobs in 1996, when the newsroom was shut down over a dispute with Saudi officials about the airing of a documentary on executions in Saudi Arabia. Determined to find a way to report uncensored news to the Middle East, many of those

The executioner
Video of Saddam's hanging showed many people in the room, what didn't it show?

Iranian Santa
Iran v the IAEA, who will be the winner?

journalists helped launch the new satellite channel Al Jazeera, funded by the Emir of Qatar.[4]

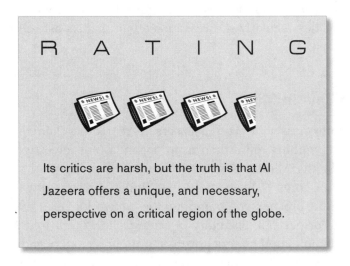

RATING

Its critics are harsh, but the truth is that Al Jazeera offers a unique, and necessary, perspective on a critical region of the globe.

Endnotes

1. From Aljazeera.net, Jan. 8, 2006.
2. From the *Washington Post*, reprinted at www.jihadwatch.org, Nov. 23, 2005.
3. Both Powell's comments and the quote from the *New York Times* were reported by www.inthesetimes.com on April 4, 2003.
4. Michael Moran, "In defense of al-Jazeera," MSNBC, Oct. 18, 2001.

3

allAfrica

www.allafrica.com

Overview

Once upon a time, Africa was referred to as "the dark continent." Though exploration, cultural exchanges, robust international reporting, and geo-political alliances have heightened its profile in recent decades, many contemporary Web users might still know little about this complex and critical region of the globe. And what they do know probably amounts to a litany of well-rehearsed themes that have come to dominate mainstream reporting about Africa: famine, civil war, brutal dictatorships, and crushing poverty.

No one disputes the region's long and troubled history, but reducing the continent to its most significant and public setbacks does a disservice to Africa's vibrant and significant contributions. What's needed is a forceful voice for the good, the bad, the ugly, and the wondrous that emerges from "the dark continent." Such a voice would, ideally, be comprised of many perspectives spoken with many accents. In other words, what's needed is allAfrica.com.

This news service boasts one of the most engaged and committed group of working journalists on the Web today, and the beneficiaries include everyone from armchair tourists to die-hard policy wonks with an interest in Africa's affairs. It's a journalistic diamond mine with riches that are available to anybody with a browser and a little curiosity.

What You'll Find There

The main news page of allAfrica.com boasts the usual icon of "Top Headlines" that most sites do, with the caveat that these stories all deal in some way with Africa.

Just underneath this list of headlines is another selection of stories, each accompanied by a photo or graphic, dealing in greater depth

9

with an African issue in the news. The advantage here is depth: For every topic covered in this section, there might be as many as a dozen related stories and additional material about that topic, from U.N. resolutions to speeches by world leaders and from analysis by policy experts to congressional testimony. Because the site not only features reporting by its independent staff but also from major news services around the world (Reuters, the BBC, et al.), the amount and quality of news is daunting. For instance, a recent special report on democratic elections in the Congo included "backgrounders" on the history of the region, the U.N. resolution establishing a special police force to oversee the elections, BBC reports of sporadic violence at polling sites, and a survey of regional leaders about the impact the elections could have.

The site also offers an archive that—by its accounting—contains more than 900,000 articles that are fully searchable, while adding another 1,000 articles a day in both English and French. Many stories can also be found through the main page's pull-down menu where readers can browse by region, country, or topic.

Though most of the news has a serious and sober edge to it, the site contains lots of "lighter" pieces, from book reviews and arts reporting to extensive soccer coverage and travelogues. A menu of topics on the second page offers an extensive choice of African cultural reporting, from HIV/AIDS-related news and features to reviews of the latest popular African musical groups.

There are also graphics and links to take you to the Web pages of Sustainable Africa, an eco-think tank aimed at preserving the resources of the continent, Peace Africa, which is an organization dedicated to African conflict resolution, and even BizTech, a service that covers business and finance related to the African continent.

Why You Should Visit

Much of what you'll find on the site will likely strike you as new. And even if you have an understanding of African history and cultural geography, you'll discover a wealth of background material that will

TOP HEADLINES	
Niger: Government And UN Food Agency Team Up to Deliver Food to Most Vulnerable	UN News
Congo-Kinshasa: Everyone Must Respect the Democratic Process - Commission President [interview]	MONUC
Sudan: Government Asks Security Council to Be Patient On Darfur	IRIN
Burundi: Former President's Arrest Seen As Part of Pattern of Abuse	IRIN
Congo-Kinshasa: Legislative Election Results Expected Any Time, Says UN Mission	UN News
Zambia: Debt Reduction Doesn't Guarantee Debt Sustainability - World Bank	Post (Lusaka)
South Africa: Government and LEC to Assist in Second Round of DRC Elections	BuaNews
South Africa: President Proposes Deeper Interaction with Traditional Leaders	BuaNews
East Africa: COMESA Wants Tanzania Out of SADC	Mmegi
Botswana: BCP to Pull Out of Talks After November	Mmegi
Angola: Country's Exports to Reach $28 Billion This Year	ANGOP
Namibia: Bankrupt BEE Outfits Face Grilling	New Era
Namibia: New Housing Scheme for War Veterans	New Era
Africa: Renewed Efforts Could Eliminate Waterborne Diseases	SciDev.Net

help illuminate "the dark continent." Given the region's recent history of violence and social turmoil, allAfrica.com is a real gift to the curious and the under-informed. It moves beyond the grim and graphic headlines to reveal the context of this news-making region of the world.

Keep This in Mind

Because of the complexity and history of many of the stories on allAfrica.com—even the breaking news—this site is not exactly "light reading." Readers who are not familiar with the patchwork quilt of African politics might find themselves somewhat challenged by the vast amount of history that seems to inform most of the reporting. However, there is such an abundance of material available on the site to readers wholly ignorant of the region's politics that one needn't be offput by unfamiliar references.

Off the Record

allAfrica.com is the successor to the Africa News Service, a nonprofit agency that, prior to 1999, supplied prize-winning reporting to major international media outlets such as the BBC, NPR, and the *Washington Post.*

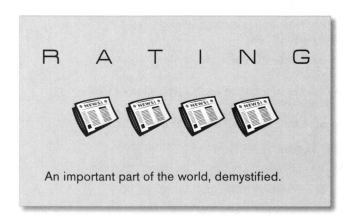

R A T I N G

An important part of the world, demystified.

4

AlterNet
www.alternet.org

Overview

When the Internet became a fully functional means of reaching people around the world directly, there must have been a number of political progressives who finally thought their day had come. So much of the progressive movement's failure to mobilize the public on a large scale has often been attributed to fragmentation. A grassroots movement, after all, can only reach other people on the same patch of lawn.

But with the Internet, politically active progressives gained the power to reach millions of people around the world; no more standing on street corners waving "Stop the War" placards, no more silent peace vigils in the local town square.

Whether the world has changed substantially now that the Internet has brought the warnings of global warming, pleas for economic and racial justice, and exposés of corporate greed to desktops across the fruited plains remains an open question. But if it turns out to be no different than the pre-Internet world, you won't be able to blame AlterNet, a site that aims to be a forum "in which key progressive ideas and strategies are echoed."

What You'll Find There

AlterNet offers a curious but engaging mix of well-known media figures (Arianna Huffington and Jim Hightower, for example), an in-house staff of reporters, columnists, and bloggers, and also total unknowns writing from the hinterland, those progressives who've just left the peace rally and are posting stories and editorials from their local Starbucks. It's a rare example of true vertical integration in the media age (as opposed to giant media conglomerates comprised of already established units).

The home page offers news and analysis with a clear left spin: Articles question various policies of the current administration and reiterate socially sacrosanct chestnuts, like our need to develop alternative energy policies or the injustice of the current minimum wage. The stories are largely written by AlterNet staff members, and most articles are clear and compelling—though with a pronounced prejudice in favor of the political left.

There's a box for "Breaking News," which is pulled from various wire services, and a list of columnists, essayists, and bloggers (with accompanying thumbnail photos) who are weighing in on the news of the day. The site also features downloadable videos from independent journalists and filmmakers and lots of message boards for their typically passionate readers.

A highlighted section on the home page called "Special Coverage" includes extended "think pieces" on everything from the constitutionality of the Homeland Security Act to critiques of the national media.

Overall, the site is a comprehensive guide to the things that are really bugging people on the left—complete (usually) with a prescription for how to set things straight. As the editors note in their

"About Us" link, "Despite the radical right's media power, progressives now have an opportunity to compete." So the battle has been joined.

Why You Should Visit

Despite the ascendancy of what many people see as a conservative ruling authority in this country, the progressive wing of the American electorate continues to play a role in shaping policy, though some say it's a greatly diminished role.

AlterNet is balm for the progressive's soul. In its passionate and well-reasoned articles and essays, it provides the intellectual heft necessary to undergird a serious political movement. Anyone who's not acquainted with the list of grievances from the political left will quickly be brought up to speed after strolling through AlterNet. And those who oppose its political posture will find a thoughtful corps of thinkers eager to engage with readers on all sides of the political spectrum.

Keep This in Mind

AlterNet is so determinedly progressive that it commits one of the most common sins of its political opponents: It often opts for only one side. If the Web site were truly dedicated to "Alternate" points of view (as the pun

Columnists The latest

Molly Ivins:
The New 'Activist' Judges

Somehow, activist judges are held responsible for gay marriage, Roe v. Wade and everything else Americans disagree about.

Norman Solomon:
The Mythical End to the Politics of Fear

Mainstream news reporting accepts and propagates the basic world view of the Bush administration.

Matt Taibbi:
Firing Squad Looms for the Dem Party Oligarchy

Establishment Dems treat their political party like a house in the fucking Hamptons. Who died and made these people gatekeepers to anything?

Arianna Huffington:
When Hillary Meets Ned

Hillary needs to leave her upcoming meeting with Ned Lamont and hit the campaign trail on his behalf -- hard, and often.

Will Durst:
Dubya's Latest Press Debacle

In an hour-long press conference, the president introduced the new official buzz phrase of the Iraqi

of its name implies), then it should welcome genuinely diverse views, from the critics of the current system who write and attack from the far right, to libertarians, to disaffected Democrats and independents, even to "neo-cons"—all of whom have something to say about the major issues under consideration at AlterNet. The site does give alternatives to the mainstream media's often-monolithic worldview, but it does so in an unsurprising way. Longtime lefties will learn little on this site, though it's certain they'll agree with most of what they read.

With that in mind, AlterNet does offer one of the widest swaths of smartly packaged progressive opinion anywhere on the Web, with a clean and clear site that is easily navigable.

Off the Record

Bad news has been good news for AlterNet, which saw its traffic spike about 40 percent during the 9/11 tragedy, the first days of the invasion of Iraq, and the unfolding misery of Hurricane Katrina.

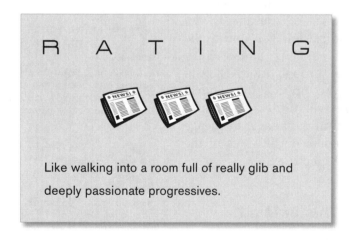

RATING

Like walking into a room full of really glib and deeply passionate progressives.

5

American Association of Retired Persons (AARP)

www.aarp.org

Overview

Though often derided by late-night television comics as a group of cranky, eccentric, and money-hording bad drivers who clog the freeways of Florida in slow pursuit of the early bird special, America's retirees are getting the last laugh. Over the past decade, their member organization, the American Association of Retired Persons (AARP), has evolved into one of the most potent political forces in Washington—and throughout the country. Founded as an organization to promote "productive aging" for retired teachers, the group has become the voice for issues affecting the senior population (though membership is available to anyone age 50 and older).

And while those wise-cracking comics still joke about seniors' befuddlement with new technology—especially the Internet—the AARP has countered those barbs by setting up a Web site that is easy to use, wildly comprehensive, well written, and engaging, even for those who have no plans to retire.

Given that the group's membership is expected to balloon from an already impressive 35 million members to an almost incomprehensible 70 million as baby boomers cash in their pensions for RVs, the AARP is well positioned to remain a potent and necessary advocate for our country's sunsetters. The group's Web site seems to be expanding as rapidly as the roster of members. This is partly to stay ahead of the many issues that are cresting on the political shore (prescription drug benefits, corporate raiding of retirement funds, etc.), but it is also because of the site's popularity and increasingly important place in the information stream.

What You'll Find There

The AARP Web site is really many sites rolled into one. First, there's the home page, which includes some highlighted feature stories on aging-related matters (such as ways to increase your brain power, where to find the best medical specialists in the country, or places to go for the perfect retired couple's vacation). Across the top of the page is a menu of icons such as "Issues and Elections," "Learning and Technology," "Health," "Money and Work," and even "Fun and Games."

Clicking on any of these icons will take you to Web pages that would shame most other organizations in their scope and accessibility. Each page offers multiple links to articles, columns, message boards, and member blogs, as well as travel agencies, car rental firms, social service agencies, nonprofit organizations, governmental offices, and hotlines of every imaginable bent (from tax preparation to gardening). Each page offers an archive of articles, essays, and editorials from any one of a handful of AARP-produced publications, such as *AARP Magazine* (formerly *Modern Maturity*), the *AARP Bulletin*, which is like a daily newspaper that focuses on retiree-related stories making news, and *Segunda Juventud*, the group's bilingual publication. And once inside these publications on the AARP site, there's a handy search engine for retrieving stories by publication date, year, or subject.

It's impossible to chronicle the extent of the information available to AARP members in this single review. It's a good thing senior citizens have a lot of time on their hands: They're going to need it if they want to read everything of interest to them on the AARP site.

Why You Should Visit

For at least 35 million people, why they should visit is obvious: to keep tabs on a group they belong to. For others who may be nearing retirement, it's a chance to discover a wealth of information that soon may be more than just a passing interest. And for younger readers who equate AARP with picking out cemetery plots and wearing your pants hitched up to your sternum, you're in for a surprise: Many of the AARP's members help shape your culture, from political figures to record company executives, movie stars, and college presidents. And for those with a naturally curious mind, the AARP's site contains hundreds of articles that are of use and interest to everybody, from profiles

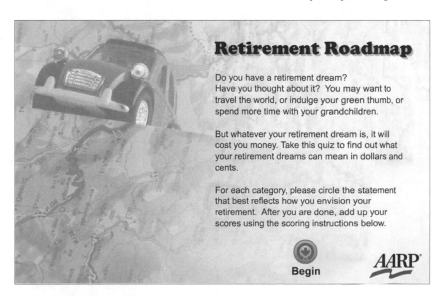

Retirement Roadmap

Do you have a retirement dream? Have you thought about it? You may want to travel the world, or indulge your green thumb, or spend more time with your grandchildren.

But whatever your retirement dream is, it will cost you money. Take this quiz to find out what your retirement dreams can mean in dollars and cents.

For each category, please circle the statement that best reflects how you envision your retirement. After you are done, add up your scores using the scoring instructions below.

Begin

AARP

of celebrities to tips about how to minimize your tax bite every April 15. (And to its great credit, the Web site contains lots of articles and interviews that are quite lengthy by Web standards: several pages worth of text rather than the 400-word, one-page fly-by typical of many popular Web-based magazines.)

Keep This in Mind

Breaking news is spotty on the AARP Web site. Some issues are covered well—and in real time. Most daily news, however, is absent. For general interest news, you'll need to bookmark another site. And not much attempt is made to entice the pre-retiree set. For those who aren't intellectually curious enough to read outside their usual sphere of publications, the AARP is likely to remain as distant and unappealing as the idea of hip surgery or a bottle of Maalox.

Off the Record

The AARP is all over every political issue that affects seniors—but as an ardent informer, not a partisan. The group does not endorse candidates or donate to any political organization.

RATING

As people continue to live longer, we'll all be looking for something good to read. Here's a Web site that informs as well as entertains.

6

American Broadcasting Company (ABC) News

abcnews.go.com

Overview

In August 2005, Peter Jennings, the longtime anchor of *World News Tonight* and the iconic face of ABC News, died of lung cancer at the age of 67. Like its two competing networks, the American Broadcasting Company (ABC) had arrived at a once unimaginable moment: It needed to replace its star power, its piece of the Big 3 anchor pie. After negotiations with Charles Gibson—co-anchor of the network's morning show *Good Morning America* who had occasionally filled in for Jennings—failed, ABC News executives named Elizabeth Vargas and Bob Woodruff (43 and 44 years old, respectively, at the time of the late 2005 announcement) as co-anchors of its flagship 30-minute evening news broadcast. In doing so, ABC seemed to make the choice with the hope of giving "the news division a decidedly younger image as it tries to expand its reach on the Web."[1] (The next month Woodruff sustained serious injuries in Iraq, and Vargas left in 2006 on maternity leave, forcing Gibson into the anchor chair.) Like their counterparts at other network news divisions, the braintrust at ABC News seems to have given a great deal of thought to how best to capture an increasingly fragmented news viewership. Their conclusion: their Web site.

What You'll Find There

The ABC News Web site does what none of its time-restricted television programs can do: It provides comprehensive coverage of the world around the clock with a depth unattainable in a two-minute broadcast segment.

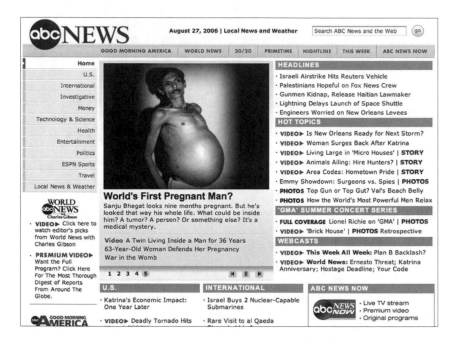

The home page is designed so that the latest and arguably the most important news of the day maintains a prominent position. In the center of the page—below the ABC News banner and horizontal menu, which includes links to the home pages of the station's familiar news programs (*Good Morning America*, *World News Tonight*, *20/20*, *Primetime*, *Nightline*, and *This Week*)—the top five stories of the moment are presented in a slideshow (a headline, photo, teaser, and usually a couple of links to other related items such as a sidebar, photo essay, or video). To the right of the scrolling display of top stories is a list of a dozen other "Top Headlines" and "Hot Topics."

A vertical navigation menu is in the far-left column near the top of the home page, guiding users to various portions of the ABC News site, including its national, international, money, technology and science, sports, health, entertainment, politics, and travel sections. The front pages of these sections (and of each ABC News program) use the same format as the home page—a consistent design that lets users quickly get acquainted with the entire site and the location of its features.

While viewers of nightly news might not expect an opportunity to help shape the network's coverage, users of ABCNews.com will find a variety of blogs—like "Inside Out" and "The World Newser"—aimed at critiquing the news, revealing how coverage is decided, and soliciting ideas, comments, and criticism from viewers. Once relegated to the obscure and undiscovered corners of the Internet, blogs—as evidenced by the "Blogs and Opinion" section at ABCNews.com—have become mainstream.

Why You Should Visit

While depending on one source for all of your information can be fraught with problems, the ABC News site can essentially serve as a one-stop shop for news consumers.

The news the site provides actually originates from various sources. Along with original ABC News reports, the site's content also consists of a healthy mix of material from credible and trustworthy news organizations, including the Associated Press and Reuters. In its "International" section, ABC News provides stories reported by the *Christian Science Monitor*, arguably one of the most reputable sources for coverage of global events, issues, and perspectives. Even the site's sports section relies almost exclusively on another source— its sister station ESPN.

Also adding to the site's allure are the many methods the site employs to deliver the news. As one might expect from a broadcast

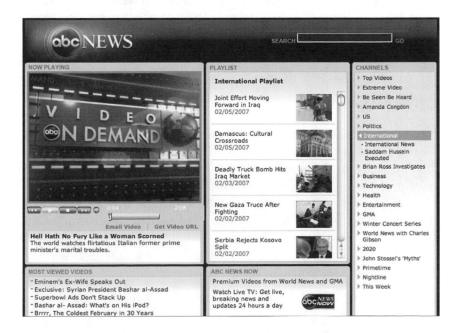

media-related Web site, video is a ubiquitous feature, which is evident by a quick glance at any of its pages (the video links are labeled as such with a red font). Most of the clips are free, provided you are willing to watch a 30-second commercial. Accompanying the video and audio features typical of broadcast news, the ABC News site delivers in-depth, thoughtful, and well-written articles usually reserved for quality print journalism. The successful blending of the two forms is quite enticing: one site with the best of both worlds.

Keep This in Mind

Disney-owned ABC News has clearly demonstrated a commitment to the Internet and embraced its potential as a means for the organization to maintain legitimate viability in a future when the citizenry will rely less and less on evening news broadcasts of the major networks for their information.

ABC News, however, still seems to be playing catch-up in the world of 24-hour broadcast outlets despite launching its own around-the-clock cable channel in July 2004. Viewers can access the site, called ABC News Now, in several ways: through select digital cable providers, through ABC News by paying a yearly $40 subscription to receive the service via computer (it is free to subscribers of a handful of Internet providers), or through most major mobile phone service providers. Because watching ABC News Now is not as simple as punching the buttons on your television remote, it is still no match for the likes of CNN.

Off the Record

In early fall 2002, a deal between AOL Time Warner and the Walt Disney Company to merge CNN with ABC News seemed likely. But after several months of talks, the idea of such a merger, which would have produced a company owned mostly (70 percent) by CNN, was officially abandoned in February 2003 because AOL Time Warner "had too much else to worry about ... to pursue the complicated negotiations."[2]

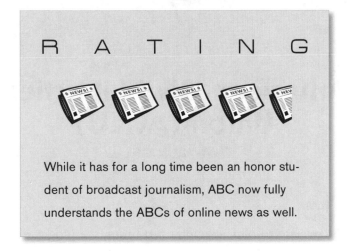

R A T I N G

While it has for a long time been an honor student of broadcast journalism, ABC now fully understands the ABCs of online news as well.

Endnotes

1. Bill Carter and Jacques Steinberg, "At impasse with network star, ABC picks 2 youthful anchors," *New York Times*, Dec. 6, 2005.

2. Jim Rutenberg, "Talks collapse on plan to merge CNN with ABC News," *New York Times*, Feb. 14, 2003.

7

American Civil Liberties Union (ACLU)

www.aclu.org

Overview

In our increasingly politically polarized times, seemingly few people feel neutral about the ACLU. Those who endorse its aims proudly flout their membership cards. These are the same people who are derided by the group's opponents as "card-carrying liberals." Because the ACLU has injected itself into today's most rancorous and divisive social issues, the group's reputation as an institutional instigator is probably well deserved.

The ACLU's scope of concern is widespread indeed, from criminals' rights and racial justice to free speech and reproductive rights. Its Web site is equally comprehensive, serving almost as much as a mini-encyclopedia for civil libertarians as a general interest Web site. Think of the site as the world's most extensive newsletter, covering anything and everything a reader might ever want to know about the organization and its causes.

But there's also quite a lot of news on the site—though not in its usual guise of objective, thoroughly reported stories. Because the ACLU is an advocacy group, the articles posted on the site reflect viewpoints that sympathize with the group's stated objectives: "To defend the rights of all citizens as enshrined in the Bill of Rights of the United States Constitution."

What You'll Find There

The top third of the home page of the ACLU site greets visitors with a boxed photo and story about a prominent civil rights issue in the news (that space recently has been filled with stories related to the war on terror, such as Guantanamo detainees and the Homeland

Security Act). If there's breaking news, such as a Supreme Court decision or act of Congress, it will be featured under the box in a bold blue (think Blue State) headline. These stories are really more like legal briefs than standard journalistic articles, with a plethora of quotes from ACLU lawyers and sympathizers.

The rest of the page is divided between a menu of "News" and "Features," which fills out the bottom of the page. Clicking on any of these headlines takes you to stories written by ACLU staff writers. All of the stories deal with civil liberty issues, with headlines such as "Librarians Gagged by Patriot Act Speak Out for First Time" and "ACLU Seeks Records on Use of Brain Scanners in Interrogation." If it's not about civil liberties—even if it's making headlines on every other news site—it's not likely to be on ACLU.org. (Nor does the site cover sports, entertainment, health, personal finance, or any of the other topics that fill most news sites.)

But the real wealth of the site can be found to the right of the page in a very unassuming menu of "Issues," beginning with "Criminal Rights," then running through more than a dozen issues, ending with "Women's Rights." Clicking on these links takes you to Web pages that are stuffed with an immense amount of information, from articles that have run on the ACLU Web site about that topic to analyses, special reports, columns, petition drives, and links to other advocacy organizations and Congressional offices, as well as ACLU hotlines and other pro-bono legal services.

And, of course, sprinkled throughout each page are ads to "Become a Card-Carrying Member of the ACLU," as well as video features with titles such as "The Spies Have It" and promos for upcoming regional ACLU conferences.

Why You Should Visit

Want to start an argument? Bring up civil liberties at your next social gathering and see what happens. Everybody has an opinion about the "big" issues that make up the battlefront for civil liberties, from affirmative action to racial profiling and unreasonable search and seizures. Checking in with ACLU.org will help you understand an issue—from one side, that is. Reading the ACLU's take on events could make you angry. If you're a card-carrying member—or wish to

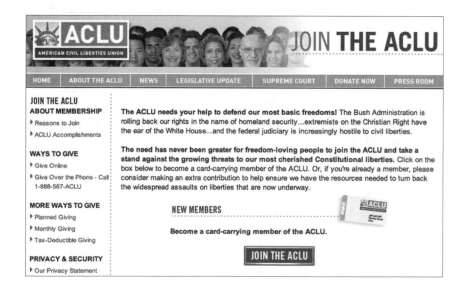

be—you'll be incensed at the way the courts and current administration appear to be trampling on our rights. If you're of the opposite political persuasion, you're likely to be incensed at the lack of balance and context on the site and the cut-and-dried presentation of complex legal issues in favor of the civil libertarian viewpoint.

Keep This in Mind

It's best to remember two things: 1) The ACLU has become, for many Americans, the last bastion of reason in a country dominated by an unchecked authoritarian law and order ethic; and 2) the ACLU has become, for many Americans, the most despised and dangerous organization in a country run amok with lawyers and victims who secretly hate the U.S. and want to bring it down.

Off the Record

The ACLU picked up all the legal bills for John T. Scopes, who in 1925 challenged the state of Tennessee's anti-evolution law in the famous "Scopes Monkey Trial" case. His lawyer was ACLU National Committee member Clarence Darrow.[1]

R A T I N G

The ACLU practices what it preaches—but preaching ain't journalism.

Endnotes

1. From "John Scopes," by Doug Linder, available at www.law.umkc.edu/faculty/
projects/ftrials/scopes

8

Amnesty International
www.amnesty.org

Overview

What does Amnesty International have in common with Mother Teresa, Martin Luther King, the International Committee of the Red Cross, Elie Wiesel, Desmond Tutu, Theodore Roosevelt, the International Atomic Energy Agency, and Mikhail Gorbachev? They all share a worthy title: winners of the Nobel Peace Prize.[1] Amnesty earned the title in 1977, only 15 years after the organization was founded by a British lawyer who "became angry after reading a report about two Portuguese students who had been imprisoned for raising their glasses in a toast to freedom."[2]

With that as its *raison d'être*, Amnesty, as the name would suggest, focused its efforts—campaigns that consisted of writing letters, publishing newsletters, applying pressure on governments—solely on helping free political prisoners. As the organization grew, Amnesty expanded its mission to include all human rights issues and abuses throughout the world.

Alarming. Disheartening. Illuminating. Challenging. All are apt descriptors of the content at Amnesty.org. While the activist organization could easily sensationalize the material it posts there, Amnesty often does the opposite. It seems to realize there's really no need to play that card: Plainly stated headlines and well-researched facts are emotive enough. Amnesty.org certainly intends to inform, as evidenced by the vast amount of press releases, articles, and reports it posts, most of which the mainstream media ignores and is "news" to visitors of the Web site as a result. The mission, however, is far from accomplished. After arming them with knowledge, Amnesty wants action.

What You'll Find There

The home page, which looks similar to a traditional news site, is divided into three columns. The middle and widest column features

about four stories—a headline/link, a blurb, usually a photograph, and sometimes a link to a related video—that, because of their placement and presentation, draw the most attention. A list of "Latest News" and "Latest Reports" fills the page's left column. In the top of the right column, Amnesty urges users to join the organization or make a donation. Beneath it, users can access the pages dedicated to specific issues of concern to Amnesty—torture, death penalty, arms control, violence against women—by clicking on the colorful graphics in the "Our Campaigns" box.

At the top of the page, visitors to the site can access various sections through the navigational menu. The "News" page consists of Amnesty press releases, which read more like commentary, or sermons, than traditional news. The headlines all begin with the area of the world being covered, for example, "Israel/occupied territories: Deliberate attacks a war crime"; "Japan: Prisoners executed without warning after decades on death row"; and "Montenegro: Amnesty International urges newest UN member state to improve human rights." Users can also search through Amnesty's "news" by clicking on the "Regional Breakdown" link in the left column, where information is presented in five categories: Africa, Americas, Asia and the Pacific, Europe and Central Asia, and Middle East and North Africa. Searching "Video and Audio"—a surprisingly extensive section that includes interviews and on-the-ground footage of areas in turmoil— is done through an interactive map of the world.

Two other areas of the site are worth checking out: "Good News" is a section where users can read about the successful results achieved by Amnesty's efforts, and the "Make Some Noise" section features a collection of exclusive John Lennon songs performed by a bevy of pop musicians and lets users view videos or buy downloadable tracks to help support the organization.

Amnesty International is a global organization, both in its coverage and in its setup. Amnesty is made up of more than 1.8 million members in more than 150 countries. Many of its international offices also maintain Web sites, many of which are accessible by scrolling through the drop-down menu on the "Contact Us" page of Amnesty.org.

Why You Should Visit

In 2005, the three major networks dedicated a total of 18 minutes of their evening broadcasts to covering the catastrophic crisis in Darfur, while allotting nearly five times as much coverage to the Michael Jackson child molestation trial.[3] You can be sure the priorities of Amnesty International, reflected in the information presented on its Web site, are exactly the opposite. If your celebrity scandal IQ is greater than your knowledge of human rights atrocities that regularly occur throughout the world, Amnesty.org will take you to school—and try to convince you to put those lessons into action.

Keep This in Mind

Amnesty International asserts that it is "independent of any government, political ideology, economic interest or religion." And its record—whether urging the United Nations in 1988 to put an end to the mass murder of Kurdish civilians by Saddam Hussein's Iraqi forces or condemning the Bush administration's use of torture in its war on terror in the post-9/11 world—supports this claim. But some governments—frequently those that have been reprimanded by Amnesty International, ranging from the Taliban and China to the U.S.—have attacked it for "alleged bias, one-side reporting, or failure to take security threats as a mitigating factor."[4]

Off the Record

In June 2006, Nicolas Cage donated $2 million to Amnesty International to help former child soldiers. Less than a year before making the considerable contribution, the actor played the role of a global gunrunner in *Lord of War*, a film about the worldwide arms market for which Cage and the filmmakers consulted Amnesty in an effort to increase the movie-going public's familiarity with its Control Arms Campaign.

Amnesty.org holds its audience captive.

Endnotes

1. See the list of all Nobel Peace Prize winners at nobelprize.org/nobel_prizes/peace/laureates/index.html.
2. From Amnesty International Canada's history overview at www.amnesty.ca/about/history.
3. Nicholas D. Kristof, "Helping Bill O'Reilly," *New York Times*, Feb. 7, 2006.
4. From the Wikipedia (wikipedia.org) article (under the heading "Criticism and response") on Amnesty International.

9

Asia Times Online
www.atimes.com

Overview

It's easy to take for granted the Western perspective that dominates most of the news people in the U.S. receive. Even if that information is sometimes skewed to the left or the right, it's usually informed by a Western point-of-view that anchors all news and commentary. So it is refreshing to come across a Web site that holds no particular reverence for deep-seated beliefs in the superiority of "The American Century" (labeled "a fairy tale" on this site) and calls into question the idea of the forceful spreading of democracy—by tank and B-2 bomber.

But it's not just its Eastern perspective that makes the Asia Times Online such a welcome addition to the family of Internet-based news agencies. It's the clear, even sparkling writing, the bold commentary, and the sense of history—and humor—that illuminate the site. Those expecting a stodgy Web site filled with the Nikkei averages and academic discussions of the North Korean nuclear situation are in for a surprise. The site features great writing about important topics in an entertaining and useful way.

"We look at these issues from an Asian perspective; this distinguishes us from the mainstream English-language media, whose reporting on Asian matters is generally by Westerners, for Westerners," according to the site. But good reporting and writing is truly international, as the Asia Times Online demonstrates.

What You'll Find There

The home page features a number of highlighted "main stories" with headlines and a brief blurb about each one. The headlines carry an almost tabloid-like style, such as "Indo-US nuclear deal blasts ahead" and "Elvis and war crimes." The stories usually begin with anecdotal

leads—stories, rather than facts and figures—and offer what will be for some readers an uncomfortable amount of commentary, even in articles that are strictly news. (This breach is perhaps forgivable because the site is trying to convey a cultural impression as much as a cut-and-dried factual account.)

The home page is divided into news, commentary, special reports such as "China and the U.S.," a business section, and—still on the front page—the book review section (a bit of a rarity to place arts reporting so high on a news page).

Along the left-hand side of the page is a menu of countries and regions (Greater China, South Asia, Japan, Korea, et al.) that offers quick clicks to additional stories and features relating to those particular places. The stories are written, largely, by Asia Times Online correspondents, each of whom seems steeped in the cultural history of the region in question. The stories are among the most user-friendly on the Web in their clarity and catchiness.

The home page also features blogs and message boards for reader comment, as well as more standard features including a currency converter and information about hotels and tours in Asia.

Why You Should Visit

If the political pundits from all industrialized countries are correct, China is going to be the major player—globally—in the coming century. The emergence of the Chinese middle class, as well as the delicate political dance toward a more open society (and all the questions of industrialization and political influence that follow in its wake), have already started to rattle the timbers of the Western world. Because so little is known about China in particular and Asia in general, having a staff of savvy experts who can dissect and interpret the events unfolding there is an immense help to Western readers.

This is a Web site that addresses those issues unflinchingly, but not in an academic "think tank" kind of way.

Keep This in Mind

Despite its growing prominence and centrality in many public policy circles, Asia is not exactly water cooler fodder for most people. And although the site does cover issues as close to home as the "war on terror" and the U.S. auto industry, many readers might be hesitant to bookmark a site with such a clear focus on such a distant place. But for those readers willing to think outside the geopolitical box, this site has much to offer.

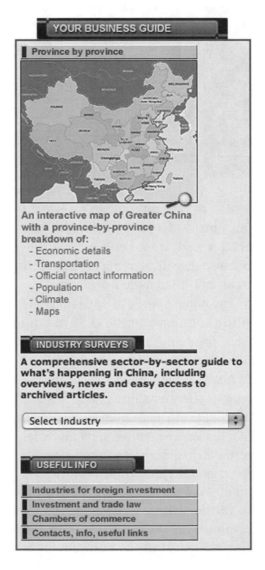

YOUR BUSINESS GUIDE

Province by province

An interactive map of Greater China with a province-by-province breakdown of:
- Economic details
- Transportation
- Official contact information
- Population
- Climate
- Maps

INDUSTRY SURVEYS

A comprehensive sector-by-sector guide to what's happening in China, including overviews, news and easy access to archived articles.

Select Industry

USEFUL INFO

Industries for foreign investment
Investment and trade law
Chambers of commerce
Contacts, info, useful links

Off the Record

Asia Times Online is a sort of media-age phoenix, having risen from the ashes of the *Asia Times* newspaper, a Hong Kong/Bangkok-based daily that folded in 1997 as a result of the Asian financial crisis that washed over the region like a tsunami of financial woe.

It makes the Asian world a lot less foreign to Western readers.

10

Associated Press (AP)

www.ap.org

Overview

The history of the world for the past 150 years is, in some way, the history as the Associated Press has told it. No news organization has come close to the Associated Press (known to most readers simply as the "AP") in its breadth of coverage. One couldn't find a major news event from any region of the globe that hasn't been chronicled by the reporters of the AP. Much of what has leeched into the history books has been pilfered from the pages of the countless newspapers that subscribe to the AP.

Founded in 1848, the AP is not so much a formal news organization as a loosely allied brotherhood (and sisterhood) of reporters in bureaus in 120 countries. More than 3,700 reporters contribute reports to the AP, which then disseminates the information to newspapers, television stations, and radio outlets around the clock and around the world.

What You'll Find There

The AP has a multi-layered Web site. The home page does not offer an at-a-glance rundown of all the stories that AP has recently issued (which would be difficult given the thousands of stories that move across AP wires each day). Rather, it offers a series of icons that lead to various AP-sponsored Web pages. For example, Web surfers can click on any of a half-dozen breaking news stories from the AP that are now appearing on "Media Sites Worldwide." There are also icons for AP-originated video of breaking news stories, news photos, streaming audio from its reporters, and separate icons for news about the media itself.

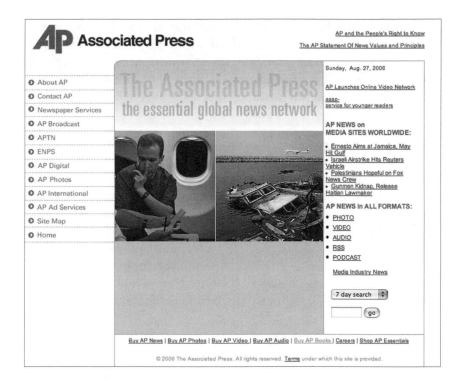

The Web site also offers lots of useful information for people in the news business, such as updates on freedom of information requests and an archive of past stories from the AP.

You'll find links on the site to purchase AP-originated products, from photos in its searchable archive to books for both professional journalists and general readers and information about careers in journalism with the AP.

Why You Should Visit

One of the aims of this book is to help Web surfers understand how Web sites gather, filter, and present the news. The AP Web site, in effect, performs that same function about itself. As one of the most important (and far and away the largest) news agencies operating today, the AP deserves scrutiny. The organization's Web site provides some information vital to understanding how it goes about its business, giving an accounting of the history and protocol of the massive AP newsgathering apparatus.

Because of its longevity, the AP site has amassed an awesome amount of first-hand historical information, from war dispatches to documentary footage. The site offers information of value to researchers as well as casual news seekers about events large and small from the pageant of world history.

Keep This in Mind

The AP Web page serves a dual purpose: to present the news of the day and also to promote the AP itself. Much of what's on the Web site is aimed at enticing other news agencies to subscribe to the AP. As a single-source news outlet, the AP site comes up a little short—though in fairness, its aim is to provide only a sampling of what the AP can do, not a comprehensive clearinghouse of everything they cover.

The AP site in particular and AP stories in general lack the kind of opinion or attitude that many readers have come to expect from

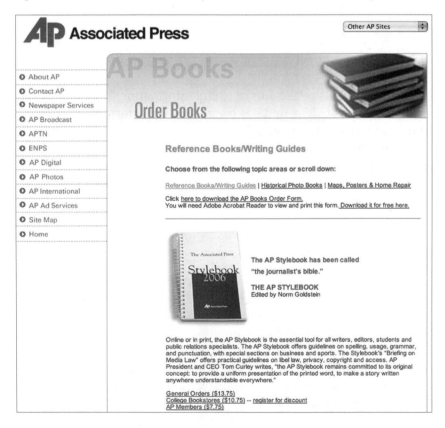

news reports. The AP is still "old school" in how it presents the news—a highly laudable objective in this climate of opinionated, talk-radio bombast. But such objective presentation of the news might leave some readers unexcited, especially younger readers who were brought up in the climate of news blogs and cable-yakfests.

Off the Record

The AP not only presents the news, but it also assists writers and editors who are thwarted in their attempts to get the story. The AP robustly defends the rights of reporters to do their jobs, sponsoring dozens of freedom of information appeals at the local, state, and national levels.

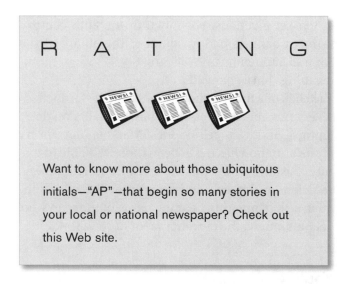

RATING

Want to know more about those ubiquitous initials—"AP"—that begin so many stories in your local or national newspaper? Check out this Web site.

11

Bloomberg
www.bloomberg.com

Overview

Most people who actually know what "ticker tape" is have probably only encountered it at a parade for some military hero or sports rally, where tons of the stuff is shredded and rained down upon the celebrants. But once upon a time, ticker tape served a valuable function. It was the quickest and most efficient way to convey financial data to the business community. Rivers of thin strips of paper sputtered out the latest market gyrations. For much of the 20th century, brokers and investment bankers had to squint at this financial spaghetti to learn what was happening on Wall Street.

My how things have changed.

With the click of a mouse, the latest numbers—crunched and analyzed in every possible permutation—are available on desktop computers, laptops, and even cell phones. Markets move every second, and timely information has never been more valuable to the financial community. Cashing in on that new reality is Bloomberg, a monstrously efficient and hugely successful provider of online financial data—which also happens to bear the name of the man who founded it, Michael Bloomberg, the current mayor of New York City.

What You'll Find There

On Bloomberg.com's home page, you'll find a quarter-page chart indicating the latest moves in the Dow Jones Industrial Average. The multicolored graph abuts a news box that highlights three or four major news stories impacting the business community (corporate earnings reports, government policy changes, pronouncements by political figures, etc.). Across the top of the page run a half-dozen icons that take you further into Bloomberg's exhaustive world of financial news.

These icons include "Market Data," "News and Commentary," "Charts and Analysis," "Bloomberg Media," and "About Bloomberg."

The bottom half of the home page is comprised of a grab bag of market data, such as foreign currencies or prices in the oil market, teases of recently posted opinion columns or analysis, and "editor's picks," a potpourri of items such as dispatches from the auto show or ads for the latest tech upgrades.

The site has a ton of information but is clean, clear, and easily navigated.

Most of the information, even on the pages buried deep within the site, seems fresh and relevant. All of the content is labeled clearly and blurbed in a reader-friendly way. In addition to financial news, the site contains some cultural reporting and even a sports page for those cyber-jocks who are a little bit of both.

Why You Should Visit

There are two answers, really, to why you should visit the site, depending on the kind of person you are. For the professional investor or member of the business community, Bloomberg.com qualifies as a "must-see." Its breakout charts on individual stocks, trends in the market, and in-depth analysis would keep even the wonkiest market watcher enthralled for hours. The site provides customizable stock and bond charts for individual investors and an archive of market data in every conceivable trading category.

The site also features a highly impressive array of dozens of columnists from various economic sectors—from the home mortgage industry to political pundits—who weigh in on topical issues in an informed and authoritative way.

It is these columnists, in fact, who offer the greatest value to the non-serious investor who just wants to know a little bit about the world of finance and its eminently mysterious ways. Bloomberg has assembled an A-list of financial gurus who cover the world—but not just in jargon-laced tirades. Most of the writing, such as that on U.S. politics, general news, foreign affairs (and even a New York dining column!), is clear and engaging.

Keep This in Mind

This is a site primarily for serious investors, so much of what's posted is phrased in the shorthand of the financial community. The site's "top stories" are often of interest only to the financial community. Much of what one would find on mainstream news sites is absent from Bloomberg, which knows its audience and caters to it ferociously. This is to be expected from a site that was started by a former general partner in the investment firm Salomon Brothers back in 1981—the infancy of real-time financial news.

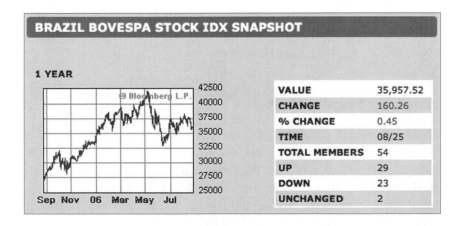

BRAZIL BOVESPA STOCK IDX SNAPSHOT

1 YEAR

VALUE	35,957.52
CHANGE	160.26
% CHANGE	0.45
TIME	08/25
TOTAL MEMBERS	54
UP	29
DOWN	23
UNCHANGED	2

Off the Record

Bloomberg has become a many-headed hydra in the financial world. The company has successfully branched out into the radio business, as well as magazine and book publishing and even 24-hour-a-day business and financial news television. Always anticipating its readers' needs, the company has recently begun promoting its podcasts, ensuring that future market obsessives will never be more than a click or beep away from the tidal Wall Street backwash.

R A T I N G

For people who mean business, this is the site to visit.

12

British Broadcasting Corporation (BBC) News

news.bbc.co.uk

Overview

The Internet, being a relatively new development in the history of news reporting, doesn't generally conjure up much nostalgia. Most news sites are far younger than the people signing on to them. Trolling through most URLs doesn't usually bring to mind much more than the most recent headlines. But there's a grand exception.

Just the mention of the "BBC" summons a certain image of paternalistic journalism, a static-punctuated sobriety amid the noise of war and riot. Perhaps because it's so very British, the BBC inevitably brings to mind those well-worn clichés so many Yanks have about the Brits: tweed-suited patriarchs enjoying brandy by the hearth, radio tuned to the BBC as the newsreaders exhort in their best "stiff-upper-lip" style. It strikes one as all so very proper.

But the BBC News site is not, as they say, your father's BBC. It's thoroughly modern in all the best ways, while remaining grounded in the BBC's long tradition of seriousness and comprehensiveness.

What You'll Find There

The BBC has a Web presence for its extensive television and radio station networks, but it's the news site that really brings the world, quickly and comprehensively, to a user's computer screen. Graphically clear and simple, the page for BBC News arranges stories according to importance at the moment (the banner at the top of the page proclaims "Updated every minute of every day") and region of the globe (Africa, Middle East, the Americas). Each of the main stories is teased with a headline, a meat-and-potatoes news lead, a thumbnail graphic, and, in most cases, links for streaming video from all

around the world. (For viewers interested only in news from the United Kingdom, a strictly-U.K. version is available through a prompt on the news main page.)

There are also a number of icons for audio feeds from both the television and radio wings of the BBC, where surfers can eavesdrop on such broadcasts as the *BBC Newshour* or the *World Today* program. Soccer and cricket fans can also hear updated match reports from European and World league play. (The BBC covers U.S. pop culture pretty well, but U.S. sports don't get much play on the site.)

Behind the headlines on the home page and the prompts that run along the border ("Business," "Health," "Science/Nature," and "Technology") are the stories, each of which usually includes a couple of imaginatively chosen hyperlinks, providing the background on the news of the day. For example, a breaking story about a coal mine collapse in West Virginia included links to the U.S. Federal Mine

Safety guidelines page and a profile of the international conglomerate that owned and operated the mine. While many sites would be
content simply to dredge up stories of other recent collapses, the BBC
sent its readers to source material that offered a larger understanding
of the issues.

Why You Should Visit

In the myopic world of mainstream news, where international coverage is often seen as a delicacy rather than a main course, the BBC
puts the whole world on the menu. The depth of coverage in areas
that many news organizations couldn't even pronounce—let alone
send a reporter to—is impressive and laudable. In general, the style of
reporting and writing on the site reflects the fabled sobriety of the
British Broadcasting Corporation, eschewing the breathless exclama-
tions of many other, nosier news sites.

   Although not without its quirkier side—a recent story featured a
close-up photo of a two-headed snake for sale on eBay—BBC News
is about as reliable and serious a news site as is likely to appeal to a

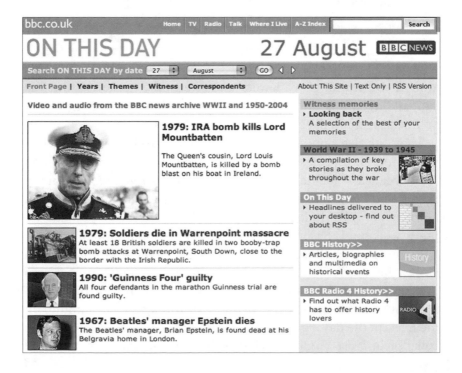

garden-variety Web surfer who's trying to learn a little more about the world in which we live.

Keep This in Mind

For all its history and tradition, the BBC is not immune to charges of political bias and journalistic massaging. It has been assailed by critics mostly on the political right—both in Britain and in the U.S.—for its promotion of an anti-Western ideology. Its intense focus on issues such as global warming, Third World poverty, the war in Iraq, and even the relief efforts in the wake of Hurricane Katrina (which reportedly caused Tony Blair to label the BBC "full of hatred of America"[1]) led some to conclude the BBC is interested in remaking the world, not just covering it. One disaffected bloke has even set up a Web site to chronicle the news organization's alleged bias: Check out his site at biased-bbc.blogspot.com.

Off the Record

It was none other than the father of commercial radio, Guglielmo Marconi, who was one of the founders of the BBC. In fact, the very first broadcast by the BBC, on November 14, 1922, originated from Marconi's London studio.

The BBC remains the benchmark against which most other news reporting could be measured.

Endnote

1. James Robinson, et al., "Blair attacks BBC for 'anti-US bias'," *The Observer*, Sept. 18, 2005 (rpt. at politics.guardian.co.uk/media/story).

13

Cable News Network (CNN)

www.cnn.com

Overview

Is there anyone in the free world who is not familiar with the news gathering juggernaut known as CNN? Not only has the Ted Turner-originated network come to define cable news, but it has also been the subject of books, copycat Web sites, parodies—and even a feature film.

You can close your eyes and hear James Earl Jones' stentorian bass proclaiming "This is CNN"—one of the many ways Turner has sought to emblazon the brand on the news-watching public's consciousness. Another way is through the network's Web site (which, when it debuted in 1995, was simply called CNN Interactive).[1] But can a Web site possibly replicate the legendary broadcast outlet in its brashness, topicality, and self-promotional pomp?

Well, TV is TV, and the Internet is the Internet. But CNN.com takes a backseat to no broadcast outlet in its scope, comprehensiveness, and timeliness. Like its more heralded parent, the site is a standard setter.

What You'll Find There

On CNN.com, you'll find the news of the day, of course, and lots of it: in print, video feeds, and pictures. CNN.com is a full-service Web site, covering everything from politics to international news, money and finance, and sports (though clicking on the "Sports" icon promptly leads off-site to *Sports Illustrated*'s Web page).

The main page boasts the usual variety of "Breaking News" stories as well as a generic link to "More News," most of which is listed in surprisingly tiny type. The major story of the day is usually teased with a

splashy photo or graphic, accompanied by the lead paragraph of the story, with prompts to go further into the story or veer off into related stories or background information.

Throughout each of the stories, which are credited to CNN writers (with an occasional nod to contributions from the Associated Press), there are numerous hyperlinks, leading readers to sidebar stories and "backgrounders," as well as streaming video highlights, timelines, and photo galleries. CNN reporters do their homework. The stories are brief enough to appeal to the ever-shortening attention span of the average Web peruser but packaged in a way to provide context for the deeper reader.

There's also the unavoidable smattering of self-promotional fare: boxed ads promoting CNN broadcast shows, links to *Time* magazine and *Sports Illustrated* (both products of Time Warner, parent company of Turner Broadcasting), and even a blog maintained by Anderson Cooper, CNN's anchor/boy-wonder.

The site also provides links to CNN's broadcast channel Headline News as well as an International Edition and a searchable archive of stories from CNN.com.

Why You Should Visit

Anybody who cut his or her news teeth during Gulf War I or Gulf War II will always think of CNN when it comes to breaking news around the globe. Ditto 9/11. The broadcast outlet has monopolized our early-warning responses to national disasters and unfolding tragedy. And the Web site is right there, drawing on the strength of dozens of worldwide bureaus and well-placed reporters, feeding information almost instantaneously to the site and providing surprising depth for a mostly TV-based operation.

In addition to breaking news, the Web site offers lots of neat little features for people clicking on the news icons. The "Health" news page not only provides the latest medical findings, but it also offers a comprehensive health library; the "Education" page covers all the usual studies and reports making news, but there's a CNN student news section with news and information relevant to those actually in the educational system, not just readers of press releases from the education department. Even the "Politics" page has a link to a gallery of political cartoons.

Keep This in Mind

CNN is corporate, with a capital C. The site is not known for its challenges to orthodoxy. It's a mainstream site, which means that the envelope-pushing reporting and really tough questions that make journalism exciting—and essential—is often left to other, less patrician Web sites. (And any network that would jettison the thoughtful, probing Aaron Brown opens itself up to questions of its journalistic commitment.)

360° Blog

Follow along on the blog as Anderson Cooper and his team take you behind the scenes of "Anderson Cooper 360°." You'll hear about stories as they are developing and get Anderson's unique take on the day's events.

Today's Headline: Cluster bombs raising troubling questions

CNN is also about ratings. Much of the Web site contains not-so-subtle previews, ads, and promos for upcoming CNN shows. And CNN.com is not immune to that virus of popular news sites, the "Instant Viewer" poll, which asks readers to weigh in on some topic of the moment—and then makes a "View Results" button available to see how firmly you are (or aren't) in the mainstream.

Off the Record

CNN, the broadcast channel, seems to have lost some of its footing recently. Once the bastion of much-watched political fight-fests such as *The Capital Gang* and *Crossfire*, these shows—and several others with a political focus—have been canceled. Critics, and viewers, are feeling the growth of rival Fox News as it continues to chip away at CNN's hold on American cable viewers.

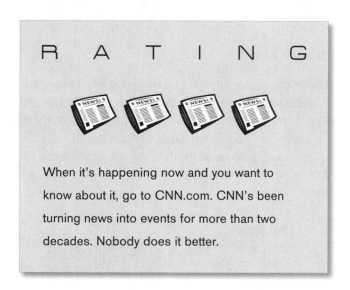

R A T I N G

When it's happening now and you want to know about it, go to CNN.com. CNN's been turning news into events for more than two decades. Nobody does it better.

Endnotes

1. From the Wikipedia (wikipedia.org) article on CNN.

14

Cable-Satellite Public Affairs Network (C-SPAN)

www.cspan.org

Overview

At first glance, C-SPAN seems like a cable network dreamt up by an insomniac. A closer look at C-SPAN reveals an invaluable public service. Born out of an idea to televise—live and gavel-to-gavel—sessions of the U.S. House of Representatives, C-SPAN made its first broadcast on March 19, 1979, when it aired a speech by Congressman Al Gore. Since then, the network—a nonprofit funded solely by cable companies—has expanded exponentially: Coverage has broadened to the Senate, the White House, think tanks, and media and publishing, but the thrust of the network remains the same, airing unfiltered sessions of Congress, along with unedited press conferences, panel discussions, and interviews.

Along with three cable channels and radio stations, the Internet has enabled C-SPAN to expand its reach. Launched in 1997, C-SPAN.org has maximized recent developments in the online world. While most of its content is derived from the network's television programming, users are able to fast-forward video clips and select specific segments—both enticing reasons to visit the site. If you can't spend more than a few minutes with C-SPAN on the TV screen (the programming, after all, is not the most dramatic or dynamic force on cable television), C-SPAN.org is a useful and important substitute.

What You'll Find There

The C-SPAN.org home page is divided into three columns and is entirely ad-free. In a narrow strip down the left side of the page, you will find a comprehensive list of links to various sections within the

C-SPAN site and to the home pages of several other sites run by the cable network. Six "Featured Topics"—links to pages that focus on specific, timely topics—top that list, followed by links to sections of the site that complement C-SPAN television programs. Under the heading "Other C-SPAN Sites," you can access C-SPAN's niche sites (mainly educational or historical in nature), including American Presidents.org, AmericanWriters.org, and BookTV.org.

On the opposite side of the home page, the site alerts users to the upcoming C-SPAN coverage schedule. In the narrow right column, visitors will find a catalog of "Web Resources," an invaluable service that allows you to quickly and easily access hundreds of important political and media sites, from those related to all three branches of the federal government to state legislatures and governments throughout the world, from think tanks and blogs to media organizations and special C-SPAN online productions. For a full directory, click "All Web Resources" at the bottom of the column.

Logically positioned in the dominant middle column, the meat of the page—timely and regularly updated content of C-SPAN.org—garners the most attention. A teaser to a broadcast of a Congressional hearing or press conference typically receives the top spot, where a still image of the video is joined by a headline, a brief description, and a "Watch" link. A section titled "CapitalNews" (C-SPAN's news service) follows and presents about five recent headlines, which usually link to wire service or mainstream media stories. Click "More Headlines" to visit CapitalNews.org. Below three "Featured Links," visitors can explore the site's video archive by using the search tool, scrolling through the "Recent Programs" section, or wandering through the "Video Library" (which is divided into a dozen topical sections). Video is the predominant feature at C-SPAN.org, and the site is smart to provide users with links to free downloads of the necessary software. Just below the "Video Library" section, you can watch "Live Streams" of the programs currently airing on one of C-SPAN's three networks.

Why You Should Visit

C-SPAN's site yanks open the curtains of the political stage. Granted, the show might not always be the most riveting production. But if the American democracy is indeed a government "of the people, by the people, and for the people," those people need access to the political process. C-SPAN offers unfiltered glimpses of the world and workings

MOST WATCHED C-SPAN VIDEO

[WATCH] Pres. Bush Press Conference (8/21/2006)

[WATCH] Pres. Bush Press Briefing from Camp David (8/18/2006)

[WATCH] White House Press Briefing with Tony Snow (8/17/2006)

[WATCH] Lawrence Wright, Author, *The Looming Tower* (8/18/2006)

[WATCH] American Perspectives: African American Men & Dole

inside the Beltway, and there's probably no better way to become an informed and active citizen. For those who have struggled to stay tuned into the C-SPAN television networks—a four-hour Congressional subcommittee meeting on appropriations can be a bit tedious—the Web site turns over the controls, letting you watch what you want, when you want. It's the ultimate reality show.

Keep This in Mind

These days, it seems every media outlet is accused of bias. One might think C-SPAN would be immune to such criticism because the network's programming consists mainly of unedited footage of Congressional sessions. Think again. Fairness & Accuracy In Reporting (FAIR) released a study in 2005 asserting that C-SPAN's *Washington Journal*—a talk show that usually airs for three hours every morning—lacks the balance the network's founder, chairman, and CEO said is "one of our main goals in life."[1] After looking at who appeared as guests on the show during a six-month stint, FAIR concluded that the program overwhelmingly featured Republicans and conservatives while often overlooking Democrats and liberals, minorities, and women.

Off the Record

When the City Club of Cleveland honored U.S. Supreme Court Justice Antonin Scalia with its Citadel of Free Speech Award in 2003, he refused to let C-SPAN cover his acceptance speech—an ironic but not-so-unusual occurrence. While C-SPAN, despite numerous requests, is not permitted to televise live Supreme Court sessions, the network often broadcasts speeches given by the justices. Except Scalia: "We don't have this problem with any other Supreme Court justice," a C-SPAN executive said, according to the Poynter Institute. "We have even covered panel discussions and the screen goes blank when he begins to speak."

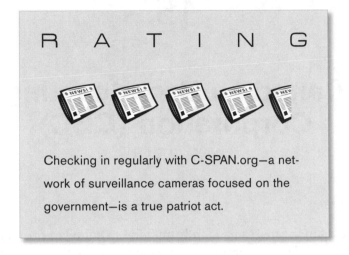

R A T I N G

Checking in regularly with C-SPAN.org—a network of surveillance cameras focused on the government—is a true patriot act.

Endnote

1. From a speech by Brian Lamb at the National Press Club in 1997. C-SPAN posts the transcript on the site's company page in the "About Us" section as part of a feature titled "Debunking the Myths" (www.cspan.org/about/company/debunk.asp? code=DEBUNK2).

15

Canadian Broadcasting Corporation (CBC)

www.cbc.ca

Overview

For most Americans, Canada truly qualifies as a foreign country. U.S. residents would probably be hard-pressed to name the prime minister (Stephen Harper), list all the country's provinces (there are 13), or identify its most popular cultural exports (Alex Trebeck, Dan Ackroyd, the rock band Rush, just to name a few). Some might even be surprised to learn that Canada is also divided by two languages: English and French.

For a country that shares so much border space with the continental U.S., Canada remains shrouded in mystery. Yet in the age of readily accessible global media, this need not be the case. The best place to start to acquaint oneself with our neglected neighbors is a Web site that will not only shine the light into the Canadian hinterlands but also will teach you a few things about the rest of the world—including what's happening south of the Canadian border (that would be the U.S.).

A model of thoughtful, meat-and-potatoes journalism, the Canadian Broadcasting Corporation (CBC) offers a wealth of information about the goings-on in that enigmatic country.

What You'll Find There

Because the CBC's Web site also serves as a daily menu for the corporation's television and radio programs (CBC operates two television networks and four radio services), viewers first encounter a "What's on CBC today?" icon, offering a comprehensive look at entertainment and cultural programming for the coming day. Once that little bit of parochialism is bypassed, you'll find a site that offers at-a-glance

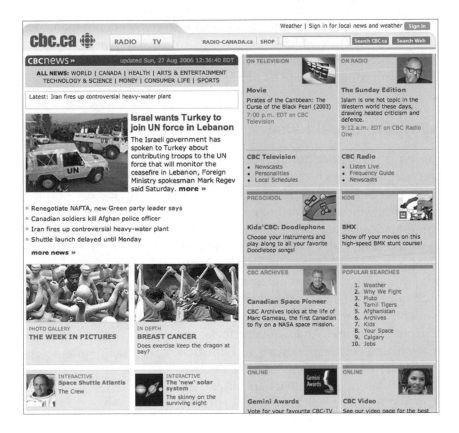

overviews of the biggest news stories in Canada, revolving mostly around the Canadian Parliament, the Supreme Court, and the oil industry (which is big business in provinces like Newfoundland).

And, of course, there's the requisite hockey story, as well as reporting about the Canadian Football League, the Arts scene in Montreal and Quebec, and news of interest to hunters and fishers. So far, very Canadian, eh?

But there are also comprehensive, updated news reports from international bureaus in the Middle East, London, Paris, and Washington D.C. Some U.S. news is covered (though not as prominently on the site as the local fare), with an emphasis on U.S. international policy and business news. There are in-depth reports, often lifted from the CBC's evening news broadcasts or radio reports about the war in Iraq, violence in places such as East Timor and the Sudan, and even forays into pop culture, with streaming audio/video available on everything from the Cannes film festival to Jennifer Aniston's love life. Most of these reports tend to go into greater depth than a lot of other news sites, which are often only interested in headlines and at-a-glance news. (In this, the CBC appears to share much of its in-depth reporting style with its better-known U.S. counterpart, PBS.)

Why You Should Visit

As with any other foreign-based news service, it's always useful to see the world from someone else's perspective. And while you wouldn't think that a country so geographically close to the U.S. could have a significantly different take on world events, a quick scroll through the CBC Web site would reveal a different story. Canada's odd and sometimes explosive blend of socialism and capitalism, French Europeanism and America-centric fascination, and cosmopolitanism and frontier mentality make the Canadian perspective quite different from anywhere else. The CBC's strong record of honest reporting of those flashpoint areas of social collision as well as thoughtful commentary and historical overviews make the site a real education. And while public broadcasting in every country tries to shake its mantle of being "good-for-you" rather than entertaining, CBC's site is both.

Keep This in Mind

Though you can't blame a site for catering to its primary audience, the CBC is mostly concerned with Canada. As a result, many of the stories require some familiarity with Canada's cultural and political systems. Readers who don't understand the history of tension between the French- and

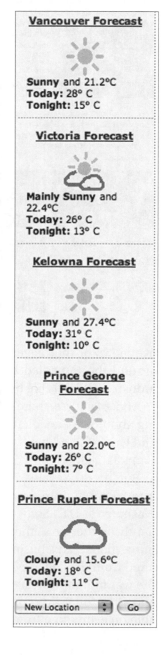

Vancouver Forecast

Sunny and 21.2°C
Today: 28° C
Tonight: 15° C

Victoria Forecast

Mainly Sunny and 22.4°C
Today: 26° C
Tonight: 13° C

Kelowna Forecast

Sunny and 27.4°C
Today: 31° C
Tonight: 10° C

Prince George Forecast

Sunny and 22.0°C
Today: 26° C
Tonight: 7° C

Prince Rupert Forecast

Cloudy and 15.6°C
Today: 18° C
Tonight: 11° C

New Location   Go

English-speaking Canadian communities might not be able to understand what much of the bickering in the Canadian political system is about (or even how a parliamentary system operates). And for those who think sports is a diversion from life, welcome to Canada, where hockey is the one uniting national religion that borders on civic obsession.

Off the Record

Public broadcasting often does its best work in the area of "service journalism" (stories that have great impact on the world but little commercial value). In 2003, the CBC's Web site won an Online News Association award in the "service journalism" category for its coverage of the SARS epidemic.[1]

RATING

Robert Frost once wrote, "Good fences make good neighbors." So do good Web sites.

Endnote

1. See a complete list of the Online News Association winners at www.journalists.org.

16

The Center for Public Integrity

www.publicintegrity.org

Overview

When Charles Lewis—after working as an investigative reporter at ABC News and an award-winning producer for Mike Wallace at CBS's *60 Minutes*—decided to leave the broadcast news industry in 1988 to start a nonprofit investigative journalism organization, some people questioned his sanity.[1]

But the limitations of network television, and daily journalism, prevented him from doing the type of investigations he wanted to conduct—those neglected by the mainstream press but absolutely necessary to the health of democracy. So he left, heading to Washington D.C. with limited capital and no independent means of circulating the reports his organization—funded almost entirely by foundations—would produce. Along with a newsletter called *The Public i*, the Center for Public Integrity regularly issued press releases and held press conferences to announce its findings (a practice that continues and has resulted in the center being cited in more than 8,000 news stories in the last decade and a half).

But as the organization grew, so did the Web. In 1996, the Center for Public Integrity's first Web site simply consisted of biographical information about itself. Three years later, it developed into much more than that: a forum that allowed the center's often-lengthy investigative reports on the actions of Congress members, the White House, the lobbying industry, or state legislatures to be delivered directly to the public—lessening its dependence on the mainstream media to disseminate its "news" through summarized mentions in an article or broadcast. As a repeat winner of online reporting awards, the Center for Public Integrity's Web presence has changed

its identity from a source for investigative journalists to a go-to source for the entire electorate.

What You'll Find There

The home page of the Center for Public Integrity, which automatically adjusts to fill the screen of the user's computer monitor, is sparse. While such an uncluttered design results in minimal strain on the eyes, it could also potentially mislead visitors into thinking the content of the site is limited. Don't be fooled: This site is overflowing with information; it just requires a bit more willingness to explore past the home page.

The site first draws users to the organization's latest report, which is featured at the top center of the page in the only colorful, graphically designed portion of the screen. Below it, under a heading of "Latest Reports," several other headlines/links (accompanied by a blurb and a date stamp) related to the site's current top project are posted.

You can find the Center for Public Integrity's "Featured Projects" in the left column of the home page, where a half-dozen links are listed. To access all such investigations, even those dating back several years (some of which are still frequently updated), click the "More Projects" link at the bottom of the column. These "Featured Projects" cover a range of topics: private military companies, local prosecutors, political nonprofits (or 527s), telecommunication corporations, the pharmaceutical industry, lobbyists, private travel sponsors of elected officials, private interests of state legislators, the oil industry, U.S. contractors in Afghanistan and Iraq—and how all the aforementioned and others influence political leaders, government, and public policy. Each investigative project occupies a section of the site that functions like a separate niche entity with navigational menus down the left side, letting you access features that typically include multimedia and interactive components, searchable databases, and original documents used in the center's investigation.

Back on the site's home page, the right column consists of links to the center's News Room, where you can access abridged versions of its reports in press release style. At the bottom of the column, you can select any state from a drop-down menu for in-depth information about the workings of its government and influential private interests. Because the site is so expansive and there's no navigation tool on the home page, you might find it helpful to locate the "Sitemap" by clicking on the "Site Search" link in the upper left corner of the home page.

Why You Should Visit

The Center for Public Integrity has accurately been dubbed "the Paul Revere of our time,"[2] and PublicIntegrity.org is its galloping horse. Abiding by the old adage of investigative journalism, it follows the money and takes you for rides along the maze of trails from corporate suites to legislative chambers.

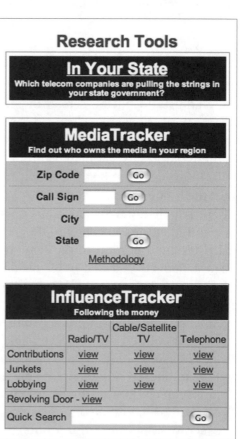

While the writing is often lackluster, the nuts-and-bolts approach works, helping to clearly explain to lay readers often complicated issues. One of the most notable aspects of the site is its nonpartisan disposition: Right and wrong mean more here than right and left. For a democracy to function properly, government must be held accountable. This site does that better than any other, empowering the voting public with information about how money and private interests are influencing elected officials and the public policy they pursue.

Keep This in Mind

Through its investigative research and reporting, the Center for Public Integrity insists that government and public leaders act with a high level of transparency and accountability. But what's great about PublicIntegrity.org is that it demands the same of itself. The Center for Public Integrity posts various items on its Web site that ensure its credibility, from policies and ethics to lists of financial backers and bios of staff members. Most importantly, each report is accompanied by a "Methodology" link, where the organization discloses the measures it took throughout the particular investigation and names the participants of the "Team" who contributed to the project. Its willingness to be held accountable is equally admirable: publicly correcting inaccuracies regardless of how minor they might be (see the site's "Corrections" page).

Off the Record

The Center for Public Integrity has published more than a dozen books since 1990. The most successful, *The Buying of the President 2004* (it also released similar titles in the presidential election years of 1996 and 2000), instantly became a *New York Times* bestseller.

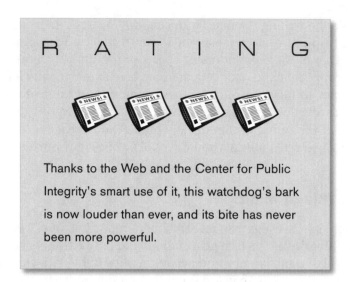

R A T I N G

Thanks to the Web and the Center for Public Integrity's smart use of it, this watchdog's bark is now louder than ever, and its bite has never been more powerful.

Endnotes

1. Mark Glaser, "Center for Public Integrity leading the way for serious online journalism," Online Journalism Review (www.ojr.org/ojr/glaser/1077668140.php), Feb. 25, 2004.

2. From caption of Karen Ruckman photo of Charles Lewis that accompanied a Nat Hentoff article ("Red Alert for Bill of Rights!") in the *Village Voice* on March 7, 2004 (www.villagevoice.com/news/0311,hentoff,42448,6.html).

17

Central Intelligence Agency (CIA)

www.cia.gov

Overview

It sounds like the stuff of black-and-white spy movies: trench-coated secret agents skulking around foreign embassies in exotic locales, cavorting with shadowy figures, and exchanging code words in the dead of night. The image of the spy is a hybrid of half-truths gleaned from real intelligence-gathering agencies and healthy dollops of invention from Cold War-era pulp novelists. Much of what we think of as the idiomatic "spy" comes from the workings of the Central Intelligence Agency (CIA)—a schizophrenic agency that maintains a globally prominent presence and a huge, impressive public head-quarters while trying to remain, essentially, invisible.

No wonder no one's really sure what to make of the CIA. Thank goodness they have a Web site.

What You'll Find There

The CIA's Web site is filled with dozens, perhaps hundreds, of facts you never knew you didn't know. For an agency that is so famously guarded, the Web site provides an immense amount of information.

The home page has a clean, clear look, with the center column dedicated to a handful of recent stories collected under the banner "What's New at CIA.gov." These stories include statements by CIA officials, updates on legislative action on matters of intelligence gathering, and announcements of personnel changes at the agency.

The real treasure trove runs along either side of the page, with captions offering everything you could ever want to know about the agency: "About the CIA" sits atop a dozen subheads including "The CIA Today," "The CIA Museum," and "Virtual Tour of the CIA" (which

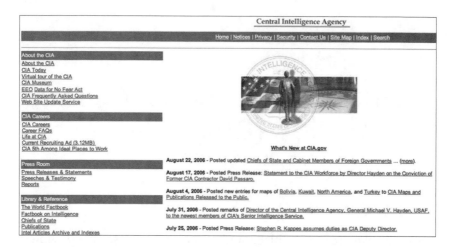

is a bit of a disappointment, as it's mostly just a collection of stills of the exterior of the agency's Virginia headquarters). Other headlines offer information about "CIA Careers," "Press Room," "Library & Reference," and a "CIA Homepage for Kids," which features games, quizzes, word puzzles, and age-appropriate discussions of the agency's mission, all presented in language that teeters dangerously close to parody: "Well, first let's look at how we are asked to do a job. We call it 'tasked.' Just like anything in life, there is a way or procedure for how things are done; we call this the intelligence cycle."

The dozens of links on the home page take you to pages filled with history, reports, articles, testimony transcripts, FAQ pages, geographical encyclopedias, and other U.S. government agency Web sites. It's bizarrely captivating and dauntingly impressive.

The site also serves as a repository of historical documents (none classified, of course) about the CIA, as well as an archive of reports and congressional testimony from CIA directors and operatives. Other useful links include the "Freedom of Information Electronic Reading Room"—which offers tips for filing FOI requests and an overview of the material available under that statute—as well as the Office of Science and Technology and the policy wonk's wonderland, the Center for the Study of Intelligence.

Why You Should Visit

Fair is fair: The CIA is watching all of us, so why shouldn't we spend a little time looking at the CIA? (Though the agency claims it is only watching us if there's a compelling national security reason.) And the CIA has given us all something to look at in its comprehensive, well-organized site. The agency, which made headlines recently with a politically explosive change of directors, has lost some clout as a result of the expansion of the Department of Homeland Security. But its powers—and its impact on the domestic *and* foreign policy of the U.S.—are considerable. So it's good to pay attention.

Beyond that, there's a mercenary reason to check in with the site from time to time: You might end up working there. The site has a "CIA Careers" section (including a fun personality profile quiz you can take online to figure out the kind of spying you're best suited for) and extensive information including news releases, which trumpet the CIA as one of the country's "Ideal Places to Work."

Keep This in Mind

It's not likely that the CIA will ever shake its reputation as a shadowy, James Bond-type operation. Some critics of the agency—and there

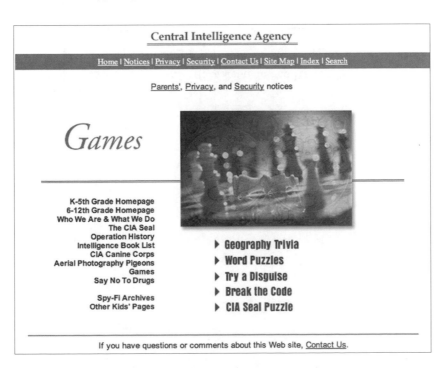

are many—continue to question its very existence, charging that its spy vs. spy tactics haven't been relevant since the end of the Cold War.

Off the Record

In certain books and in articles in the periodical press, the CIA has been charged with involvement in such things as drug trafficking and political assassinations. The CIA's official, succinct response to these charges can be found on the Web site: "It does neither."

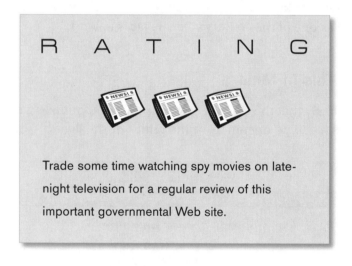

R A T I N G

Trade some time watching spy movies on late-night television for a regular review of this important governmental Web site.

18

Chicago Tribune
www.chicagotribune.com

Overview

The notion of "vertical integration" is a fairly recent concept in telecommunications. The idea is that a cable television station, say, will purchase a radio station, a newspaper or magazine, or even an Internet company so that its programming (or "content," to use the current buzzword) can be accessed in a variety of media.

That new idea is old news to the Tribune Company, which pioneered the concept in 1924 when it purchased radio station WGN as a companion to its highly successful and influential newspaper, the *Chicago Tribune* ("WGN," by the way, is an acronym of the paper's long-standing slogan, "World's Greatest Newspaper"). Two decades later, it established WGN television as a key player in a partnership that stands to this day, supplemented by the *Chicago Tribune*'s CLTV, a 24-hour cable channel covering the Chicago area. The highly profitable WGN-TV, sometimes called a "superstation," can be seen on cable outlets nationwide, and, in a sign of the times, has combined with its print counterpart to collaborate on investigative journalistic pieces and sponsoring of debates for public office seekers.

The *Chicago Tribune* remains an important voice on the American journalistic landscape, and, in the age of digital communication, its Web site continues the tradition of solid, public service journalism, smartly written and up-to-date.

What You'll Find There

The home page of the *Chicago Tribune* is not the most visually striking newspaper site on the Web. Rather than attempt (as many papers do) to reproduce the look of the front page of the print edition, the *Tribune* site forgoes style for substance, using small photos and even smaller type to proclaim the day's news. The tradeoff is more stories

listed on the page than just about any other major newspaper site. Perhaps in a nod to its storied conservatism and Republican roots, the *Tribune*'s Web presence is rather understated.

Icons not much bigger than the text font itself lead readers to the usual array of sections: "Latest News," "Sports," "Opinion," etc. The *Tribune* has a robust local section that has produced some important investigative journalism, and the editorial page is considered a must-read for those taking the political pulse of America's heartland.

Though lacking in self-congratulatory graphical excess, ChicagoTribune.com offers readers a thorough immersion in the day's events, from breaking coverage of world events to in-depth local sports (though it seems, curiously, to favor still photos over streaming video). The home page also offers readers a chance to do a little job searching through the CareerBuilder network, check the latest stock quotes, and even go shopping online for a car, a mortgage, or a mate.

Why You Should Visit

The *Chicago Tribune* has won two dozen Pulitzer Prizes, unseated countless public figures exposed in scandals, and helped guide political movements and voters for generations in its well-reasoned and sober editorials. It has also been—and continues to be—home to some of the best and most significant columnists writing today. What else would one expect from the longtime home of columnist and beloved curmudgeon Mike Royko? Pulitzer-winning Clarence Page, a fixture on cable television talk-fests and in opinion journals, still writes for the *Tribune*, as does Bob Verdi, one of the deans of baseball writing. The writings of these columnists, and dozens of others, are available on the Web site.

ChicagoTribune.com continues to showcase lots of terrific investigative reporting on issues ranging from public health to the death penalty to scandals in the governor's mansion. And though Republican in roots, it maintains a stubborn Midwestern independence: In 2004, it endorsed George W. Bush for a second presidential term and Democrat Barack Obama for U.S. Senate. A widely acknowledged opinion shaper, the editorial page is distinguished by its thoughtful, weighty arguments on matters large and small. People

---

Opinion   08/27/2006 01:04 AM

Editorials

Cashing in on the calendar
More than 80 companies have come under scrutiny in federal investigations of possible stock option fraud, and you can't help but wonder if we're on the verge of Enron/WorldCom/Tyco revisited.

State Street? Still standing
Many Chicagoans expressed outrage when Federated Department Stores bought Marshall Field's and announced that, come September, the venerable Field's name would disappear--even on the State Street store--and Macy's would take its place. Shoppers vowed their loyalty to a Chicago icon. Many insisted they would cut up their credit card and never again set foot inside the soon-to-be formerly Field's.

WHAT OTHERS ARE SAYING
Despite huge subsidies and tax breaks, the only thing ethanol seems to be accomplishing is eating up the corn supply. Consider that one tankful of ethanol could feed one person for a year.

A Berlin tightrope
A strange thing happened after Angela Merkel squeezed Gerhard Schroeder out of power last fall in an election that was as bitter and as close as the U.S. presidential race in 2000. Her popularity soared. Germans took to Merkel, though she often comes across as a dour technocrat.

Davis' marvelous adventure
At least Tom DeLay found some legitimate-sounding benefactors to pay for his junkets. Danny Davis? The U.S. government says his overseas hosts were terrorists who have to rely on suicide bombers and child soldiers to do their bidding when no member of the U.S.

Bloggers
Recent posts from Chicago Tribune news, features and sports reporters

Columnists

Clarence
Page
Anti-poverty victories
have to begin at home

Steve
Chapman
Paternalism without the
nanny state

John
Kass
It's wheeler-dealers'
choice at Judy's

who read the *Tribune*'s editorials will always learn something about an issue.

Keep This in Mind

ChicagoTribune.com is not the sexiest Web site; it lacks the breathless presentation and vigor of many other newspaper Web sites. Graphics are kept to a bare minimum. The site offers little hype and won't do much for younger surfers who are unaware of the company's long tradition of journalistic bona fides. (And it certainly lacks the visual slickness of its neighbor across Michigan Avenue, the *Chicago Sun-Times*.)

Off the Record

Well, if you're going to make a mistake, at least make it memorable: The *Chicago Tribune*'s famous headline and story, "Dewey Defeats Truman," from the 1948 presidential election, has entered the annals of American history as, perhaps, the most famous flub in journalism.

RATING

Proving that sense and sobriety can thrive, even in the cyber age.

19

Christian Science Monitor

www.csmonitor.com

Overview

Although its name might imply such, the *Christian Science Monitor*, based in Boston, is not the local church bulletin. And while the weekday newspaper is published by the Church of Christ, Scientist, readers would be hard-pressed to make the connection if it weren't for the masthead.

In 1908, church founder Mary Baker Eddy started the newspaper—a revolutionary endeavor for a woman during a time when women were still denied the right to vote. The year before, then 86-year-old Eddy was the target of the relentless Joseph Pulitzer and his *New York World* after writing a bestselling book about her unorthodox religious beliefs. Then came Mark Twain's *Christian Science*, a searing critique of the new religion. That, combined with a disdain for the notorious "yellow journalism" of the early 20th century, prompted Eddy to create her own media outlet to counter the sensational tales that populated the rags of her time. Ironically, Eddy's enterprise eventually went on to win seven Pulitzer Prizes for excellence in journalism. And the tradition continues online.

What You'll Find There

The home page of CSMonitor.com maintains a design that is easily navigable and allows users to find the top stories of the day quickly. The print edition of the *Monitor* includes a different feature section each weekday ("Work & Money," "Learning," "Homefront," "Ideas," and "Arts & Leisure"). On the site, a navigation bar beneath the masthead lets visitors search a number of sections—"World," "USA," "Commentary," "Work & Money," "Learning," "Living," "Sci/Tech," "A & E," "Books," and "The Home Forum"—any time they please. The day's lead story is typically packaged with a photo at the top left of the

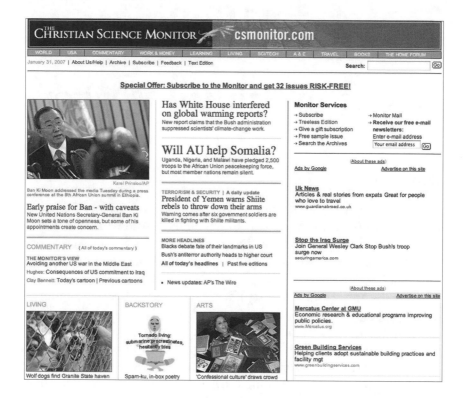

page just below the navigation bar. Within each section, visitors can use sub-categories to easily focus in on a particular topic or region. For example, the "World" section is divided into regions of the globe from the Americas to the Middle East to Asia Pacific; the "USA" section is divvied up into topical categories: "Domestic Politics," "Economy," "Foreign Policy," "Justice," "Military," and "Society & Culture."

The *Christian Science Monitor* depends heavily on its staff writers, who are based in 11 countries and the U.S., for its content—rather than wire services used by most metro dailies. Its stories are often long but well written, in-depth, and contextually rich. The site contains, in addition to the staff-produced material, a section of news updates called "AP's The Wire," which features briefs of the Associated Press' top stories of the day, with links to full-length AP articles and a wealth of other offerings from the organization.

In a column that runs down the left side of the bottom of the home page, users will find graphic links to the *Monitor*'s special projects—a bevy of thorough, and often interactive, stories on wide-ranging issues, from the future of passenger trains in America to how Americans can bridge the red-blue divide—that alone are worth the trip to CSMonitor.com. Another must-see is the work of Clay Bennett, the Pulitzer Prize-winning editorial cartoonist.

Why You Should Visit

The *Christian Science Monitor* reports stories from across the globe that are too often overlooked or underplayed by the mainstream media—stories that are *actually important* to understanding the world in which we live.

The objectivity of the *Monitor* is superior. In fact, its accuracy, combined with the global perspective it offers, have reportedly earned the paper avid readers in the intelligence sectors.[1] As a *Boston*

Globe columnist wrote, the *Monitor* produces a "distinctive brand of nonhysterical journalism." And that is certainly a welcome contribution now more than ever.

Keep This in Mind

Neither the *Christian Science Monitor* nor its Web companion is a propaganda arm for its patron church. It has, however, been criticized at times for avoiding stories that deal with "controversial and unfavorable issues involving the church."[2]

In an effort to combat declining readership, the *Monitor* turned to the Web to disseminate its global news. In 1996, it became one of the first newspapers to put its text online. Five years later, it pioneered another technology when it launched a PDF edition. Again, it took the lead in using RSS (Really Simple Syndication) feeds—articles automatically downloaded from the site; in May 2005, it sent out 6.4 million such files. By that time, CSMonitor.com was also doing relatively well in attracting browsers, receiving nearly 2 million different visitors to the site each month (while the *New York Times* receives about 10 million, according to Nielsen/NetRatings).

Off the Record

Jill Carroll, while working as a freelance reporter for the *Christian Science Monitor*, was kidnapped in Baghdad, Iraq, in 2006. She was released after spending 82 days as a hostage. The *Monitor*, which worked vigorously for her release, hired Carroll as a staff writer about a week after her abduction to guarantee that she would receive full benefits and support, according to editor Richard Bergenheim.

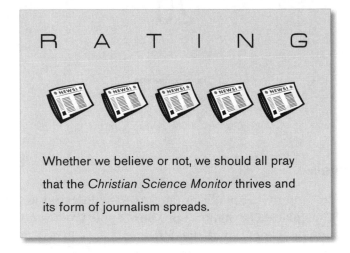

Endnotes

1. From the Wikipedia (wikipedia.org) article on the *Christian Science Monitor*.
2. Ibid.

20

CNET

www.cnet.com

Overview

PC or Mac? Internet Explorer or Firefox? Sony Ericsson K800i or LG VX8500 Chocolate? PlayStation 3 or Xbox? Apple iPod Nano or iRiver Clix? Canon or Nikon? What's the difference between an 8-megapixel SLR and a 5-megapixel wallet-sized point-and-shoot digital camera? How do I transfer my files from an old computer to my new one? What's all the hype about Bluetooth? What's the best free Web-based e-mail service? ...

For technophiles and technophobes alike, the questions facing those in the market for a new piece of technology mount up quicker than you can say "Bill Gates"; finding the right answers, however, often seems to take longer than reading his autobiography. But in a tech-obsessed world where fashion frequently eclipses function, shoppers who need (or more likely want) the latest innovations— from large equipment (i.e., plasma televisions and desktop computers) to tiny gadgets (i.e., PDAs and MP3 players)—would be wise to do their homework before strolling the aisles of an electronic superstore. Luckily, CNET provides an online classroom geared toward the tech-wary in need of introductory tutorial, tekkies already in possession of an advanced degree, and everyone in between. Part *Consumer Reports*, part news service, CNET.com is a technological guru with all the answers—often to questions you didn't even know you needed to ask.

What You'll Find There

On CNET.com, you'll find just about everything you need to become a smarter consumer of the new technology on your wish list and a wiser user of what you've already checked off. The usefulness of CNET.com, along with its broad coverage and application of multimedia, is evident

on the home page. At the top center of the page, a Flash presentation continuously scrolls through the site's top four headlines (accompanied by a blurb, graphic, and link), which typically include a wide range of technology-related topics: "The self-parking Lexus," "Top 10 must-have gadgets," "PC buying guide," "Hottest games," and "Best phones for each carrier." Below the attention-grabbing feature, another 18 headlines fill two columns under the heading "More Stories." An alphabetically arranged list of product category links— from camcorders to TVs—fills the narrow column on the left side of the page. In the upper-right corner, you can access CNET TV video clips—a major component of the site.

Midway down the home page, headlines of recent postings from the site's many blogs reveal the latest in technology news and rumors. Below that, users can learn what products the site's editors endorse and what the site's members most want to get their hands on ("Most Wanted"). To the right of these features, users can listen to any of several CNET podcasts, including the popular "Buzz Out Loud."

A menu of the site's sections ("News," "Reviews," "Compare Prices," "Tips & Tricks," "Downloads," and "CNET TV") spans the top of the home page, designed to look like file folder tabs. After clicking on any of the tabs, you are taken to the corresponding section front, where another horizontal navigation bar features several subsections.

In the "Reviews" section, which is arguably the site's must useful feature, reviews are sensibly categorized by product type, making navigation quite simple. Each review consists of a rating (on a 10-point scale); short blurbs highlighting "the good," "the bad," and "the bottom line"; a full-length, detailed critique; a photo gallery; "Buying Choices" with prices from and links to reputable online stores; the ability to compare with similar products; a list of product specifications; and opinions about the product from fellow site users. Many reviews also include a video component—usually the reviewer toying with and talking about the product.

Why You Should Visit

Purchasing high-tech merchandise is an expensive endeavor—and often a confusing one. That's a dangerous combination. But with a little help from CNET, you'll know all of your options and the pros and

cons of each. While CNET.com is an invaluable resource for would-be consumers, it also keeps you up to speed on news and developments in the technology sector better than most sites. Along with its an easy-to-navigate design and all its multimedia tools, CNET avoids the trap of catering only to tekkies. Because the site limits information-age jargon to a minimum, even users who don't work for Microsoft or Apple can find CNET.com beneficial.

Keep This in Mind

These days, it's common practice for television news programs to drive viewers to its Web site. CNET, however, was truly the first to integrate broadcast and online mediums. *CNET Central*, a weekly television series that began airing on USA Network and the Sci-Fi Channel in April 1995 (at about the same time CNET Online launched), used onscreen icons to alert viewers that more information was available at the CNET Web site. During the next few years, CNET developed and aired several other television shows, including *CNET News.com* on CNBC (which debuted in 1999). But by 2001, CNET abandoned broadcast television to focus solely on the Internet and the increasing video capabilities it offered. Those broadcast roots, however, remain evident online at its CNET TV site (go to www.cnettv.com or use the link on the CNET.com home page), which functions essentially as its own cable channel and is where you'll find some of the best original video content produced exclusively for the Web. And by concentrating strictly on its online presence, CNET Networks has expanded its domain and now controls dozens of sites: MetaCritic.com, GameSpot.com, mySimon.com, Search.com, TV.com, Webshots.com, MP3.com, and a host of others.

Off the Record

In 1994, Microsoft cofounder Paul Allen realized the potential of CNET, investing $5 million in CNET before it even aired any of its television programming or launched its Web site.

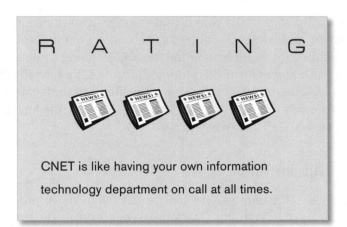

RATING

CNET is like having your own information technology department on call at all times.

21

Columbia Broadcasting Service (CBS) News

www.cbsnews.com

Overview

If there ever was truly a "golden age" of broadcast journalism, then the Columbia Broadcasting Service (CBS) was its royal court. From the infancy of television news in the early 1950s through the next tumultuous decade, figures such as Edward R. Murrow and Walter Cronkite became journalistic icons, and CBS (which was known as "The Tiffany Network") was seen as the gold standard in this increasingly omnipresent medium.

To repeat a cliché, times have changed. "Broadcast journalism" has morphed into a many-headed hydra of television networks, cable stations, Internet news providers, radio (free and satellite subscription), and even podcasts. The days when one company or broadcast outlet could dominate the news business are long gone.

And yet, despite the encroachment of competition from all sides—and even the head start many news agencies have had in adapting to new technology—CBS News offers a Web presence that is, in many ways, still the gold standard. Its site is one of the most comprehensive, extensive, and innovative of any major media outlet.

What You'll Find There

There are really two levels of the CBS News Web site: what you'll see when you sign on and what awaits you as you click further into the news and features on the main page.

The site carries all of the news of the day, of course, from updates on the war in Iraq, political races, and breaking stories around the country to lifestyle features, sports, and entertainment. Each of these stories is usually presented in a standard text article, with most

accompanied by a video clip and streaming audio. What makes the site such a delight is the depth of coverage available to Web surfers. Many of the stories posted on the site include links to sidebars that present things like historical timelines, opinion columns, photo galleries, and even blogs. The site's coverage of Iraq, for example, is remarkable, featuring detailed geographical overviews of the relevant Middle East countries, stories about the Muslim world and its people, cultural commentary, timelines of the war and benchmark events in Iraq's past, blogs by Mideast correspondents, and an archive of speeches from world leaders about the Iraq situation. There are also links to opinion columns and editorials of a wide political stripe.

Such depth is not uncommon for many of the subjects covered on the site, from bird flu to the NFL draft. With first-rate, first-hand reporting, video, background stories, "readers reply" message boards, and extensive archives of related material, the site is a news junkie's bonanza.

Why You Should Visit

Perhaps the single best feature of this impressive Web site is the section called the "Public Eye," a hybrid of in-house commentary and public ombudsman. Set up to look like a blog, the "Public Eye" offers insights on the news—and the compiling of the news—that are truly original and useful. The mission of the "Public Eye" is described in the following way on the site: "Public Eye will be run by a team of independent and experienced journalists. They will take questions, criticisms and observations from our vast and articulate audience to the people of CBS News and try to come back with some answers, explanations and analysis." That description does little justice to the smart and savvy commentary that awaits the reader of this surprisingly entertaining and informative blog.

Keep This in Mind

The once-proud reputation of CBS News has been somewhat sullied by some high-profile screw-ups, most notably the controversial 2004 report about President George W. Bush's record of service in the Texas National Guard, which suggested the president had missed much of his compulsory service. Former anchor Dan Rather was forced to apologize on air for his reliance on documents that later turned out to be forgeries.

Off the Record

CBS News watchers—and media commentators around the world— reacted with surprise (and, in some venues, outrage) to the announcement that Katie Couric, the popular co-anchor of NBC's

CBS NEWS BLOGS

PublicEye
INSIDE THE NEWS, INSIDE CBS.

Public Eye looks inside CBS News and the rest of the press.

Today Show, was to succeed the veteran Rather in the anchor chair. Questions centered on whether Couric had the experience to front a news division of such journalistic distinction and tradition. (CBS countered by reminding critics that Couric worked as NBC News' Pentagon reporter in the 1980s.[1])

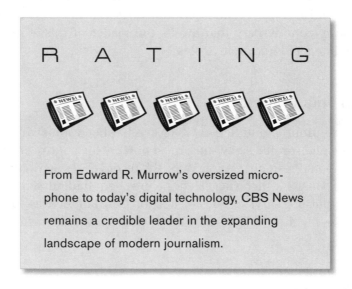

From Edward R. Murrow's oversized microphone to today's digital technology, CBS News remains a credible leader in the expanding landscape of modern journalism.

Endnote

1. From CBS Press release announcing Couric's appointment (www.cbscorporation.com/news/prdetailsphp?id=463)

22

Congressional Quarterly

www.cq.com

Overview

Say what you want about the U.S. Congress—and much has been said about it, from Mark Twain to Will Rogers to Maureen Dowd—there's no doubt that what happens in the halls of Congress usually becomes front-page news.

That fact wasn't lost upon newspaperman Nelson Poynter, who with his wife Henrietta founded a news service in 1945 called the *Congressional Quarterly*, with the aim of helping local newspapers stay on top of the legislative comings and goings in our nation's Capitol. Poynter (who lent his name to the journalistic organization the Poynter Institute) might never have realized that his modest aim of reporting on Congress would result in one of the most respected and valuable vehicles in modern journalism.

The *Congressional Quarterly* Web presence is impressive. If you're a policy wonk who lives for legislative updates or a fed-up citizen who lives to rail against political chicanery, CQ.com is for you.

What You'll Find There

On the home page of CQ.com, you'll find several news stories dealing with—what else?—the U.S. Congress. These include analytical pieces dealing with the prospects of a bill's passage, reports about grass-roots efforts to support or enact certain legislation, and interviews with senators, congressional members, and governors about pending legislation.

Aside from those fairly traditional political stories, the CQ.com page also offers plenty of links for people who like their politics served in a deeper dish. These include "CQ Politics," a collection of news articles, profiles, analyses, and even "political trivia" about the workings of Congress; "CQ Midday," which provides daily updated

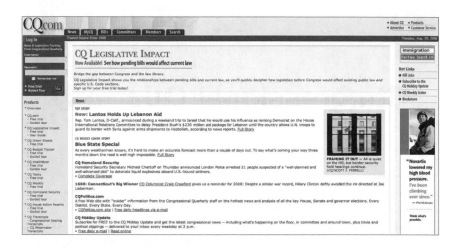

congressional news "including what's happening on the floor, in committee, and around town—delivered to your inbox every week-day at 2 PM"; "CQ Budget Tracker," for die-hard money people who like to follow the byzantine budget appropriation process (and, per-haps fittingly, requires a subscription fee); and even more specialized services such as "CQ HealthBeat" and "CQ Green Sheets," a special-ized service that covers environmental and energy policies.

Additional links will take you to other niche areas dealing with Congress—from a service that provides transcripts of hearings and committee meetings to a listing of "Hill Jobs," featuring ads for every-thing from summer interns to senior communications directors for prominent lawmakers. And if all that reading online isn't enough to slake your political thirst, there's a bookstore, "CQ Books and Special Supplements," that offers *Congressional Quarterly*-produced titles like *The New Congressional Demographic* and *Politics in America* for the truly politically inclined.

Why You Should Visit

Any random flip through a basic cable package of channels will reveal that politics and inside-the-Beltway maneuvering is the No. 1 topic for the media-chattering class. The last decade has seen an explosion of pundits, pollsters, and political prophets opining about the future of our democracy and the men and women who seek to move up within the congressional hierarchy.

Is it a good development that politics is now covered like a horse race, light on substance but heavy on speculation and strategizing? Likely not. But rather than lament the passing of "serious journalism," it's probably better to educate oneself about who the players are and what they're really up to rather than to throw up one's hands and stop paying attention altogether. *Congressional Quarterly*'s Web site might be top-heavy with an eye-glazing amount of political minutiae, but at least somebody's paying attention. You probably should be, too.

Keep This in Mind

You won't get news about Madonna—unless she's testifying in front of a congressional committee. Nor will you find news about sports (unless it's a hearing on illegal steroid use) or natural disasters (unless there's a pending vote on a disaster relief package). *Congressional Quarterly* has an unrelenting focus on the echo chamber of Capitol Hill. It covers Congress with the kind of focus that makes Poli-Sci professors' hearts palpitate. But for an overview of what's going on in the wider world, you'll have to go elsewhere.

Off the Record

Although it's called *Congressional Quarterly*, the publication was only published on a quarterly basis during its first year of operation in 1945. After that, it began publishing in weekly installments, and then, finally, in daily form.[1] Today, its Web site is updated regularly with flashes, bulletins, and legislative alerts issued around the clock.

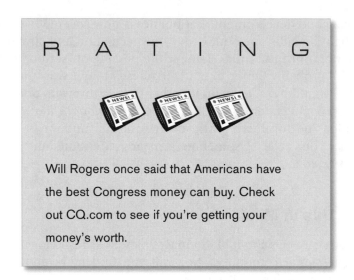

RATING

Will Rogers once said that Americans have the best Congress money can buy. Check out CQ.com to see if you're getting your money's worth.

Endnote

1. From the Wikipedia (wikipedia.org) article on the *Congressional Quarterly*.

23

Consumer Reports
www.consumerreports.org

Overview

If there's one quality that defines America—notwithstanding its diversity and cultural diffusion—it's probably consumerism. This is a nation of buyers. You can buy stuff at 24-hour convenience stores and department stores, through catalogs, over the phone, and, of course, on the Internet. Everyone, it seems, is comparing prices, shopping, or returning something they bought—creating an endless capitalistic loop of searches and purchase.

How informed all these buyers are is anybody's guess. Given the long return lines at most customer service counters, there are apparently a lot of dissatisfied consumers. Well, not everyone knows a real bargain when they see one. If they did, they would be taking advantage of a great bargain—largely free, in fact—for all consumers: the online version of the buyers' bible *Consumer Reports*.

The Internet incarnation of the famously meticulous magazine is a different publication, to be sure, with almost none of the specific product ratings available to non-subscribers. Yet there's still a good deal of useful information that will raise your shopping IQ and teach you a few things about the products and services you're already using. If you're willing to navigate around the many "Subscriber Only" articles on the Web page—a bit of an annoyance—you'll emerge a wiser consumer.

What You'll Find There

The home page for ConsumerReports.org is divided fairly evenly among dozens of traditional product reviews (marked with a parenthetical "R"), which you have to subscribe to get, and lots of articles under the more generic "Consumer News" icon. But don't despair: There's some really great stuff stowed away in the "free" section of the

Web site. Take water heaters, for instance. If you're not a subscriber, you won't get the specific ratings and energy efficiency data on any of the major brands available, but you will find informative articles about *how* to shop for water heaters—what questions to ask, how to gauge the size of the unit you'll need, what the standard industry efficiency ratings are, and how to spot a lemon.

This is the modus operandi of most of the articles in this section, providing highly informative "how-to" guides, whether you're looking for lawn care services, exterior paint, computers, or an automobile. The free articles tell you what to look for, in general. If you want to know, however, whether a particular make and model rates in *Consumer Reports'* eyes, you'll have to subscribe (though the dirty little secret here is that most public libraries carry *Consumer Reports*, so you can save the subscription fee simply be visiting your local library).

Lots of general interest-type articles are available on Consumer Reports.org. Across the top of the page runs a list of links to the following categories: "Cars," "Appliances," "Electronics and

Computers," "Health and Fitness," "Personal Finance," "Babies and Kids," "Travel," and "Food." Each of these links takes you to a page that, again, is divided between subscriber-only ratings and broader articles aimed at making you a more savvy consumer of these particular goods and services.

Why You Should Visit

Why should you visit ConsumerReports.org? It's always buying season, that's why. And it's unrealistic to expect anyone to be an expert on everything—from just what to pack if you're traveling with an infant on a plane to determining which kind of mulch might be harmful to household pets. The articles in the "Babies and Kids" section are particularly useful and plentiful—offering tips on everything from childproofing your home to baby shower checklists.

There's no shortage of places asking for your money, and no paucity of products that claim they will change your life. Even though the particular ratings would be nice to have by merely clicking, everyone can benefit from a good, basic consumer education.

Keep This in Mind

You have to take what they're offering. If you're looking for information about buying caulk for your tub, and the site doesn't offer such information, you're once again on your own. In almost all the areas where Consumer Reports. org offers general information, there are many other Web sites that also offer similar information— sometimes including more detailed, step-by-step information. This site is a great place to become

Conditions & Treatments from **Consumer Reports**

MedicalGuide.org

- *ConsumerReportsMedical Guide.org Home*
- **Conditions A-Z Index**
- **Drug reviews A-Z Index**
- **Natural medicine ratings**

ConsumerReportsMedicalGuide.org provides trusted, fact-based, straight forward Ratings for thousands of treatment, drugs, and natural medicines.

▶ **Take tour**
▶ **Join now!**

more familiar with many goods and services, but only as a first step. You might still have some homework ahead of you (depending, of course, on how deeply you wish to get into a subject).

Off the Record

Perhaps not unexpectedly, *Consumer Reports'* verdicts on some products have irked certain manufacturers. In one celebrated case, the Bose speaker company challenged a 1984 article that negatively rated the speakers. Bose claimed that the wording of the rating was libelous. The court agreed—though the $210,000 monetary judgment against the magazine was eventually overturned.[1]

R A T I N G

Want to remain at the mercy of a fast-talking salesperson? If not, your shopping spree begins here.

Endnote

1. From the Wikipedia (wikipedia.org) article on *Consumer Reports*.

24

Democratic National Committee (DNC)

www.democrats.org

Overview

During the past three decades, the Democratic Party has played the role of little brother in the world of the two-party system in America. While the Democrats have struggled to find their way in the political landscape of the late 20th and early 21st centuries, the well-oiled Republican machine has cruised through the country, painting it red along the way, fueled by the fire of talk radio.

With a Republican monopoly controlling the AM dial, some Democrats looked to capitalize on the uncharted territory of the Internet. During the Democratic presidential primary in 2003, Howard Dean turned the World Wide Web into a virtual ATM by attracting streams of small donations (on average, less than $80 each) from individual supporters—"a strategy that transformed a former governor from the 49th-largest state with no national fund-raising network into the best-financed Democrat in the presidential campaign."[1]

A pioneer of Internet campaigning, Dean's use of the Web not only raised record funds but also helped galvanize support. While the Dean campaign eventually ended before a single primary win, many experts credit him with revolutionizing the Internet's function and purpose in political campaigns—one saying "[H]e's going to be a milestone in the history of the Internet"[2] and another calling his legacy of teaching "people how to use the social networking piece of the Internet ... permanent and lasting."[3]

Tapped in 2005 as the new leader of the Democratic National Committee (DNC), it's no surprise Dean has emphasized the organization's Web site and fundraising forces in tandem from early in his tenure.

What You'll Find There

The first item visitors to Democrats.org will usually see is a banner graphic that spotlights the site's current top feature. This link, which seems to change quite often, can range in topic from an ad soliciting funds during election season to a special report on the anniversary of a major event, from a recap of a Democratic convention to profiles of important figures during Black History Month, and from a message about the party's agenda to a strong statement on the war in Iraq.

Between the Democratic Party masthead and the aforementioned banner is a horizontal navigation tool listing the site's various features: a blog titled "Kicking Ass"; a section called "Our Party," which highlights the organization's current setup, its leaders, and its history; a place to take "Action," from donating funds and volunteering time to registering to vote and writing a letter to a newspaper editor; the Democratic "Agenda" detailing the party platform; a "Local" section with links to state party Web sites and local contact information; a "People" page focusing on minority and under-represented communities; and a "Press" section that includes the latest news releases, DNC research and special reports, and transcripts, along with the actual audio, of the weekly Democratic radio address.

At the bottom of the home page (below the site's two featured articles), the top headlines are listed in each of four sections—"the blog," "national," "local," and "communities"—to make navigation of the site even easier. Much of the site's content—its blog included—is derived from news reports (the DNC adds its thoughts) and from the editorial pages of the *New York Times*, *Washington Post*, and *Los Angeles Times*. When such items are cited or excerpted, the DNC provides links to the full article. From the DNC's blog page, users can link to several dozen other blogs—mostly those with a similar mindset as the Democratic Party.

Down the right side of the home page are several logos that link to special sections of the site. In the past, these sections have included a "Republican Culture of Corruption" dossier, designed to look like a file folder with tabs for "Corruption/Abuse of Power," "Cronies," "Smear Campaigns," and "Coverups/Stonewalling"; an "Information Resource Center" for the war in Iraq, featuring a timeline of events, news, blogs, troop deployment by state, maps of Iraq and the region, and regularly updated statistics on the money spent and lives lost in Iraq; and, of course, the requisite "Contribute" prompt.

Why You Should Visit

While much of the content of Democrats.org naturally focuses on what's wrong with Republicans and their actions, the DNC also wisely

uses its Web presence to clearly (and often specifically) elucidate its alternative agenda. Despite an abundance of content, the site maintains a clean design, allowing visitors to search and read with little strain. Although partisanship will largely determine who visits this site, Dean's mission to revitalize the party at every level is largely reflected in its overhauled online endeavor—reason enough for those on the other side of the fence to log on and take note.

Keep This in Mind

¿Usted habla Español? By simply clicking on the "Español" link prominently located at the far right of the horizontal navigation menu, users are taken to the Spanish-language version of Democrats.org (El Partido Demócrata)—a completely separate section of the Web site, not simply a conversion of the entire site from English to Spanish. The format of the section is nearly identical to the rest of the site; it also includes a blog, along with stories of interest to the Hispanic community—typically a Democratic stronghold.

Off the Record

The Democratic Party is one of the oldest political parties in the world. Established by Andrew Jackson in the 1820s, the Democratic Party can trace its roots even further back in history to Thomas Jefferson's Democratic-Republican Party of the 1790s. The Democratic Party held its first national convention in 1832, but the DNC was not formed until 16 years later during the 1848 national convention.

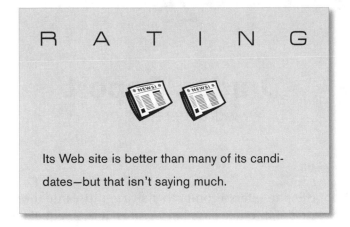

RATING

Its Web site is better than many of its candidates—but that isn't saying much.

Endnotes

1. Glen Justice, "Howard Dean's Internet push: Where will it lead?" *New York Times*, Nov, 2, 2003.
2. Todd S. Purdum, "The Dean comet: So what was that all about," *New York Times*, Feb, 22, 2004.
3. Ibid.

25

Drudge Report

www.drudgereport.com

Overview

The Drudge Report offers a comprehensive glimpse into the very best and very worst of Internet-based news sites. It is, in equal measures, timely and premature, informed and purely speculative, comprehensive and narrow-minded, user-friendly and totally unwieldy. How can one site represent the extremes of both heroic "citizen journalism" and irresponsible rumor-mongering drivel?

Welcome to the world of Matt Drudge, an innovator (and gadfly) as visionary as he is obnoxious. His site is like nothing else on the Web. Probably that's a good thing. In addition to his Web site, Drudge has carved out a niche for himself as a radio talk-show host and even as—gulp!—an author. His lone book, *Manifesto*, is much like the Drudge Report—large chunks of it utterly unreadable, interrupted by thoroughly fascinating insider tidbits about Washington culture. If Drudge wasn't so infernally knowledgeable about Washington politics and culture, he'd be easy to dismiss. But in his scattershot approach to covering the world, he sometimes gets it right. He's living proof of the axiom that even a blind squirrel finds an acorn now and again.

What You'll Find There

Visitors to Drudge's Web-based news rodeo will find a roundup of the latest headlines from all over the world—with a strong emphasis on U.S. politics—accented with a smirky, semiformal headline style reflecting Drudge's semi-distrust of authority (he regularly refers to the U.S. Supreme Court as "The Supremes"[1]). Drudge, who made his reputation in the late 1990s with a series of scoops (he accurately predicted that Bob Dole would pick Jack Kemp as his running mate in 1996, and he tipped off the world to the Monica Lewinsky scandal

while *Newsweek* was dithering over the alleged diddling), provides hundreds of links to other newspapers, news services, columnists, and Web sites, varying from the highly reputable to the conspiratorial. He's as likely to feature a lead story about a presidential campaign bid as he is to discuss the ratings of a TV movie about incest. You're as likely to get a graphic illustrating a Mideast peace proposal as you are to get an illustration of Ted Kennedy's colonoscopy. Drudge is not so much a reporter as he is a carrier pigeon, flying around the world, peeking at everything, squawking about it, leaving you to figure out what it all means and whether it's really true or a case of mistaken identity (he's been named in some high-profile libel suits).

Why You Should Visit

If people are talking about it, Drudge has it. Even in a cyber-paced world, Drudge moves fast, posting information gleaned from the network of computer, radio, and TV outlets he monitors from his Florida office/condominium.[2] He not only has a network of well-placed spies feeding him information around the clock, he also solicits stories from his readers, guaranteeing an uncensored egalitarian dialogue (that's good) and a high degree of speculative lunacy (that's bad). Drudge serves as a fitting pioneer of the movement toward "citizen journalism," a trend that has spawned readily available first-hand accounts, uncensored and unmediated, but also far too many unsubstantiated, rumor-filled subjective reports masquerading as journalism. Many bloggers owe their very existence to the success of the Drudge Report—a legacy of dubious distinction to be sure.

Keep This in Mind

Drudge has often been linked to the conservative movement in American politics. His gleeful shredding of Bill Clinton did little to dispel this connection. Drudge, however, continues to maintain that he is more libertarian than authoritarian, and there may be something to that. Though he once hosted a TV show on the conservative Fox News channel, he left after a dispute with his bosses that some say proved his independence. Still, our read of his site shows a strong rightward tilt in most headlines and "news" stories. Drudge remains the darling of some conservatives, and we get the impression that the feeling remains mutual.

Off the Record

The chattering class can't seem to reach any agreement about Drudge's worth. He's been called "an idiot with a modem" by newsman/commentator Keith Olbermann and "the kind of bold, entrepreneurial, free-wheeling, information-oriented outsider we need far more of in this country" by culture critic Camille Paglia.[3]

VISITS TO DRUDGE 8/29/06

014,304,340 IN PAST 24 HOURS
337,524,008 IN PAST 31 DAYS
3,529,175,738 IN PAST YEAR

DRUDGE ARCHIVES

DRUDGE REFERENCE DESK

EMAIL: DRUDGE@DRUDGEREPORT.COM

BE SEEN! RUN ADS ON DRUDGE REPORT...

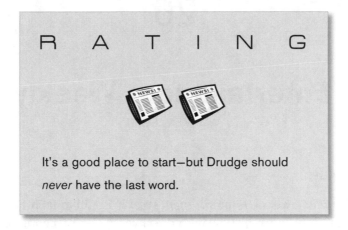

RATING

It's a good place to start—but Drudge should *never* have the last word.

Endnotes

1. See the Drudge Report for April 4, 2004.
2. See the Wikipedia article on Drudge at wikipedia.org/wiki/MattDrudge; for additional background, see *Drudge: Manifesto* (New York: New American Library, 2000).
3. Ibid.

26

Entertainment Weekly

www.ew.com

Overview

In print media years, *Entertainment Weekly* is still in its infancy. But the magazine—born in 1990 with the silver spoon of a conglomerate parent (Time Inc.) in its pages—is as well known, if not more popular, than other pubs with an eye on Hollywood's doings. The magazine's younger Web sibling, however, is already an Internet veteran: "Entertainment Weekly Online was one of the first major editorial Web sites when it debuted on Time Inc.'s Pathfinder Network in October 1994."[1] EW.com has undergone major surgery a couple of times during the past dozen years and has experimented with content offerings and access restrictions (i.e., magazine subscribers only). For EW.com, however, older does not mean wiser.

What You'll Find There

The most noticeable element of the home page is a large vertical (and colorful) box presenting the day's "Photo Gallery," which links users to a series of related photographs of the publicity sort or to one of the site's many "lists." To its left, several stories are teased under the "Today's Latest" heading, complete with a small thumbnail pic, headline, summary, and "Read More" link. On the top of the home page, sandwiched below the masthead and above the aforementioned teaser, a navigation bar lets you easily select one of seven clearly demarcated sections: "News & Notes," "Movies," "DVD & Video," "TV," "Music," "Books," and "Pop Culture."

After clicking to one of these departments, you are greeted by lots of headlines and photos that link to usually brief articles, reviews, the day's "News Roundups," interviews with Hollywood elite, and previews of upcoming entertainment. Each section features a chart—

box office figures, DVD rentals, most-watched shows, top albums, and best-selling fiction—at the top right of the page.

EW.com is review-heavy, but the e-zine is equally in love with lists—from the most memorable Super Bowl commercials to the 10 most surprising Oscar snubs to the 10 best Bond girls. These lists are usually presented in a photo slideshow format. No matter where you click, you can count on finding a list of something, be it top music downloads, top DVD rentals, top book sales, or anything else that can possibly be ranked. And then, of course, there is "The Must List"—a top-10 list of entertainment recommendations for each upcoming week that commonly consists of a hodgepodge of media choices ranging from a video clip download suggestion to a DVD box set of a long-forgotten season of a long-forgotten television show.

Why You Should Visit

A 21st-century interactive experience is not the reason to head to EW.com—though the site has slightly increased its video/audio content of late. Despite its claim of being one of the first "major editorial Web sites," the site has not progressed at the same rate as the Internet. But even EW.com now has a blog. EW.com once boasted on its "About Us" page that in October 2000 *Women's Wear Daily* said the site "is like *Entertainment Weekly* after two martinis." And that is exactly the right moment to actually enjoy this e-zine. Then, at least, "PopWatch"—a daily blog where a somewhat predictable roster of writers post off-the-cuff comments about the latest Hollywood gossip—can be enjoyed. The writers often end with a prompt, hoping readers will post a comment. And many do. So while the world is on the brink of full-blown bedlam, users can chime in on the ultimate question of the day: "Who's your favorite American Idol of all time?"

But visiting EW.com has its benefits. Unlike some entertainment-focused publications geared toward the Hollywood "insider," *Entertainment Weekly*, and its online companion, fashions its content for a more general reader—and largely succeeds. Through clear, brief, and simple (though sometimes overly so, often eliminating any depth and context) reviews, it appeals to *anyone* who wants an idea on how best to spend their entertainment-allotted allowance, be it at the box office, the video game store, or the bookseller. Plus, fans of Stephen King—and there are, based on his sales, many—are in for a treat. In his somewhat irregular column, "The Pop of King," the horror master provides his take on pop culture, from his favorite TV shows to his disgust with *Headline News* anchor Nancy Grace, and yes, even Britney Spears.

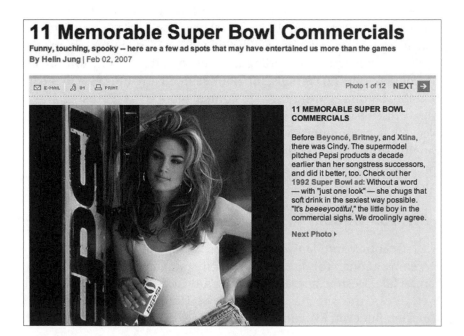

11 Memorable Super Bowl Commercials

Funny, touching, spooky — here are a few ad spots that may have entertained us more than the games
By Helin Jung | Feb 02, 2007

E-MAIL   IM   PRINT   Photo 1 of 12   NEXT

11 MEMORABLE SUPER BOWL COMMERCIALS

Before Beyoncé, Britney, and Xtina, there was Cindy. The supermodel pitched Pepsi products a decade earlier than her songstress successors, and did it better, too. Check out her 1992 Super Bowl ad: Without a word — with "just one look" — she chugs that soft drink in the sexiest way possible. "It's *beeeeyootiful*," the little boy in the commercial sighs. We droolingly agree.

Next Photo ▶

Keep This in Mind

A small percentage of EW.com's content is Web-exclusive. Save for "The Q&A" interviews, such as the one in January 2006 with former *Nightline* host Ted Koppel or an exclusive with the subject of the magazine's most recent cover story, its claims of producing an abundance of online-only material seems a bit over-hyped. But you can access the site's complete "Magazine Archive" of issues dating back to the publication's debut in 1990 (if, of course, you feel the need to read about k. d. lang or recall what movies had success more than 10 years ago).

Off the Record

Logging on to EW.com can sometimes seem like opening your mailbox to find a slough of subscription solicitations. Thanks to a heavy dose of ads offering two free trial issues and promoting the print edition, the site seems to want its users to sign off and sign up.

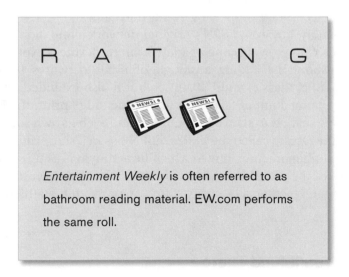

R A T I N G

Entertainment Weekly is often referred to as bathroom reading material. EW.com performs the same roll.

Endnotes

1. www.ew.com/ew/aboutus, Jan. 13, 2005

27

ESPN
espn.go.com

Overview

On the seventh day, God created ESPN. Well, not exactly. But it was on the seventh day of September 1979 that an all-sports-all-the-time cable network called ESPN debuted on American television sets. While sports had always played an integral part in American life—a religion of sorts—ESPN eventually became the house of worship for millions of fanatical followers. By the time it celebrated 25 years of existence, ESPN had expanded into a mega-church. Building on the widespread popularity of its cliché-riddled sportscast, ESPN filled the time between the repetitive airings of *SportsCenter* with other sport-specific studio programs, original movies, ongoing series, and even reality shows (along with actual coverage of sporting events and games).

Ultimately, however, ESPN's original network alone did not fulfill the needs of its growing congregation of sports devotees. Not only did ESPN respond by adding a slough of other networks including ESPN2, ESPN Classic, and ESPNEWS, but it also extended its reach beyond the medium of television to include radio, print, the Web, a cell phone service, a chain of restaurants, and even its own sports version of the Oscars called the ESPYs. ESPN has in a short run become a cultural phenomenon, one in which its acronym is as recognizable as those of the professional sports leagues it covers, its cast of characters often reaching a celebrity status on par with the athletes they observe.

What You'll Find There

The design of ESPN.com can be perceived in one of two ways: Either it appears overcrowded or it contains no wasted space. The latter proves to be the case. That's because the wide world of sports in the 21st century is vast, and ESPN.com seems to be making an implicit

vow to cover it *all* for the tens of millions of people who sign on every month.

It leads with an attention-grabbing package—a bold, catchy headline, action photo, a blurb, and links to related articles, commentary, and video—at the top-left third of the page just below the masthead and horizontal navigation bar. The top-middle third of the home page is filled with the latest sports headlines (which also act as links to full stories) that typically include game previews and recaps but can also frequently read like the police blotter. Most of the stories included in the "ESPNEWS Headlines" section are concise, non-bylined stories from either the Associated Press or ESPN.com wire services. Its emphasis on video content is evident as soon as you arrive. Receiving prominent placement on the home page is "ESPN Motion," which consists of broadband video clips derived from ESPN's many networks and usually includes game highlights, news read by its anchors, or commentary from its analysts. Many of the site's written pieces are accompanied by related video.

Some of ESPN.com's content (blogs, real-time scores, recruiting and scouting information, the latest rumors, analysts' insights, fantasy-league tools, and podcasts of the top ESPN Radio shows) is restricted to users with "Insider" access. This exclusive material is clearly labeled with an orange "in" icon. Insider access requires a subscription to *ESPN The Magazine*, which has quickly become to sports what *Rolling Stone* is to music. But a majority of the site's content is available to anyone who logs on.

Why You Should Visit

Saying that ESPN.com's coverage is average is like calling Michael Jordan a decent basketball player. If it's sports, it's here in some form—straight news-style stories, thoughtful pieces of analysis from one of ESPN's many "experts," biting screeds from its sizable stable of voices, and, of course, video features (just in case you miss one of the many reruns of *SportsCenter* on any given day).

ESPN.com, just like its namesake network, is the definitive source for sports information, covering everything from the NFL to professional rodeo (giving every sport a "Front Page" and what seems like its own site). There's also EXPN.com, treating extreme sports with the same seriousness and importance as America's pastime. And for those who want more than standings, statistics, and scores—all of which can certainly be found at ESPN.com—the site's "Page 2" section, for which Hunter S. Thompson wrote regularly before his death in early 2005, offers offbeat perspectives. "SportsNation" is the site's main interactive component, letting you chat with ESPN personalities, participate in polls that post

results in a fashion similar to state-by-state electoral maps, and even become a "talking head" yourself. And as an antidote to a sports world plagued by sound bites and highlights, be sure not to miss ESPN.com's "E-Ticket," an ongoing series of magazine-length feature stories with multimedia tools that look behind, and often beyond, the headlines. The latest installment of "E-Ticket" is featured midway down the middle column of the home page, along with a link to the archive. From profiles to investigations, "E-Ticket" is an all-access pass to the best sports journalism being practiced today.

Keep This in Mind

ESPN.com has garnered numerous honors for its work—and popularity—on the Internet. In 2002, it won the Society of Professional Journalists' Sigma Delta Chi Award for online investigative reporting—a sports reporting rarity—for a series about the torture of athletes and other allegations of abuse by the Iraqi Olympic Committee called "Blood on the Rings." The following year, the Online News Association awarded ESPN.com with a general excellence award. During a seven-year span beginning in 2000, it won the International Academy of Digital Arts & Sciences' Webby Award for best sports site four times and captured the People's Voice award (chosen through a public vote rather than by the academy's judges) for best sports site each of those seven years.

Off the Record

ESPN.com is the most visited sports site on the Web, destroying all of the competition month after month. In March 2006, ESPN.com attracted more than 18 million people to its site, nearly 4 million more than the next closest sports site (Fox Sports) and 13 million more than the venerable *Sports Illustrated*'s site. Not surprisingly, 82 percent of its visitors are male.

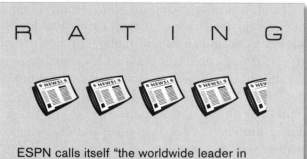

ESPN calls itself "the worldwide leader in sports." More often than not, that's exactly what it is, thanks in large part to its strong presence on the Web and the comprehensive coverage it offers online.

28

Federal Bureau of Investigation (FBI)

www.fbi.gov

Overview

From its very inception, the Federal Bureau of Investigation (FBI) has been making front-page news. Some of the most historically significant events of the 20th century—the pursuit of John Dillinger, the clandestine surveillance of Martin Luther King Jr., the infiltration and prosecution of the Mafia—were the result of FBI activity. And the roster of notable personages who have been associated with the FBI is just as daunting (beginning and ending with the monstrously influential J. Edgar Hoover). From special agent and famed gangland G-man Melvin Pervis to the controversial recent director Louis Freeh, most Americans have some knowledge of this world-renowned investigative force.

One might think a special investigative agency like the FBI would desire secrecy, but in many ways the agency has always sought an elevated public profile. From holding press conferences during the Chicago crime syndicate wars in the 1930s to its latest publicity tool—a Web site—the agency seems eager for Americans to know what it's doing (at least the stuff the agency *wants* you to know).

And what the agency wants you to know is vast. The Web site covers every imaginable aspect of the agency, from its day-to-day operations to its history, hiring practices, and long-term crime-fighting plans. There are quizzes, "Most Wanted" updates, crime alerts, and a trove of material for researchers. The site is packed. It's every junior G-man's dream.

What You'll Find There

As with most news and information Web sites, the FBI's main page begins with a "Top Story" icon. But there's a difference here. The FBI's

"Top Story" is just as likely to be a user-friendly feature—such as its recent "Are You Crime Savvy? Quiz Yourself on Recent FBI News"—instead of actual news.

Just below the "Top Story" is a list of headlines under the banner "FBI in the News." This is mostly a press release-type roster of stories about arrests of prominent criminals, new initiatives to fight corruption in the corporate sector, or announcements of plea agreements in cases of fraud or money laundering.

A fairly generic-sounding "More Stories" section includes stories that might not have made the newspaper or television news, such as the introduction of new safety protocols for FBI agents or quirky criminal-related stories (a recent posting boasted of the "Case of the Concrete Conspiracy"). And, of course, just as a reminder that the FBI is out there, protecting us all, there's a regularly updated FBI "Gotcha" story about the apprehension of a long-sought criminal.

The rest of the page consists of what can mostly be considered public service-type stories, dealing with in-depth looks at how the

agency does its job, from fighting terrorism and public corruption to policing white-collar crime and engaging in counterintelligence. Clicking on any of these areas, which can be found in the "What We Investigate" section, leads you to separate pages filled with case histories, background on each of these specialized areas, a Q&A section, more quizzes, hotlines, and information to help citizens report any unscrupulous or suspicious activity.

And, of course, there's the famous "Most Wanted" list, complete with photos and descriptions of fugitives (there's a separate list for terrorists) who are on the lam and awaiting capture by the feds. There's also a list of current kidnappings under investigation, as well as an updated roster of missing persons and even information about sexual predators.

Why You Should Visit

Hopefully, you'll never need the services of the FBI—nor be sought by any of their agents. But just because your brush with the Bureau might never be closer than your local cineplex or television rerun of *The Untouchables* doesn't mean you shouldn't try to understand more about this influential and historically important agency. And in an era when the erosion of civil rights and the limits of individual freedom have become hotly debated points of contention, it's good to know what the most powerful law enforcement agency in the country is doing.

It's also worth noting that, for such a serious agency, the Web site is actually kind of fun. From learning about fingerprint technology to how to submit crime tips, from a highly useful "Internet Safety for Kids" tutorial to the crime quizzes, the site is more engaging than its foreboding namesake might suggest.

Keep This in Mind

The FBI has come under harsh criticism during the past decade for a number of public missteps. In the 1990s, it was assailed for its role in the catastrophic Waco incident involving the Branch Davidian separatist group, as well as for its erroneous leaking of Richard Jewell's name as a suspect in the bombing at the Atlanta Summer Olympics in 1996. Early in 2001, longtime FBI agent Robert Hanssen was caught selling secrets to the Russians. More recently, the agency was criticized by the 9/11 Commission for not pursuing intelligence leads that might have prevented the tragedy.

Off the Record

In his book *The Secret Life of J. Edgar Hoover,* author Anthony Summers claims that J. Edgard Hoover and Clyde Tolson, assistant director of the FBI, were lovers, carrying on a secret homosexual relationship for decades.[1]

RATING

Do a little investigating of your own.

Endnote

1. From www.spartacus.schoolnet.co.uk/USAhooverE.htm

29

First Amendment Center
www.firstamendmentcenter.org

Overview

After more than 200 years, you would think there'd be *some* agreement about what the First Amendment means—or at least what it's supposed to do. Yet legal scholars, journalists, politicians, and citizens' groups continue to wrangle about just what freedoms this oft-cited paragraph ensures. On the surface, this should be a simple question. The rights themselves are named clearly and specifically: religion, assembly, speech, press, and petition.

Yet the debate has never been more heated—and the stakes have never been higher. In this era of governmental eavesdropping, the expansion of police powers, and the ever-growing war on terror, the power of the First Amendment—and its traditional role as the freedom of first resort for civil libertarians—is under perpetual scrutiny.

Perhaps not unexpectedly, there is a Web site dedicated entirely to the First Amendment that explores this bedrock constitutional precept from just about every conceivable angle (and doing it in language that is clear and accessible to non-scholars of constitutional law).

Want to find out more about the First Amendment than you ever thought was worth knowing? Have we got a Web site for you: the First Amendment Center.

What You'll Find There

Much like other Web sites, the First Amendment Center is organized according to the hierarchy of "Top News," "Other Headlines," "Analysis," and "Commentary," as well as an archive of Supreme Court decisions and congressional action on First Amendment issues. The leading news stories tend to revolve around issues such as the jailing of journalists or a pending court case about the First Amendment. In many ways, the site could be just another news site.

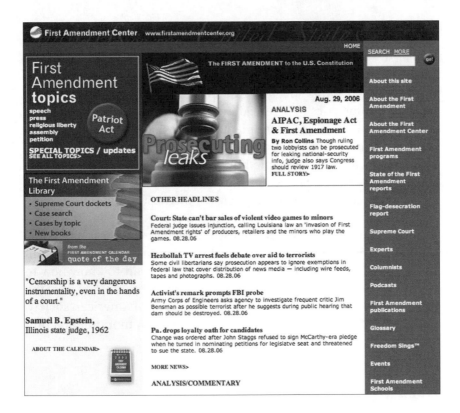

But the First Amendment Center goes deep—much more deeply than most "news" Web sites—looking at all the ways that the rights and limits of the First Amendment impact our society. The "news" stories are written with an awareness of the amendment's history and permutations, usually by experts on staff who have the constitutional grounding to provide the necessary context to make sense of the story (though they also pick up stories from the Associated Press wire).

The columnists include Nat Hentoff, a nationally recognized commentator and journalist affiliated with publications as different as the *Wall Street Journal* and the *Village Voice*. Other columnists include Paul K. McMasters, the ombudsman for the First Amendment Center, and Charles Haynes, author of numerous books and a national lecturer on First Amendment rights.

The site provides a sidebar menu linking to articles and other sites about everything from flag desecration to lesson planning for secondary school teachers. And many of the site's news stories offer links to "related" stories, which expand even further on the issues in question.

Why You Should Visit

The First Amendment has become a hot-button issue, with many of the most urgent social upheavals of the day revolving around the various interpretations of the document. From cases involving "obscene" song lyrics to the freedom to wear a Muslim headscarf to a public school, the First Amendment is increasingly being put forth as the Rosetta Stone of wide-scale civic disputes. One look at almost any other news site will reveal a plethora of First Amendment-related stories, but this site goes beyond the headlines and offers interested, curious readers a primer in the basics of the First Amendment.

There aren't too many Web sites that can serve everyone from junior high school students doing a research paper to professional journalists wanting a crash course on the amendment's history, from lawyers studying case law to citizens who just want to know how to file a Freedom of Information request. It's hard to overemphasize the importance of the First Amendment in the fabric of American society, but it's easy to appreciate a site that makes such a monumental precept so accessible.

Keep This in Mind

OK, so the First Amendment makes news—but it's not the only news. Like many other single-issue Web sites, this one tells you everything and nothing—everything about its chosen subject, nothing about the

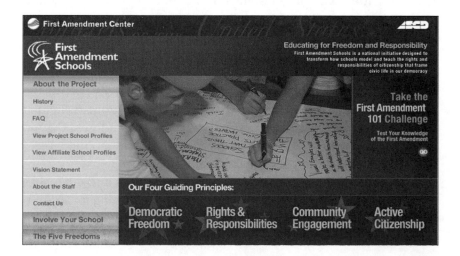

news of the day involving the usual stuff: political scandals, war, celebrity gossip, sports, or health and lifestyle. You can't fault the site for doing what it does well, but you'll definitely have to bookmark other sites if you want to consider yourself truly informed.

Off the Record

The First Amendment has been invoked in some high-profile—and rather bizarre—cases. In 1988, the Rev. Jerry Falwell sued *Hustler* magazine over a satirical ad that claimed Falwell had sexual relations with his own mother in an outhouse. Falwell was understandably outraged, but the U.S. Supreme Court ruled that the First Amendment allowed such parody under the right to free speech.

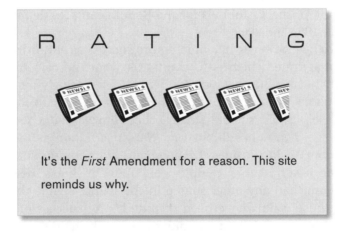

R A T I N G

It's the *First* Amendment for a reason. This site reminds us why.

30

Forbes
www.forbes.com

Overview

The dynasty started quite simply: In 1917, a leading business columnist for Hearst newspapers decided to start his own publication, using the family name for its title. Nearly a century later, *Forbes* is no longer just a surname—it's a brand name. Now running the empire—best known for its business magazine—is the founder's great-grandson, Malcolm Stevenson Forbes Jr. (better known as Steve Forbes), who made unsuccessful bids for the Republican presidential nomination in 1996 and 2000.

Forbes has, however, had much more success as editor-in-chief of *Forbes* magazine, which is to capitalists what the calculator is to mathematicians. But this tool has become increasingly more useful and valuable—for everyone from the casual investor to top executives in the business sector—since Forbes.com was launched about a decade ago. *Forbes* has dubbed its Web incarnation as the "Home Page for the World's Business Leaders" and promotes the site through ads that assert "more people get their business news from Forbes.com than any other source in the world." While the figures behind those claims have been disputed,[1] the success of the site, thriving both financially and popularly, is hardly in doubt.

What You'll Find There

Users who log on to Forbes.com will find what looks like a traditional business news site. Divided into two columns, the home page's left side contains links to five stories, each featuring a headline, byline, thumbnail photo, and three related links (usually to video and commentary). The topics covered here are generally unsurprising, but whether it's happening on Wall Street or at corporate headquarters, Forbes.com will fill readers in with original reporting, analysis, and

commentary. In the right column, you will find five headlines/links to the moment's "Top Stories" (usually business-related content from the Associated Press wire, although an occasional breaking news article may appear); two features from Forbes.com's extensive "Video Network"; two links under the heading "Faces in the News" (where familiar names like Gates and Buffet are the first word of the headline); and the latest fluctuations of the "Markets."

Across the top of the page, a menu of the site's sections—"Business," "Tech," "Markets," "Entrepreneurs," "Leadership," "Personal Finance," "ForbesLife," "Lists," and "Opinions"—hints at the depth of Forbes.com. When users roll the cursor over any of the menu headings, a second level of choices appears, displaying links to more specific—and diverse—subsections, from "Bonds" to "Philanthropy" to "Wine & Food."

Forbes magazine is best known for its various lists: the world's billionaires, the most powerful women, and the top 100 celebrities. So for those logging on to check out these famous rankings, Forbes.com doesn't disappoint. Scrolling through its "Lists" page, users will discover a peculiar collection: hundreds—each including an article, slideshow, and video—organized into about a dozen categories ranging from "Companies" and "Personal Finance" to "Health & Style" and

"Sports." So whether you're looking for the "best blended scotches," the "most luxurious spas in the world," or the "top topless beaches," Forbes.com provides the listing—and searching through them all is oddly addictive.

Why You Should Visit

If you want to learn how to make lots of money, or if you already have it but need ideas on how to spend it, Forbes.com is a valuable resource—it's part straightforward business news coverage, part shopping guide for the super rich, and part *Lifestyles of the Rich and Famous*. One user could be checking in on the S&P 500 while another is searching for the world's most expensive hotel room while still another is left spellbound by "The Hottest Billionaire Heiresses." With its broad coverage of all things "green" (and here the color refers to

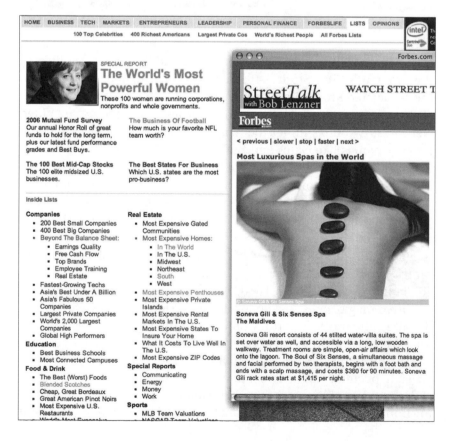

money, not the environment), Forbes.com manages to appeal to the wealthy, those who aspire to be, and anyone just obsessed with those who are.

Keep This in Mind

In the early days of the Web, questions about reliability reigned supreme. So when Forbes.com exposed the fraud perpetrated by Stephen Glass through his reporting in the *New Republic* in 1998, not only did the scoop draw attention to the Forbes.com site, but it also forced old media to take immediate notice of this new form, which had previously been looked at through a prism of skepticism. But as a result of the commendable work done by those at Forbes.com, all of Internet journalism stood to gain from the fall of one "traditional" journalist. And every news site in business today can thank Forbes.com for lending some credibility to "new media."

Off the Record

In August 2006, Forbes sold 40 percent of the company to Elevation Partners for a reported $300 million. Forbes.com was a major reason Elevation Partners, a private equity group that gets its name from the title of a song by one of its managing directors (Bono of the band U2), made the investment, saying that the site will be its central focus.

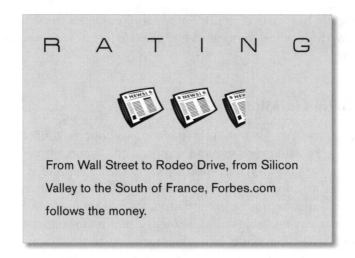

RATING

From Wall Street to Rodeo Drive, from Silicon Valley to the South of France, Forbes.com follows the money.

Endnote

1. Peter Edmonston, "At Forbes.com, lots of glitter but maybe not so many visitors," *New York Times*, Aug. 28, 2006.

31

Foreign Affairs
www.foreignaffairs.org

Overview

How you view the Web site of the venerable publication *Foreign Affairs* will depend a lot on how you answer the following question: Does size matter?

If you happen to believe it does, then you'll be favorably impressed by the publication's commitment to length. Most of the content of the Web site (gleaned largely from its print counterpart) far exceeds the length of your average news site offerings. *Foreign Affairs* is nothing if not thorough in its presentation of the events making news—and the context for understanding those events.

Those who favor a "quick hit" when checking in with their online news provider will find the *Foreign Affairs* site to be rather unaccommodating. There are none of the usual attractions of the more "mainstream" Web sites, such as snappy headlines, news digests or lifestyle featurettes, and there is no color or photographic embellishment.

So does that make the site good or bad? And, to return to our original question, does size matter?

What You'll Find There

A handful of articles offer clear (though generally uninspired) headlines. The home page features the top three articles from the most recent print issue of the publication in the upper portion of the page, running right down the middle, and a host of other articles, columns, and essays, in smaller-sized headline font, filling out the rest of the page.

Web surfers can expect each of these lengthy news essays to be about rather weighty issues, such as the instability of political leadership in sub-Saharan Africa or the decline of the radical left in Central

America. *Foreign Affairs* promises what it delivers: thoughtful, prob-ing diagnosis of the world's geopolitical temperature.

Most of the writers featured on the Web page know the terrain they write about very well. The roster of *Foreign Affairs* contributors is a Who's Who in American foreign policy over the past several decades: former secretaries of state, highly placed diplomats, academic experts, and journalists who've covered various political "hot spots" for major news organizations.

The site has an exceedingly useful "Background on the News" sec-tion, which contains articles and essays that have run in previous edi-tions of the journal but are relevant again because of some recent development on the world stage. There are a number of book reviews about works that address the foreign policy arena, from academic tomes to popular histories and best-selling policy analyses.

And, finally, the "Browse by Topic" feature allows you to call up a region of the globe and read all the relevant material published recently about that area. For die-hard policy wonks—the hardcore crowd that watches C-SPAN and can name the U.S. ambassador to most major industrialized nations—this site is nirvana.

Why You Should Visit

You won't hear most of the stuff on the *Foreign Affairs* site on the nightly news. The kind of depth and context featured on the site flies in the face of most "re-packaged" mainstream news. If it can be said in a sound bite, it won't be found on this site. Instead, Foreign Affairs.org offers challenging and occasionally dry overviews of some of the world's more complex problems. If you want simple answers that can be delivered between commercial breaks on your favorite talk radio station, don't bother bookmarking this site.

Keep This in Mind

Because most of the material is written by experts who have had genuine experience in the realm of foreign affairs, the site reflects a pronounced institutional bias. Few of the ideas encountered there represent much of a departure from the staid and steady policies of the U.S. administration. The analysis is sober, the articles

well-reasoned. But *Foreign Affairs* seldom proposes an idea that hasn't already been floated at one time or another at the State Department or the U.N. General Assembly. (This is no doubt due to the publication being an offshoot of the Council on Foreign Relations, an 80-year-old think tank with a membership that comprises a litany of well-placed Washington insiders.)

Off the Record

The Web site of the Council on Foreign Relations (www.cfr.org) is, surprisingly, much more entertaining and user-friendly than its offspring, ForeignAffairs.org. CFR.org offers daily updates on the news, analysis of breaking stories, online debates, and even podcasts. Who knew that robust global perspectives on the news could be so engaging?

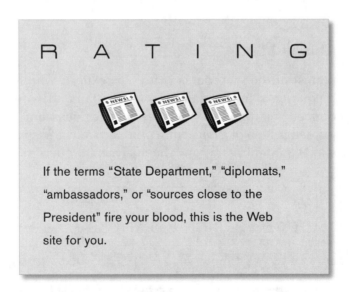

R A T I N G

If the terms "State Department," "diplomats," "ambassadors," or "sources close to the President" fire your blood, this is the Web site for you.

32

Fox News

www.foxnews.com

Overview

In October 1996, Rupert Murdoch launched the Fox News Channel in an attempt to counter a news media he viewed as dominated by liberal interests. As CEO of the News Corporation, Murdoch already controlled many major media outlets throughout the globe, including the conservative-leaning *New York Post*. But he longed for a 24-hour cable news channel, and Murdoch tapped Roger Ailes, who had experience running CNBC and America's Talking (a predecessor to MSNBC), to create and captain his broadcasting flagship. In the decade since its debut, Fox News has surpassed the viewer ratings of CNN and MSNBC combined (although in 2006 CNN still attracted more unique viewers each month), and eight of the 10 highest-rated cable news programs belong to Murdoch's network, with its nightly talk show hosted by Bill O'Reilly, currently the Fox News Channel's most identifiable figure, topping the list.

But along with the popularity attained by Fox News during its meteoric rise has come a cornucopia of criticism, much of which alleges—often accurately—a conservative bias in its "news" coverage and sometimes goes as far as to describe the channel as a propaganda arm of the Republican Party. While there is widespread belief that Fox News clearly supports, at a minimum, a conservative point of view, that alone is not the cause of the fervent debate over the brand of journalism practiced by the organization. Rather, it is Fox News' zealous denial of such bias—hiding behind a cloak of deceptive slogans such as "We Report, You Decide" and "Fair and Balanced"—that is the more disturbing aspect of the Fox News Channel. Although a place certainly exists within American journalism for opinion and commentary, by disguising its broadcasts as objective rather than disclosing its coverage as ideologically driven, Fox News is a detriment to the overall health of the news media.

What You'll Find There

Like most Web sites connected to major media outlets, FoxNews.com reflects the personality of its big brother, the Fox News Channel. The site is as loud, visually speaking, as the shouting pundits who fill its channel's lineup. And as a result of all the design noise, you will have to navigate through a site that's as chaotic as a Jackson Pollack painting (the color palate for FoxNews.com is, of course, red, white, and blue).

Above the masthead are two horizontal navigation bars stacked on top of each other. The first consists of headings typical to news sites, including "U.S.," "World," "Politics," "Business," "Health," and "Entertainment." The second menu lists links to the pages of several Fox News Channel programs—each of which consists almost entirely of video clips from recent (and in some cases, not-so-recent) broadcasts.

Under the masthead, which reserves a spot for upcoming television program notes, Fox News features its top stories, usually between one and four headlines, one of which is accompanied by a large photo. Listed in a box below are more than a dozen other headlines. While many of the stories posted in this top section of the home page are pulled from the Associated Press, FoxNews.com is often guilty of sensationalism in its selection, placement, and presentation of "top stories" (local or regional stories get top billing if they are gruesome or juicy—and not only during slow news cycles).

About six stories "Only On Fox" are featured below the top-stories section, followed by a section of lifestyle and entertainment items (many more are available on the site's "Foxlife" pages). And, of course, opinion certainly has a home at FoxNews.com. "Fox 24/7" includes video clips from several of the channel's programs during which the hosts (Neil Cavuto, John Gibson, Bill O'Reilly, and Brit Hume) offer their thoughts on issues. Links to their blogs are provided here as well, and about 10 more blogs are accessible near the bottom of the home page.

Why You Should Visit

Fox News is the most highly criticized news organization in America—so much so that a 77-minute documentary (*Outfoxed: Rupert Murdoch's War on Journalism*) condemning Fox's practices garnered much attention even without a theatrical release. But

FOX 24/7

THE O'REILLY FACTOR
Talking Points

Either Iran stops threatening the world or nobody does business with it. Period.

THE O'REILLY FACTOR
Anti-War Celebs

Raw and unfiltered: 'The Factor' confronts Fonda, Penn, Sarandon and Robbins at D.C. anti-war rally

• Read 'The Factor' transcript

YOUR WORLD W/ NEIL CAVUTO
Common Sense

Why President Bush is a Wall Street rock star

THE BIG STORY W/ JOHN GIBSON
John Gibson's My Word

Democrats are back in charge. Let the festivities begin

• Read Neil's Common Sense

• Read John's My Word

FOX BLOGS

GRETAWIRE
Embargoed speeches take the fun out of big political events

FRIENDS INSIDER
Do airline passengers need a bill of rights?

despite the criticism, it is the most-watched television news channel and one of the most visited online news sites, wielding influential power in Washington and on society as a result—reasons enough to possess an understanding of Fox News.

Keep This in Mind

"I challenge anybody to show me an example of bias in Fox News Channel," Rupert Murdoch told Salon.com in March 2001. Well, let's start with its staff. From top to bottom, Fox News is dominated by conservative voices, including its CEO, chairman, and president Roger Ailes. Ailes, who once served as a producer for Rush Limbaugh's short-lived television show, worked as a key political strategist for the presidential campaigns of Richard M. Nixon, Ronald Reagan, and the elder George Bush. Tony Snow, who was employed by the ultraconservative *Washington Times* as editorial page editor from 1987 to 1991 before becoming the chief speechwriter for the first President Bush, hosted *Fox News Sunday* (the Fox News Channel's equivalent of NBC's *Meet the Press*) from 1996 to 2003. After years of guest hosting Rush Limbaugh's radio show, Snow hosted his own talk show on Fox News Radio from late 2003 until April 2006, when President George W. Bush named him his press secretary.

Off the Record

According to an October 2003 study,[1] people who used Fox News as their primary source of news were much more likely to believe at least one of the following misperceptions: Evidence of links between Al Qaeda and Iraq were found; weapons of mass destruction were found in Iraq; and world public opinion favored the U.S. war with Iraq. Among respondents who rely primarily on Fox News, 80 percent believed at least one of these inaccurate assertions—a percentage 25 points higher than that of its main competitor (CNN), nearly double that of print sources, and about four times more than that of PBS or NPR. And yet, according to a 2006 poll conducted by Reuters and BBC, 11 percent of Americans called Fox News their most trusted news source—a higher percentage than any other news outlet in the country received.

R A T I N G

Fox News insists that it reports and then commands that we decide. Well, we've decided:
"Fair and Balanced" would be right at home in
George Orwell's dictionary of doublespeak. So
unless you want neo-con spin and Republican-
driven opinion, FoxNews.com belongs in the
no-visit zone.

Endnote

1. "Misperceptions, the media and the Iraq War," The Program on International Policy
   Attitudes at the University of Maryland and Knowledge Networks, Oct. 2, 2003
   (www.worldpublicopinion.org/pipa/articles/international_security_bt/102.php?
   nid=&id=&pnt=102&lb=brusc).

33

Globe and Mail

www.theglobeandmail.com

Overview

The *Globe and Mail* has long been considered the yardstick by which all other Canadian media are measured. Founded as a weekly in 1844 to promote the politics of the country's Reform Party, the Toronto-based newspaper soon became a respected independent daily. Eventually establishing itself as Canada's newspaper of record, it is still viewed by critics as an arm of the liberal caucus.

Enter media baron Conrad Black, who launched the conservative-leaning *National Post* in 1998 to challenge the *Globe and Mail* as the nation's newspaper. While the new competition spurred the older newspaper to make changes, namely through adding color and more content to its pages, the *Globe and Mail* had no need to alter the slogan—"Canada's National Newspaper"—it carries on the front-page banner. Throughout the national newspaper war, the *Globe and Mail* has prevailed as the circulation leader (although it continues to trail the local *Toronto Star*).

Two decades before it went online in 1995, the *Globe and Mail* established itself as an innovator of electronic information services when it became the first newspaper to create a commercially available full-text database of its print stories called InfoGlobe. While that pioneering plunge into "new media"—coupled with its visually appealing print edition (twice named the "World's Best Designed Newspaper" in the mid-1990s)—would seemingly position the *Globe and Mail* to fully exploit the medium of the Internet, neither asset has translated into an inventive and imaginative Web site, where its cornucopia of content is devoured by its unruly design.

What You'll Find There

Let's start by stating that GlobeandMail.com will not be crowned the "World's Best Designed Internet Site" anytime soon. There is, however, much content to be had if you have the stamina to outlast the visual assault, which begins immediately upon arrival to the home page. A number of ads—some marketing products, others luring readers to one of several sister sites (globeauto.com, globeinvestor.com, workopolis.com) or to a special feature of GlobeandMail.com itself—can have an off-putting effect and make navigation tougher than it needs to be.

A menu of the site's sections spans the home page under the main banner and consists of headings you might expect: "National," "World," "Business & Investing," "Opinions," "Sports," "Arts," "Technology," "Health," and "Auto." Just move your mouse over these links for the subsections to appear.

The page is divided into four columns, one of which is noticeably wider than the rest. There, a crawl of the latest headlines is followed by the site's four top stories—a mix of international, national, and regional news. A photo and related features are usually packaged with the first headline, while the remaining three consist of a headline/link, a one-sentence summary, and perhaps a related multimedia feature. The rest of the column is comprised of sections similar to those in the navigation bar. Each of these sections posts between two and five headlines. Users have the ability to change the display: headlines only, headlines and summaries, or headline and summary for the top story of each section and headlines only for the rest. In the narrower column to the right, the site displays teasers to features ranging from "Day in Pictures" and special series to "Web-Exclusive Comment" and blogs.

While many of the main stories on the home page come from the Associated Press and the Canadian Press, users can click on the speech-balloon icon after the headline to view comments posted by the *Globe and Mail*'s predominantly Canadian readership.

Why You Should Visit

The *Globe and Mail* is Canada's national newspaper of record. That alone makes it worth a visit. When you do stop by, probably not for

FRONT PAGE

Falling gas prices reflect break from adversity
PATRICK BRETHOUR

Polygamous 'prophet' nabbed in a red Caddy
PETTI FONG

Ottawa voids Khadr decision
COLIN FREEZE

Chinese dissident disputes organ-harvest allegations
GEOFFREY YORK

A shopping list for the collegian who needs it all
CAROLINE ALPHONSO

long, look for the "print edition"—a section of the site accessible from midway down the left column on the home page. This "Headline Index" lists links to stories, which are often staff-originated, that appeared in that day's newspaper (along with an image of the front page), providing a quick, easy, and enlightening tour of this important newspaper and, as a result, this important—but often neglected—country.

Keep This in Mind

For those who want to broaden their perspective by checking in with a newspaper that doesn't land at their doorstep every morning, you'll get a little bit of a chance to do so by logging on to Globeand Mail.com. The keyword being *little*, thanks to the newspaper erecting the Great Wall of Payment between its columnists and users of the site. The only way to scale it, save for a 14-day trial, is to open the wallet. This disappointing strategy, which is labeled "Insider Edition" and dominates the right column of the home page (look for the color red and a padlock icon—no kidding), eliminates a top reason to visit a news site outside one's own borders—views of the world in which we live through a much different lens.

Off the Record

In 2004, as the Canadian cable industry attempted to include the Fox News Channel as an option for its viewers, John Doyle, a TV critic for the *Globe and Mail*, wrote an incendiary column: "Bring it on, I say. We're all in need of a good laugh. ... We'll find out if this Bill O'Reilly fella is as stupendously pompous and preening as he appears to be in the rare clips we see of Fox News." The column provoked, quite unsurprisingly, Bill O'Reilly to respond on his nightly show: "Hey you pinheads up there, I may be pompous, but at least I'm honest." The spat prompted ranting Fox News fans to inundate Doyle's e-mail inbox with hundreds of expletive-filled messages.

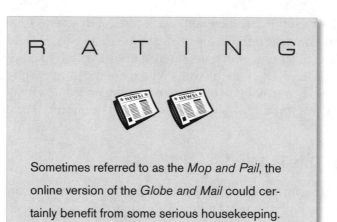

R A T I N G

Sometimes referred to as the *Mop and Pail*, the online version of the *Globe and Mail* could certainly benefit from some serious housekeeping.

34

Google News

news.google.com

Overview

Even if you've never turned on a computer, you have probably heard of Google. The growth of the search engine, which was started in crude fashion in 1996 by two Stanford University computer science graduate students in their early 20s, is simply astonishing. Now the largest, and most popular, search engine on the Web, the company's odd name has become part of the English vernacular—literally. In July 2006, the *Merriam-Webster Dictionary* added "google" (with a lowercase "g") to the lexicon as a verb; a month earlier, the *Oxford English Dictionary* added the commonly used word (meaning to search the Internet for information) to its online dictionary but preserved the brand's capitalized first letter.

In September 2002, Google entered the news business, sort of, as it continued to lengthen its list of search services. The company didn't hire journalists; the goal was not to produce original editorial content but to collect and organize news from other sources (about 4,500 of them, from respected newspapers to unfamiliar trade journals) on the Web. As an aggregator of news, all the stories posted on Google News can be found elsewhere. And while it's functional, the experience is as exciting as reading a company newsletter.

What You'll Find There

The Google News home page is divided into nine sections: "Top Stories," "World," "U.S.," "Business," "Sci/Tech," "Sports," "Entertainment," "Health," and "Most Popular." At the top of the page, which is updated every 15 minutes, Google News posts two top stories. To the right, it lists about five other headlines and a list of 10 people, places, things, or events that are currently "In The News." To the far left, links to each section enable users to open a page dedicated to that topic.

Each of the two top stories include a headline (in blue font and underlined) that acts as a link, the source, how long ago it was posted, and a portion of the lead. Below that are two other headlines/links (also in a blue font, but in a smaller size) to a similar story from different sources. Then, Google News provides more links to four other sources—only their names (in green underlined fonts)—reporting on the topic and another link to "all related" stories.

The rest of the site is divided into a two-column, eight-box grid. Each section consists of three stories (although users have the ability to "show more stories" or "show fewer stories"), presented in the same manner. By clicking on the story link (the headline), you are taken to the source's Web site to read the full article.

You can personalize the Google News home page by rearranging the order of the sections, by adding sections from one or more of its three-dozen international editions, and by creating custom sections based on keyword entries. You can also get "recommended stories," provided you register for a free Google account and create a profile.

Why You Should Visit

Without doubt, getting your news from multiple sources is the best way to stay informed. In fact, relying exclusively on one source could prove detrimental to fully understanding the world in which we live. Google News enables users, with ease and speed, to access a wide

variety of news organizations, allowing them to see how these different sources handle the same story. Users who have limited time to
access the day's top news will find Google News helpful. So will those
who know what news they want but don't know where to find it—the
Google News search tool will likely produce the right responses.

Keep This in Mind

Much of Google's success can be attributed to the minimalist design
of its home page. Consisting of only the colorful but simple "Google"
logo and the search tool on a white background, the page is refreshingly uncluttered and clean. The same, unfortunately, cannot be said
of the Google News home page, which looks more like Bourbon Street
during Mardi Gras and can have a dizzying effect on the visual senses.

And while Google has been successful, it has also been the center
of controversy on more than one occasion. Numerous lawsuits have
been filed against the company in recent years, most alleging copyright infringement. Agence France-Presse sued Google News for
$17.5 million for posting headlines, stories, and photos from the
news agency without permission. Google News has also been
accused of bias, "putting too much emphasis on small conservative
fringe sites."[1] But Google News has rebuffed the criticism: "The truth
is, Google News doesn't have a point of view. It's a computer, and
computers do not understand these topics the way humans do and
can't be systematically biased in any direction."[2] Ultimately, however,

users will have to decide if a certain bias exists—and if so, decide whether or not that bothers them.

Off the Record

Although "google" has become entrenched in our vocabulary, it certainly was not when the search engine's founders chose such a strange word to name their Web site and company. In fact, it wasn't even a word; it's a play on the term "googol," which represents the number 10^{100} (a 1 followed by 100 zeros). Quite fitting for a company with a mission "to organize the immense amount of information available on the Web."

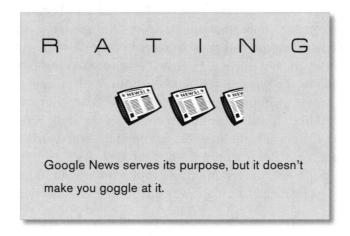

Google News serves its purpose, but it doesn't make you goggle at it.

Endnotes

1. Jonathan Dube, "Is Google News biased?" Cyberjournalist.net, Dec. 4, 2004 (www.cyberjournalist.net/news/001759.php).

2. Ibid.

35

Guardian Unlimited
www.guardian.co.uk

Overview

"The world is shrinking. Space is every day being bridged. … Physical boundaries are disappearing." While those words sound as if they are the thesis of a best-selling book in the 21st century, they were actually written in 1922 by Charles Prestwich Scott, who edited the *Manchester Guardian* for 57 years beginning in 1872 and bought the newspaper 35 years into his reign. Founded in 1821, the British newspaper, along with other media properties in the country, is now owned by The Scott Trust, a nonprofit foundation dedicated to maintaining financial and editorial independence.

Scott's prophecy took a step toward fulfilling itself in 1959 when the newspaper dropped the regional reference in its name and became a national news broker in the U.K. Already producing an international weekly edition for the better part of the 20th century, the longtime editor seemed to understand the potential for disseminating news from and to the world outside of the U.K. While he couldn't have imagined the World Wide Web and the possibilities it would offer newspapers like his, the Internet has indeed caused the world to shrink. And no other newspaper has capitalized on its capabilities better than *The Guardian*.

Winner of the 2005 and 2006 Webby Awards for best newspaper and a number of other honors, Guardian Unlimited, which debuted in 1999, has attracted readers from around the world—nearly half of the site's visits originate in the U.S.[1]—for several reasons: its depth and quality of coverage, its varying but always appropriate tone (in contrast to a stuffiness one might expect of a British newspaper), and mainly its ability to engage readers in ways unavailable to its or any print edition.

What You'll Find There

It will not take visitors long to learn what's in store at Guardian Unlimited: a myriad of pages—featuring wide-ranging information presented in various forms through a variety of media—that create arguably one of the most comprehensive online news sources.

A double-deck menu spans the home page below the Guardian Unlimited banner. Clicking on any of the two-dozen options—including "Arts," "Books," "Business," "Comment," "Education," "Film," "Football," "Life & Health," "Jobs," "Media," "Money," "News Blog," "Observer," "Politics," "Science," "Society," "Sport," "Technology," "Travel," "UK News," and "World News"—opens a section of Guardian Unlimited that could stand alone as a completely fulfilling niche site in and of itself.

A banner, which includes three teasers to features within the site and resembles the area above the masthead on many newspaper front pages, is positioned below the main menu. The rest of the home page is divided into three columns—a wide middle flanked by two narrow strips. Dozens of links—to the site's numerous blogs, "Today's Picks," talkboards and forums, and other sections of the Guardian Unlimited Network—fill the left column of the page. The right consists of services provided by the site (typically subscription-based content), ads, "Sponsored Features," "Events & Offers," and links to learn about or contact the site. The middle, and main, column begins

GuardianUnlimited **blogs**   The sharpest writing, the liveliest debate

Home   news   comment   arts   education   podcasts   sport   travel   media   Greenslade   technology   games   ask jack

Latest from all blogs   WEB FEED

newsblog

Fat or fiction?
The British Fertility Society's guidance does not say that fat women should be barred from IVF, writes David Batty.

comment is free...

Drawing distinctions in Darfur
Daniel Davies: There is an important difference between the humanitarian lobby for Darfur and the military intervention lobby....

culturevulture
'I feel like an old man in a hurry'
Calm before the storm: Abelard and Heloise share a tender moment in Howard Brenton's In Extremis. Photograph: Stephen VaughanSex, death, religious fundamentalism and castration ... not obvious ingredients for a medieval love tale, perhaps, but with playwright Howard Brenton that's...

technologyblog
Target shipment of Sony PS3 may be halved
"Sony's target shipment volume of four million PlayStation 3 (PS3) consoles by the end of this year is likely to be cut to two million units because volume production is not set yet, according to sources in Taiwan's game console...

gamesblog
Crysis too big and powerful for next-gen consoles
There seems to be a macho philosophy underpinning PC game development: if your current project runs on a majority of PCs it is, by definition, lame. To be hotly anticipated it must only be playable on the highest spec...

ask**jack**
Charles Ely on Making the web easier to read
Charles Ely, Assistive Technology Adviser for the South Lakes Society for the Blind in Kendal, responded to one of my answers (below) with some practical advice in a letter he acknowledged would be too long to print. Fortunately the blog...

organgrinder
Cistern failure
It is a newsreader's worst nightmare. Taking a loo break and not realising your microphone is still on. Just ask CNN's Kyra Phillips....

mortarboard
Martin Sheen shows way back to the classroom
For once real life has managed to imitate the warm glow of a West Wing plot line - President Bartlet quitting the Oval Office to go back to college in Ireland. But in another way life with President Bartlet is better than real life - education for his fellow pensioners in Britain at least is facing its own apocalypse as the government cuts back on subsidised classes to concentrate money on work

travelog

with the date and a news ticker that rotates through six headlines. Three top stories follow, each accompanied by a small photo. A main headline also serves as a link to the full story; a brief description of the story is followed by links to other related content, including more headlines/links, audio reports, photo essays, special reports, and associated sections. Below links to the many multimedia and interactive components that make the site more than merely an online newspaper, nearly three dozen other articles—news, features, and opinions—comprise the rest of the page, presented in much the same way as the lead stories. Other section fronts on the site mirror the design of the home page. So do full story pages, minus the thin right column. Along the left side of the story's copy and below the end of the text, Guardian Unlimited provides users with a vast amount of related resources available somewhere within the depths of its site.

Why You Should Visit

Guardian Unlimited couldn't possess a more proper name. While many newspapers and magazines use the Web to post an online version of their print editions, Guardian Unlimited is more than a mere reproduction and repackaging of content from a traditional medium. Instead, Guardian Unlimited seeks to take advantage of what the Internet allows—an unlimited, infinite news hole—rather than simply maintaining a presence on it. From podcasts and blogs to multimedia features and interactive experiences to original reporting and inspired writing (primarily relying, thankfully, on its talented staff rather than on monotone wire services), Guardian Unlimited combines a perfect mix of new and old journalistic tools to fulfill the pledge invoked in its name.

Keep This in Mind

Nearly all of Guardian Unlimited's content is free, but some sections require users to register (at no cost) before gaining access. A few services—digital editions of the newspapers and e-mail digests of the day's top news—are available for a fee.

For those who log on outside the Britain, remember this is a British publication: There is extensive coverage of the U.K., and there are certain stylistic and spelling quirks present throughout the site that will require some acclimatization on the part of some Americans.

Off the Record

Ricky Gervais, co-creator and star of *The Office,* a hit U.K. television comedy series that found a following on the other side of the pond and led to a U.S. version on NBC, landed in the 2007 *Guinness World Records* by way of Guardian Unlimited. A record number of listeners downloaded Gervais's 12-part weekly podcast, The Ricky Gervais Show, available for free through the site: an average of 261,670 downloads per episode during its first month (earning the Guinness) and more than double that by the end of the show's three-month run.

RATING

The Guardian, thanks to its "Unlimited" online powers, will protect you from being perilously uninformed.

Endnote

1. Eric Pfanner, "*Times of London* to print daily U.S. edition," *New York Times*, May 27, 2006.

36

Hispanic News
hispanic.cc

Overview

Thanks to the Internet, the role of news provider is no longer solely the province of media moguls and mammoth corporations. A computer, a modem, and a reason—that's all one needs to publish these days. Jon Garrido, a former economic developer for two Arizona cities and later a real estate developer, had those "qualifications." A fourth-generation American Hispanic, Garrido launched his Hispanic News site, aimed at English-speaking American Hispanics, in April 2003.

By 2006, Garrido (who now operates a network of 45 sites, including Latin America News, which features stories from and about dozens of countries) began promoting the site—a mix of aggregated mainstream media articles relevant to his audience and his own opinion pieces—as Google's top-ranked site for Hispanic news.

What You'll Find There

Hispanic News is a simple site that consists largely of text rather than photos and graphics. At the top left of the home page, you will find four to five main headlines that link to a variety of stories, from a feature about Spanish soap operas to a hard-news piece about the lack of a surge in voter registration of Hispanics. On the opposite side of the page, a list of about a dozen smaller headlines, typically linking to news articles ("Census shows growth of immigrants" and "Hispanics are 33% of uninsured"), is provided.

Below, the two left columns are filled with small headlines under various headings, including "Jon Garrido Writes," "Facts Center on Undocumented," "Demographics," "Immigration," "Education," "Health," and "Hispanic Market."

Users only discover the source of the articles once they click on a headline on the home page and arrive on the story page. In the

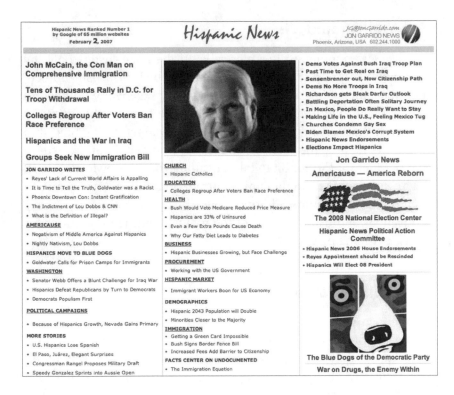

dateline of the story, the site provides the names of the writer(s) and publication in parentheses. Many of the articles—all of which deal with issues of interest to or about Hispanics—come from sources including the *New York Times*, the *Washington Post*, *USA Today*, the Associated Press, and *Newsweek*, as well as regional and local press. Some content, mostly opinion pieces written by Garrido, is original to Hispanic News.

The site's main liability is the lack of clear demarcation between news and opinion. All coverage—whether it's a *New York Times* op-ed piece or an Associated Press front-page news article—is presented in the same manner, leaving the reader with the task of having to decide. And after reading Garrido's own contributions on issues like immigration and politics, his selection of stories certainly seems biased.

For those who want to explore Garrido's other sites—Arizona News, US Times, World News, 51 Plus, and others—links are provided at the bottom of the home page.

Why You Should Visit

The Hispanic population in America is on the rise—faster than any other minority group in the U.S., according to the U.S. Census Bureau. Since 1990, the estimated Hispanic population has nearly doubled to more than 40 million and is expected to more than double again by 2050. With that comes greater influence and a larger voting bloc, and Hispanics—usually the focus of the hot-button immigration issue— need pertinent information to take advantage of this newfound clout. And Anglos benefit from remaining current on topics of importance to this growing community. Although flawed, Hispanic News does have its advantages: most, if not all, of the mainstream news about or for Hispanics in one place.

Keep This in Mind

Garrido formed the Hispanic News Political Action Committee and strongly supported Democrats using his network of Web sites, including Hispanic News and godem.org (a domain he purchased specifically for this reason), in the months leading up the 2006 midterm elections. Describing himself as a "lifetime Republican," Garrido endorsed Democrats in the hopes that they would win control of the U.S. House of Representatives and be "more receptive to approving legislation allowing all the 12 million undocumented [illegal immigrants] to become Americans."[1]

Jon Garrido Network

JonGarrido.com   JonGarrido.net
Corporate Website   Jon Garrido Network

Hispanic News
Ranked number 1 by Google of 65 million websites.

ARIZONA NEWS
Ranked number 9 by MSN.

The US Times
Ranked number 1 by MSN.

LATIN AMERICA NEWS
Ranked number 1 by MSN.

WORLD NEWS
New website.

51 Plus
Ranked number 1 by Google of 236 million websites.

Off the Record

In 2006, Garrido called for Hispanics to boycott CNN and AOL in an effort to force the media conglomerate to fire one of its news anchors, Lou Dobbs, whom Garrido has fiercely criticized for what he deems to be strongly biased "reporting" on the immigration issue. Dobbs later aired a story about Garrido's efforts, but Garrido declined to be interviewed.

RATING

Jon Garrido's site is an up-and-coming Drudge Report for Hispanics.

Endnote

1. Jon Garrido, "American Hispanics move to Democrats," Hispanic News, May 23, 2006, article available at hispanic.cc/go_dem.htm.

37

Irish Times

www.ireland.com

Overview

For those who like to be fully informed, publications that originate from foreign locales can provide invaluable context and insight. There's nothing like seeing how an event looks from a culturally different perspective. Even different countries that share the same language often have radically different views of the news. Which brings us to the *Irish Times*, a newspaper that is not quite European in sensibility, certainly not American (though sympathetic to many American interests), and not even particularly Irish—if what you think of as Ireland is limited to "Danny Boy" and the Lucky Charms leprechaun.

Ireland might be noted for its leisurely pace and pastoral languor, but the *Irish Times* was the first newspaper in Britain and Ireland to publish a Web site. In the past 10 years, the site has grown in importance and in visitors (more than 850,000 monthly). In 1999, the site became known as Ireland.com, now consisting of certain stories and features from the *Irish Times* as well as links to tourist-related sites and Irish-based businesses.

There is much to like about the site—except the annoying (and increasingly bothersome) trend toward charging viewers for information that has traditionally been available for free.

What You'll Find There

Visitors to Ireland.com will find what looks like a fairly traditional Web news page under a surprisingly small "Irish Times" banner. The first full Web page features only three or four stories, with the headline and the first paragraph reproduced in full, and the entire text of the article available by simply clicking on the link. Graphically, the page is quite simple and clutter-free, with the stories running down

the middle of the page and icon/photo boxes on the left featuring services such as photo archives and "Premium Content," a subscriber-only perk that provides access to additional stories and features. On the left side of the page is an index box to that day's edition of the *Irish Times*. Unfortunately, much of what's listed there is not available to the Web user. Clicking on any of the indexed items leads you to a page that solicits subscriptions. No subscription, no content. This invidious practice is, one supposes, economically defensible, yet nonetheless annoying. (As more sites grapple with the emerging business model for generating profit in the digital age, Web users can expect to continue to encounter such blocks in their quest for full-text access.)

The rest of the page is filled out with a hodgepodge of items, such as crossword and sudoku puzzles, weather forecasts, TV listings, birth and marriage announcements, death notices, and a daily interactive news poll. Other items, such as editorials and opinion columns, are only available to "Premium Subscribers" (these are marked by a red "P").

In an exception to the full-text freeze out, you can access the section called "The Ticket," which is a weekly entertainment guide with full-length features and dozens of listings for theater, music, and the spoken word throughout the Erin Island.

And, in a journalistic throwback to the age of Charles Foster Kane and the great early 20th-century press barons, the *Irish Times* lists a sort of declaration of principles on its site, reminding readers of the *Irish Times'* commitment to "publish an independent newspaper primarily concerned with serious issues for the benefit of the community throughout the whole of Ireland free from any form of personal or of party political, commercial, religious or other sectional control."

Why You Should Visit

In the last 10 years, Ireland has become one of the most potent economic engines driving the European economy. A surge of growth in

the computer sector has reversed what, for decades, was an infamous "brain drain," with Ireland's best and brightest going abroad for employment. As a result, the business and political communities have an increasing interest in what's happening in Ireland. Add that to the traditionally close relationship that has always existed between the U.S and "the old sod," and you have a Web site that will appeal to many U.S. readers.

Keep This in Mind

There are, of course, the annoyances (for U.S. readers) of having to deal with British spellings and idioms—as well as all those Euro dollar signs in front of numbers that require a working knowledge of the exchange rate to understand. And there's also the frustration of not being able to read the majority of each day's newspaper unless you're willing to subscribe. But in exchange, you do get a quick feel for how one of Europe's most potent and popular locales views the events parading by on the world stage.

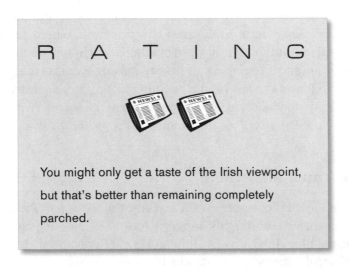

R A T I N G

You might only get a taste of the Irish viewpoint, but that's better than remaining completely parched.

38

Jerusalem Post
www.jpost.com

Overview

It would be hard to argue that any region of the world has arrested people's attention more than the Middle East. From the perspective of a news agency, the region has everything: disparate cultures living side by side, deeply rooted ancient traditions wrestling with modernity, international cities that attract tourists from around the globe, and—regrettably—an all-too-familiar heritage of violence and warfare.

In other words, a pretty important place in terms of news.

No Mideast city has had more of an impact on the world scene than Jerusalem, which (if the *New Testament* is to be believed) has hosted some of the most significant news events in human history. Has there been a time in the past two millennia when some great social and cultural upheaval wasn't taking place in Jerusalem?

Recording and interpreting the history-making events of the past half-century in Jerusalem has been a daunting task, to say the least. One of the leaders in that effort has established itself as the voice of Jerusalem—the one-time *Palestine Post*, now known as the *Jerusalem Post*.

What You'll Find There

For a publication covering an ancient city, the *Jerusalem Post*'s online presence has a thoroughly modern look. The home page, which promises "Breaking News 24 Hours A Day," offers a menu of top stories of local interest to Jerusalem residents, as well as a couple of highlighted international stories and features under the icon "Jewish News," which aim clearly at the target audience of Jewish readers (a recent feature addressed the controversial subject of whether Harry Potter's wizardry represented an affront to the Jewish faith).

In addition to news on Israeli government and politics, the Web site includes a "Talkback" section for readers who want to add their thoughts about recently published stories, functioning more like a message board than a traditional "Letters to the Editor" page, allowing anyone and everyone to vent and respond to previous posters. (A recent posting from an angry reader addressed a story about a European Community conference on racism: "The most ugly form of racism is anti-Semitism … How hypocritical are the Europeans, when they try to discuss racism without discussing anti-Semitism? Or is this denial a new form of anti-Semitism?") Blogs are maintained by *Jerusalem Post* staffers, as well as a variety of columnists from the paper's largely right-of-center political perspectives. A small entertainment section consists largely of an events calendar featuring cultural events in and around Jerusalem, as well as business and real estate news.

The Web site features "E-Paper" exclusives—that is, stories that appear only in the online edition. Readers can also browse (at a small subscription fee) the recently created "Christian Edition" of the *Jerusalem Post*, which features such items as a column by a Catholic priest, a profile of the Archbishop of Canterbury, and Christian-informed Bible commentary.

The site also includes the requisite ads—with a decidedly Semitic twist: a dating service for Jewish singles and travel agencies specializing in tours of the Holy Land.

Why You Should Visit

The U.S. and Israel have long had what many politicians and pundits call "a special relationship." The *Jerusalem Post* provides a window into the thinking of this strategically significant political ally. In addition, because the Middle East is such a cauldron of regularly clashing cultures, it's helpful—essential, really—to understand the perspectives of each of its cultural blocs. The *Jerusalem Post* represents the majority culture in a city that has often been a flashpoint throughout the 20th century.

Keep This in Mind

The focus of the newspaper and its Web site is fairly narrow. The *Jerusalem Post*—despite the recently introduced but limited "Christian Edition"—provides almost exclusively the viewpoint of Israeli Jews. Stories and columns feature headlines like "In the Diaspora," "Pilgrims' Progress," and "Olmert [Prime Minister] Promises Extension of Tal Law"—stories that most "secular" news agencies would blanch from publishing.

Off the Record

The *Jerusalem Post* began as the *Palestine Post*, a newspaper founded in 1932 by Gershon Agron, an American journalist and editor. The paper, which changed its name in 1950, was considered a liberal publication for most of its existence—though in the past two decades, it has endorsed a more right-of-center political agenda (coinciding with its purchase in the late 1980s by conservative media magnate Conrad Black).

The *Jerusalem Post* is a publication that asks you to read it religiously. It offers a useful voice, but worshipers should remember it's only one editorial pew in the journalistic cathedral.

39

Library of Congress
www.loc.gov

Overview

The vast, inestimable value of the holdings of the Library of Congress can't be discussed in common, everyday language. No dollar amount can be put on the collection's worth, no equivalency can be found for its 130 million items taking up more than 500 miles of bookshelves. Perhaps the only way to convey the immensity, in size and importance, of this treasure-trove of human knowledge is to say that a collection of this magnitude can't be housed in a single building. It can only be contained by your home computer.

The Library of Congress was established in 1800, after the seat of government was officially changed from Philadelphia to Washington D.C. The collection is under the supervision of a "Librarian of Congress," who is appointed by the president and approved by the U.S. Senate.

What You'll Find There

What *won't* you find there? This is a collection, after all, that has no less an aim than the total accumulation of the available wisdom of the generations, beginning more than 200 years ago and growing as rapidly as the body of known fact. And the Web site that makes much of this information available is, as you would expect, impressively expansive.

Visitors to the Library of Congress' home page will discover a deceptively brief and streamlined page that contains only a handful of icons, including "Library Catalogs," "American History," "Exhibitions," and "Global Gateway." Not too impressive sounding or looking, that's true. But these portals are like revolving doors that lead into airplane-hangar-sized warehouses of information. Click on the "Exhibitions" link, for example, and the breadth and depth of knowledge becomes staggering clear: From rich collections of vaudeville memorabilia,

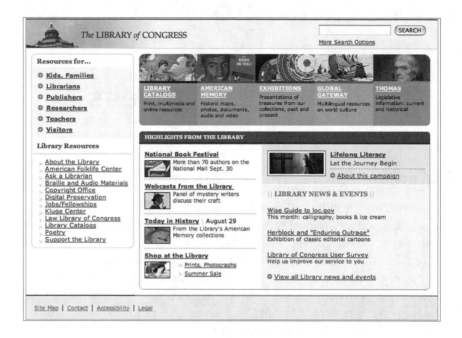

baseball, and the history of the U.S. Supreme Court, to thousands of volumes and illustrations of printmaking, French impressionism, Russian imperial history, the Dead Sea Scrolls, Frank Lloyd Wright, Walt Whitman's composition process, and early histories of woodcutting, cartooning, aviation, colonial architecture, and Jewish immigration, this corner of the Web site alone is overwhelming in its scope.

Each of the online exhibits is drawn from the on-site collection at the Washington D.C.-based institution (which is actually housed in three separate buildings). Most of the online exhibitions are presented in a surprising amount of depth (as opposed to a mere "teaser" that simply aims to entice you into the building itself), offering hours of material for browsers and researchers alike.

Why You Should Visit

The Library of Congress site provides one of the best examples of the Internet's potential, making information—from the critically important to the arcane—available in a way that would not otherwise exist. This is not just a Web site for info-geeks and die-hard scholarly types. Think of the site as a theme park for the intellectually adventurous. There's no other place like it on the Web—or in the world. The Library of Congress has the largest collection of rare books in North America. Also, the world's largest law library. Also, the world's largest film library. Also, the world's largest collection of maps. And sheet music. And sound recordings. And on and on and on.

There are separate collections on folklife, recreation, sports, performing arts, and cultural and civic history, which you can browse by subject, date, and name. There is a law library reading room, which has a massive database and links to case studies and "legal research FAQ," and a general research room, where online patrons can pose questions to the reference staff of the library.

Mostly, there's just stuff. For casual Web browsers, the site is a playground of ideas. You will always find something interesting at the Web site. It's impossible not to be drawn down some avenue of study while you're cruising through the site. Whether you're searching for the text of a pending Congressional bill that might affect your local community or seeking to discover how much that old baseball card collection in your attic might be worth, the Library of Congress will have it for you. Fast, complete, and free.

Keep This in Mind

For all its strengths, the Library of Congress is not a news site in the traditional sense. There is no page for latest headlines, breaking news, or current events. Most of what you'll learn at the site has long since passed from topical to historical. Little of recent vintage can be found in its cellar of thought. If you need to know what's going on in the world—while it's going on—then any of the hundreds of news

sites available on the Web will provide a better snapshot of your world than the Library of Congress.

Off the Record

After the original Library of Congress building was burned to the ground in 1814 by invading British forces, former President Thomas Jefferson offered his personal library—some 6,500 books—as a replacement.

RATING

If knowledge is power, then the Library of Congress is America's intellectual generator.

40

Los Angeles Times
www.latimes.com

Overview

As the news and information world of the 21st century continues to fragment, there are still a handful of names that represent the "titans" of journalism—news operations that have helped shape modern media. The *Los Angeles Times* is such a publication.

Since its founding during the fabled growth of California in the mid-19th century, its expansion in a post-war America, and its struggle to remain relevant in the digital age, the *Los Angeles Times* is an excellent mirror in which to glean a reflection of journalism's increasingly fervent quest to matter. The publication's Web site expands its award-winning coverage to an online community comprised of younger and more techno-savvy readers, as well as suburban residents who favor features and lifestyle stories over traditional "hard" news.

The Web site remains a comprehensive and useful news vehicle, comprising a nice (though light) mix of international, national, and local news. The site caters to its core constituency of Angelinos, while providing some news of interest to readers across the nation. If the *Los Angeles Times* is not quite the journalistic juggernaut it once was, it nonetheless remains a valuable voice in the national conversation and deserves a regular read.

What You'll Find There

The site is colorful and crowded, with font sizes a bit too small for most of the headlines, except for the main story, which can be found directly under the LATimes.com banner. There are two or three other major stories beneath the main story, and each offers viewers a video report as well as the traditional text article.

This being Southern California, there's a prominently placed "Entertainment News" block next to the main story of the day, and

several stories and features about Hollywood celebs help fill out the page.

There are a handful of local stories—everything from land-use disputes to immigration rallies and environmental policy reports—throughout the middle of the page, with links to corresponding columnists and editorials. However, there's not a lot of other "hard" news highlighted on the page. Most of the rest of the page consists of icon-and-image boxes for lifestyle features covering topics such as "health," "travel," "food," and (what else?) "car culture."

The site is a leader in blogs, with staffers, columnists, and even readers contributing blogs about the Los Angeles sports scene, politics, and local culture. It deserves credit for the way it reaches out to its various constituencies, offering lots of content on a range of different fronts and encouraging feedback from the online community. On the downside, the site gives fairly poor play to "hard news," listing a handful of headlines in very small type along the lower-left side of the screen and saving most of its prime real estate for lighter, reader-friendly features.

Why You Should Visit

Southern California's contributions to popular culture are innumerable. From national political figures to the movies at your local cineplex, the state is responsible for many of the country's twists, turns, fads, and fashions. The *Los Angeles Times* remains the most important voice in this state of growing power and influence. And the *Times* is still capable of some outstanding journalism, having an impressive record of netting 37 Pulitzers during its run of more than a century (five of those came in 2004).

Keep This in Mind

The melting pot that is Southern California makes an almost impossible demand on any single publication. In trying to satisfy all of its

Entertainment News

Telluride: A Film Fest That's Actually About Films
By John Horn
No deals, no cellphones. This is one event that really loves movies. >>
PHOTO GALLERY
- Six Off-the-Map Film Festivals

SPIN-OFFS

News Anchors Gone Wild
More great unplugged moments of the cable and network stars.

Jason Statham Is Up to His Old Stunts
By Susan King
The actor asked to dangle and race his way through "Crank." >>

Schieffer Ends Anchor Stint
By Matea Gold
The newsman fulfilled his dream at "CBS Evening News" and has one more in sight. >>

GM Withdraws CBS' 'Survivor' Sponsorship

PHOTO GALLERY

Celebrity Shots
A roundup of recent celebrity news and entertainment gossip.

KinseyGram
Freston-Moonves Rivalry Getting Worse?

Channel Island
Not Much Jagger in New ABC Sitcom

readers, from die-hard city residents who endorse the liberal "California" lifestyle to well-heeled suburbanites who represent a more staid, conservative approach, the *Los Angeles Times* has its work cut out for it. The Web site reflects this "all-things-to-all-people" mentality, crowding everything on the page that might appeal to anybody. The result is a bit of a jumble. Once the proud paragon of news vehicles for Southern California, the real "news" on the Web site takes a backseat to the burgeoning industry of "infotainment."

Off the Record

As of 2006, the circulation of the *Los Angeles Times* was 851,000—down more than five percent from the previous year, and continuing a trend from the mid-1990s when the paper easily surpassed 1 million readers each day.[1] Media watchers attribute this trend to an increase in the price of the newspaper and growing competition from a number of dailies in suburban Los Angeles.

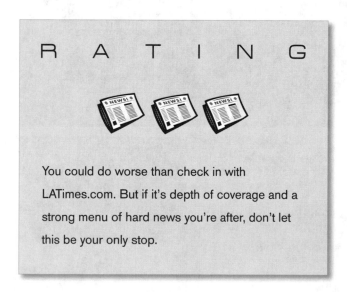

RATING

You could do worse than check in with LATimes.com. But if it's depth of coverage and a strong menu of hard news you're after, don't let this be your only stop.

Endnote

1. From the online archive of *USA Today*, June 8, 2006: "Newspaper sales dip, but Web sites gain."

41

Miami Herald

www.miamiherald.com

Overview

Trying to retain a distinctive voice in a time when more and more journalistic vehicles are aiming for the same middlebrow, mainstream reader is tough. But it is admittedly easier when you cover a part of the world that remains truly distinctive itself.

The South Florida region is, in many ways, like no other part of the country. With its famously tropical climate, its large and restive influx of Cuban-born residents, and its famous collection of migrating "snowbirds" (tourists who leave the North to winter in Florida), the region is unique. Whether that has anything to do with the Miami area's penchant for being in the eye of many international storms—both figuratively and literally—is another question. But when you think about Miami, you also think about events like the seizure of young Cuban exile Elian Gonzales by federal agents, the hotly disputed presidential vote of 2000, or the devastation of Hurricane Andrew.

What we know of such events came largely from the world-class reporting of the *Miami Herald*, an important regional newspaper. Its Web site, MiamiHerald.com, is a fitting scion to the print parent—a well-written, engaging, and user-friendly site that features stories with thorough reporting, opinion with attitude, and wide-ranging coverage of one of the most diverse places in America.

What You'll Find There

At the top of the site's home page you'll find Breaking News common to all major news sites—but in the case of MiamiHerald.com, it is largely focused on Miami-area news. The *Herald* has a reputation for dogged reporting of local corruption, environmental concerns, and regional political conflicts; each of these strains is still very much

evident on the site. Not until you've scrolled past the "Breaking News" and "Top Stories" do you come to the "Nation/World" icon, which sometimes lists as few as two stories. Yet, in many ways, even the local reporting in the *Herald* is international, given the ethnic diversity of the Miami-Dade County population.

The site provides video reports of selected news and features, as well as a full slate of the usual "lighter" stories that fill an increasing amount of the news hole in American newspapers and on news sites. There are separate sections on the site devoted to "Style," "Television," and even "Shopping."

The Web page also serves as a community-wide messaging service with icons for "Calendar of Events," "Jobs," "Real Estate," and "Dating" running down the side of the page.

Miami is a world-class sports city so there's an extensive sports section covering all the local professional teams, as well as thorough coverage of entertainment and "Tropical Life," featuring stories about the "Miami lifestyle" and the local cultural scene.

Throw in a roster of important and entertaining columnists and a readers' message board, and you've got the ingredients for a local news source that embraces its role as a servant of the people who read it.

Why You Should Visit

In addition to the great reporting and writing that has earned the paper 18 Pulitzer Prizes, the site is probably most distinguished by its roster of provocative and engaging columnists. Perhaps its showcase columnist is Leonard Pitts Jr., who won the 2004 Pulitzer Prize for, in the words of the selection committee, his "fresh, vibrant columns that spoke, with both passion and compassion, to ordinary people on often divisive issues." For those who haven't read Pitts' work, you're in for a treat. As a writer, his style is familiar, energetic, and fiercely committed. He's one of those writers who seems to leave nothing in reserve, pouring it all on the page.

The best-known columnist in this bullpen of gifted commentators is probably Dave Barry, the nationally revered humor columnist who turns the minutiae of life into 750 words twice a week (Barry won a Pulitzer in 1988). Barry's columns, which often morph into books for those outside the Miami area, comprise an opus of incredulity at the absurdities of the modern world.

Keep This in Mind

This site is so fiercely committed to local news—uprooting corruption among local politicians, exploring the development plans that impact the region's environment—that you may find yourself feeling a bit like a mildly confused tourist. To its credit, however, MiamiHerald.com covers the news that most affects its constituents. If that comes at the cost of appealing to a broader national audience, at least there's the consolation that a major news organization still takes its mission of serving the local community seriously.

Off the Record

The *Miami Herald* is owned by the McClatchy Company, which publishes dozens of newspapers including the *Sacramento Bee*, the *Star Tribune*, and the *Charlotte Observer*.

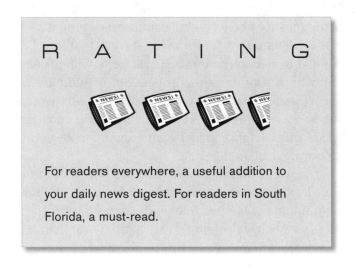

RATING

For readers everywhere, a useful addition to your daily news digest. For readers in South Florida, a must-read.

42

MichaelMoore.com
www.michaelmoore.com

Overview

If any Internet site embodies the messy but necessary function of muckraking in the age of governmental spin and concealment, it's MichaelMoore.com. The site's namesake is, himself, both messy and necessary, an eternally vigilant town crier finding fault with the administration, the media, and the pillars of modern society: capitalism, militarism, and the continued grip on power by the privileged. Michael Moore is the sharp rock in our shoe as we walk along the parade route, waving flags, and chanting "USA! USA!"

He's a real pain, but he's also a real Paine. As such, most people have strong feelings about Moore and his brand of populist agitation. Whether he's right on target—or way off—his Web site is a great example of truth in advertising, as it clearly conveys Moore's indignation, his searing intelligence, and his egomania.

Moore's site is stuffed with information, but whether or not someone finds the site credible will probably have more to do with the reader than the site itself. Moore's detractors are legion, and loud, in their denunciation of this American provocateur. His fans are just as vocal—and just as determined to see Moore's work as one of the last bastions of truth telling in an increasingly deceitful public sphere. No matter what your political stripe, you should check out MichaelMoore.com. He not only reports the headlines, he also finds his way into many of them.

What You'll Find There

Michael Moore has the courage of his convictions, and his Web site reflects his pet obsessions: the war in Iraq, the greed of U.S. corporations, the fractured U.S. healthcare system, and his own career. Readers will find a featured story (usually related to the latest war

news), with a photo or graphic, running just under a banner that offers quick clicks to Web pages dedicated to "*Fahrenheit 9/11*," "Facts in Mike's Films," "Mike's Letter," "Newsroom," "Must Read," and "Mike's Books and Films." Each of these pages offers readers information about Moore's body of work or his take on world events. Moore's writing is deceptively effective, spun out more like conversation with a really good talker than finely honed prose. His clear and casual style connects with most readers and creates a sense of familiarity and endearment. That's Moore's game: to co-opt you with his almost homey Midwestern directness and, by extension, bring you into the fold that endorses his world view.

Which is not necessarily a bad thing. You just need to be aware that Moore's take on events requires sympathy with a traditional progressive ideology. But the information on his Web site is, in most cases, thoroughly reported and accurate, and he does indeed perform the necessary function of a public scold, raising uncomfortable questions and posing alternative answers to those that flow through the authorized information pipeline.

The site also includes various stories from domestic and foreign news sites that offer information about Moore's favorite subjects, as well as essays and news analysis from Moore himself. There are links to other progressive and activist sites and organizations, a blog, a message board, and some truly moving postings from disillusioned members of the military.

Why You Should Visit

Moore's Web site is inflammatory, but so were the Federalist papers, *Common Sense*, the *Pentagon Papers*, and, well, all of Moore's films (he's far better known as a filmmaker than a Webmaster). He routinely shows up as the subject matter during the monologue of late-night talk shows *and* State Department daily press briefings. (You gotta admire that kind of range.)

In addition, Moore is an ardent supporter of voter registration, and his site is a clarion call to the unregistered to seize their share of power by becoming enfranchised. Whether or not he really is a

MIKE ALSO RECOMMENDS...

 After : The Rebuilding and Defending of America in the September 12 Era
Steven Brill

 Bush's War For Reelection : Iraq, the White House, and the People
James Moore

 Bush's Brain: How Karl Rove Made George W. Bush Presidential
James Moore

 American Dynasty: Aristocracy, Fortune, and the Politics of Deceit in the House of Bush
Kevin Phillips

 The Halliburton Agenda : The Politics of Oil and Money
Dan Briody

 Sleeping With the Devil: How Washington Sold Our Soul for Saudi Crude
Robert Baer

champion of the "little guy" is a debate best left to talk radio pundits and biographers. What matters is that he puts out important information, and he challenges people to get involved.

Keep This in Mind

Remember everything that's been said about Moore in all its contradictory miasma: He's a sell-out, a champion, a fraud, a patriot, a poseur, a pragmatist, a coward, a courageous journalist, a showman, a leader, a panderer, a decorated filmmaker, and a cheap propagandist. Keep all these things in mind, and then check out the man's Web site and come to your own conclusion.

Off the Record

When Moore was 18 years old, he ran for—and won—a position on his hometown's board of education, making him one of the youngest public officials ever to hold elective office in the U.S.

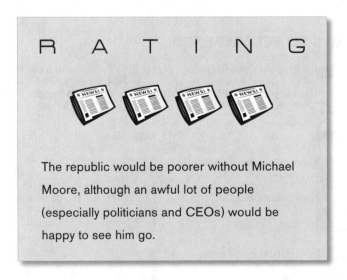

RATING

The republic would be poorer without Michael Moore, although an awful lot of people (especially politicians and CEOs) would be happy to see him go.

43

Mother Jones
www.motherjones.com

Overview

Mother Jones is not a parenting publication or a brainchild of Martha Stewart. Although the magazine's name might seem peculiar at first, it actually is quite fitting. The periodical's namesake, Mary Harris Jones (who would assume the persona of Mother Jones, "the mother of downtrodden people everywhere"), was an influential labor activist and union organizer in America during the late 19th and early 20th centuries, battling the powers that be—through marches, protests, speeches, and strikes—on behalf of working-class people. At a time when women stayed home and kept quiet, Mother Jones was a self-proclaimed "hellraiser."

The San Francisco-based magazine, founded in 1976, could certainly be called the same, abiding by the principles its namesake espoused and challenging the political and corporate establishment every two months in print and every day online. In the past 30 years, *Mother Jones* has developed a reputation for publishing hard-hitting exposés, practicing what the nonprofit magazine's founders called "a new brand of socially conscious journalism."

In attempting to accomplish that mission, *Mother Jones* realized the potential of the Internet before any other periodical—during the time when the medium was merely a narrow gravel road and not yet a superhighway. In November 1993, more than a year before most other news organizations, from *Esquire* to *USA TODAY,* shifted their cyber-vehicles into gear, *Mother Jones* launched its Web site where it posted content from the print edition. But MotherJones.com is no longer a complement to the magazine, rather an enhancement of it.

What You'll Find There

The site is easy to navigate, whether you scroll through the home page or use the menu in the left column at the top of the home page. Front and center at MotherJones.com is the "Top Story" box, which prominently displays a *Mother Jones*-produced blog or feature, but sometimes links to another source's article or op-ed. This section also includes links to other stories pertaining to the issue, along with several related headlines from previous editions of the magazine. "MoJoBlog," located below the main feature to the right and frequently updated throughout the day, is a smart way for *Mother Jones*, which publishes six issues a year, to present readers with the latest headlines.

To the left of the list of blog entries is the "Daily Jones" section, which features headlines/links, brief summaries, and the corresponding source (many of them are *Mother Jones* stories, but some originate from major daily newspapers, other sites, and even think tanks).

The *Mother Jones* content is clearly marked as "news" or "commentary" at the top of the story pages.

In the narrow left column of the home page is a menu of the site's various sections: "News & Politics," which includes original reports and investigations from the nation's capital through "Washington Dispatches"; "Arts & Culture," where you'll find "The Riff" blog and reviews of books, movies, music, and more; "Environment & Health," which features "The Blue Marble" blog and lots of information pertaining to science and medicine; "Special Reports" on topics ranging from global warming to campaign finance to domestic violence; and links to its major "Interviews," "Letters" from readers, "Photo Essays," and even "Radio" programming. The site also maintains a massive archive, which consists of everything published by the magazine since 1993 and is accessible by clicking the "Back Issues" link below the image of the current cover at the top right of the home page. Clicking the image will provide links to the stories from that edition. But be sure not to miss the content exclusive to the Web site, especially the animated editorial cartoons of Mark Fiore—a model example of how *Mother Jones* uses its site to perform feats impossible on the printed page.

Why You Should Visit

If investigative reporting demands that journalists possess the traits and tools of distinguished detectives, then *Mother Jones* is Sherlock Holmes. While much of the mainstream media seems to prefer Hannity-and-Colmes shouting to Woodward-and-Bernstein digging these days, you can still depend on *Mother*. While huge conglomerates continue to consolidate ownership of major media enterprises into the hands of a select few, you can still count on *Mother* (it's independent and likely to remain that way: "the magazine will never be part of

WASHINGTON DISPATCHES
From James Ridgeway and the Mother Jones Investigative Team

Future of Government Transparency Bill Unclear
Temporarily blocked in the Senate, a bill that would put federal contractors on notice has lost its momentum.
August 16, 2006

Government official: Explosives on planes cannot be detected
Consistent warnings about the failures of airport security systems fall on deaf ears.
August 11, 2006

VIDEO: Angry Red Team Members Speak Out
Long before 9/11, the FAA's own employees repeatedly warned the agency terrorists could penetrate the nation's air security systems.
August 14, 2006

Life As Usual in the Capital
You'd never know we're "at war."
August 10, 2006

New Conyers Report
Propaganda from the President: a step-by-step look at how Bush misled the nation into war.
August 7, 2006

AOL Time Warner," one of its founders once said). Here, the bottom line has nothing to do with dollars and cents, but has everything to do with journalism that all can profit from—often those stories that mass media outlets fail to cover, or do so less adequately. *Mother Jones'* reporting is exhaustive, its writing engaging, its Web site engrossing.

Keep This in Mind

Mother Jones, partly as a result of its "alternative" status in the media world, is regularly referred to as a left-wing publication by some critics. And while the magazine is positioned on the progressive end of the ideological spectrum (when a new editor took the helm in 2005, he promised *Mother Jones* would clearly demonstrate "why progressive ideas are right for the nation's future"), the liberal label, which often comes in the form of criticism, should not be considered a knock on the publication's credibility.

An unambiguous wall exists between news and commentary at *Mother Jones*, both in print and online. Uncensored, uncompromised, and unmatched investigative journalism takes precedence over any agenda, and the magazine's record reflects its reliability: nominated for 13 National Magazine awards in categories including reporting excellence, public service, public interest, and general excellence; won four such awards from the American Society of Magazine Editors, including general excellence in 2001; named twice by the *American Journalism Review* as the "Best in the Business" for investigative reporting; and selected as the Webby People's Voice Award winner in the politics category in 2005 and 2006.

Off the Record

In 1986, *Mother Jones* hired a little-known Michigander who had spent the last decade editing an alternative weekly in Flint to become its editor-in-chief, a post held by only one other person in the magazine's history. After a tumultuous four-month stint, Michael Moore was fired, sparking a firestorm in media circles. Moore subsequently sued *Mother Jones* for wrongful termination, eventually settling for $58,000.

R A T I N G

Visit *Mother* often? You should!

44

MoveOn.org
www.moveon.org

Overview

Most Web sites that cover the news of the day or traffic in political commentary or even titillate with scandalous headlines and blurbs, ask nothing more of their readers than to spend a few minutes perusing the site. They want to catch your attention, register a hit, and add you to their regular readership. Hopefully, you'll bookmark the site and come back. It's good for their profile, good for their advertisers, and good for the writers and designers who work on the Web site. You find, you visit, you come back.

MoveOn.org isn't like that. It's not enough for readers to take in the content of this politically engaged site. The folks behind MoveOn.org see your visit to its site as only the *first* step in a series of moves that you, the conscientious Web surfer, will take. After reading something on the site, you're encouraged, expected, and almost goaded into doing one of the following: sign a petition, organize your friends and neighbors into a discussion group, send out e-mails, host a movie screening in your living room, or attend a political rally. The key word in MoveOn.org is "Move." The site seems to have little use for people who are just trolling around the Internet, looking for news. They want commitment. To MoveOn.org, it's their way—*and* the highway (as in hit the road and get busy on behalf of a cause).

If you've been meaning to get more involved in politics at the grass-roots level—and have a reformer's soul—you've found a home. But don't move in—move on.

What You'll Find There

Rather than a list of stories, you'll find a list of causes masquerading as stories. The MoveOn.org home page looks like most news pages, with its above-the-fold photo and bold headline, followed by lots of

smaller stories accompanied by thumbnail photos and one-sentence blurbs. But each of these stories falls under a small-print logo that reads either "MoveOn.org Political Action" or "MoveOn.org Civic Action." Clicking on any of these stories (with headlines like "Save the Internet" and "Campaign for an Oil-Free Congress") takes you to a separate page that usually includes an online petition for you to sign and send electronically or a citizen's guide to mobilizing on that particular issue, as well as a list of contacts in your state or local area to link up with.

Below the main listings on the home page—the most urgent campaigns—is an archive that chronicles recent efforts on behalf of the group, from trying to derail Supreme Court nominees to protesting pending legislation on issues from cell phones and oil exploration to prescription drugs and the Iraq War. Each of these campaigns carries the requisite obligation of the readers: writing to a senator or representative, sending a donation to a political action committee, writing a letter to a local newspaper editor, or even gathering signatures on a petition in your neighborhood.

The page also includes icons for "Success Stories" where you can read about MoveOn.org's successful attempts to either block or enact various civic and political programs. This section also contains letters of support and gratitude for the organization written by average individuals sharing their good feelings about now being part of the solution, rather than part of the problem.

Finally, there are several prompts throughout the site that invite visitors to join the 3 million people who have added their names to the membership roster of MoveOn.org.

Why You Should Visit

Lots of social scientists and political operatives are keeping a close eye on the Internet, waiting to see what kind of impact this relatively new vehicle of community building will have on the political process. Much of Howard Dean's support in the early stages of the 2004 primary has been traced to the Internet in general and to MoveOn.org in particular. (Dean won MoveOn.org's first ever "online primary.")

Whether you endorse the progressive policies of MoveOn.org or are completely opposed, it's certainly instructive to see how MoveOn.org has gone about galvanizing its readership/membership. While no one knows exactly how the Web will evolve as a tool of political persuasion, it's a safe bet that MoveOn.org is going to be copied by lots of other politically-inclined Web-based organizations.

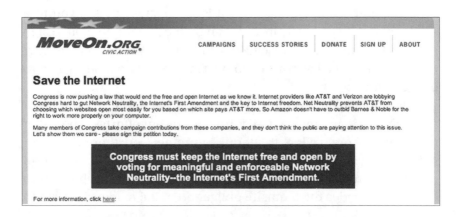

Keep This in Mind

There really isn't any "news" to speak of on this site. What you get is a checklist of steps to take as a result of news that's already happened, or is being reported elsewhere. It's not very useful for getting a sense of a story, the objective facts, or a balanced perspective filtered by professional journalists. You will definitely have to crosscheck all of MoveOn.org's postings with other, more traditional news sites.

Off the Record

MoveOn.org came into being as a result of the Bill Clinton-Monica Lewinsky sex scandal. Concluding that the Republican-led effort to impeach Clinton was a waste of time and effort, the group's founders established a site called "Censure and Move On." The site offered readers a chance to sign a petition urging lawmakers to censure the president for his behavior and get on with the business of governing the country.

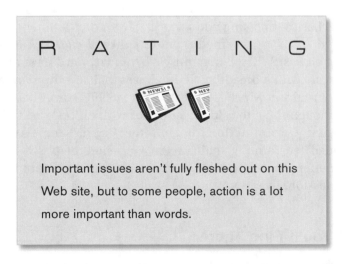

RATING

Important issues aren't fully fleshed out on this Web site, but to some people, action is a lot more important than words.

45

MSNBC
www.msnbc.com

Overview

In the landscape of cybernews, where the boundaries are drawn and redrawn with alarming frequency, bigger is not always better. Smaller, scrappier Web sites have often outperformed many of the more traditional "mainstream" news sources. And niche Web sites, aimed at covering only a small slice of the world, often scoop their better-financed rivals.

But size does have its advantages, evidenced by the online news site MSNBC. This union of Microsoft's technological stature (that's the "MS") and NBC's newsgathering capabilities has produced a truly impressive Web site, which remains one of the most visited news sources on the Internet.

And with good reason. This frequently updated site not only covers all of the basics (breaking news, world news, entertainment), but it's partnered with other media outlets like *Newsweek* and the *Washington Post*. With all that muscle behind it, you'd have reason to expect a site with a breadth and timeliness that sets the standard for online journalism, which is the case with MSNBC.com.

And though the site seldom surprises with an unexpected angle or a lengthy examination of an issue (there seems to be an unfounded fear among mainstream Web sites of posting longer, magazine-length articles), the news is packaged comprehensively and professionally.

What You'll Find There

For a site as crammed with information as MSNBC.com, you'd think the page ought to appear more crowded than it does. The site boasts a clear, colorful, and user-friendly layout that features the expected main story at the top of the page, teased with a photo and several

"related stories." There is almost always an NBC News video to accompany the story and often a *Newsweek* "Special Report," as well as other related stories.

Then there's a "More Top Stories" box, which features other top stories, and right under that, an "Also Making Headlines" section. On the right side of the page is a separate "NBC News Highlights" box, which includes video reports not only from the network's nightly news broadcast but also its quasi-investigative show *Dateline*. On the left side of the page, you'll find other headlines "In the News."

In the middle of the page is a prompt for the headlines in the "*Newsweek* Daily Edition," featuring breaking stories that the news weekly is following. Underneath, the emphasis returns to MSNBC with a roster of stories labeled "Inside MSNBC.com" and then, somewhat redundantly, "Only on MSNBC.com." It's pretty clear that this site gets lots of mileage from its news partnerships, and it's also not shy about touting its exclusives—even when those exclusives consist of only feature-type stories or photo galleries.

Running down the left side of the page is an unassuming, small-type bonanza of categories, from "World News" to "Entertainment" and a dozen others, offering readers an extensive roster of stories specific to that type of news (from weather reports to blogs). Click on these categories and dozens of stories will pop up on your screen. (If you choose not to click, you'll encounter an abbreviated list of each of those stories further down the page.)

The "Special Reports" section fills out the bottom of the page, offering not particularly insightful but mildly useful looks at some of the stories making news, often with a quirky or retrospective angle.

Why You Should Visit

A lot of the online news business is predicated upon a follow-the-leader mentality. If one site is reporting it, all the others soon will be. In this arena, MSNBC is often first with a story, and with the resources of NBC News, *Newsweek*, and the *Washington Post*, you'll remain reliably informed if you check in with this site regularly.

The site is also impressively comprehensive, covering more stories than many other sites, which quite probably fail to match up in terms of resources. And unlike some other Web sites that boast of being up-to-the-minute, MSNBC.com really does update its news pages with impressive regularity.

WASHINGTONPOST.COM HIGHLIGHTS

Bush team casts foes as defeatist

President Bush and his surrogates are launching a new campaign intended to rebuild support for the war in Iraq by accusing the opposition of aiming to appease terrorists and cut off funding for troops on the battlefield, charges that many Democrats say distort their stated positions.
● **FULL STORY**

WASHINGTONPOST.COM TOP STORIES
● **First the flood, now the fight**
   Critics say FEMA impeding Gulf Coast's recovery
● **Militias target Iraqi hospitals**
   Medical sites targeted by Shiite militiamen
● **Putin creates his own opposition**
   Move puts loyalists on both sides of aisle
● **Film counters 'Fahrenheit 9/11'**
   Conservative advocate turns to filmmaking to counter 'Fahrenheit 9/11'

MORE FROM WASHINGTONPOST.COM
● **Who's true No. 1? And nine other questions**
● **Bush, critics mark Katrina anniversary**
● **Bush priorities clash with Kazakh's visit**

Keep This in Mind

MSNBC.com can often seem like one giant commercial for its affiliated news outlets. Didn't see *NBC News*? Well, the site's Webmasters will make sure you *do* see it. Missed last week's *Newsweek* magazine? Here it is, presented online for your reading pleasure. Haven't been to the *Washington Post*'s site today? No need to bother—here's what it's reporting.

Off the Record

Although CNN and Fox News routinely trounce MSNBC's cable news channel in the ratings, the MSNBC site is routinely ranked as one of the most visited news sites. As of this writing, MSNBC.com and CNN.com remain locked in a battle for bragging rights as the Internet's most popular news Web site.

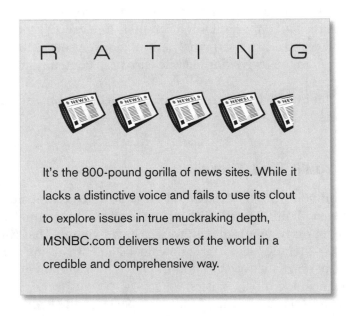

R A T I N G

It's the 800-pound gorilla of news sites. While it lacks a distinctive voice and fails to use its clout to explore issues in true muckraking depth, MSNBC.com delivers news of the world in a credible and comprehensive way.

46

MTV
www.mtv.com

Overview

Music has occupied an important place in Western civilization, from Medieval church oratories and Gregorian chants and chamber music in the salons of Vienna in the 18th century to the chronicle of woe and redemption afforded by Mississippi Delta Blues or contemporary Christian Rock. Within our culture, music seems to provide a touchstone of sorts to something central—even primal—to the psyche of humanity.

Sound a little grandiose? Well, perhaps. But there's no denying that music's charms, as noted in the *Old Testament*, Shakespeare, and Proust, to name just a few, exercise some sort of hold on people's imaginations.

If music is *that* important, shouldn't there be a way to keep up with the music world and its perpetual permutations? A source that would plug you in to the revivifying electric current of contemporary musical culture?

POOF! Your wish has been granted! (Provided your browser is set to MTV.com.)

What You'll Find There

What will you find at MTV.com? In a word, music. But not in its breadth and depth. The site, like its iconic television channel, traffics in contemporary, youth-driven, rock-inspired genres. That said, the site *rocks*—literally (with music downloads and streaming videos of musical performances) and figuratively (with imaginative graphics, video games, and movie trailers).

Icons for "News," "Games," "Music," "Style," and "Radio" lead to separate pages, loaded with clickable photos and dozens of headlines on that subject. The best and most imaginative page can be found under the "Think" icon, which offers multimedia presentations on everything from sexual health to finding ways to pay for college.

Click on the News icon and you're taken to a page that offers more music news: interviews with artists, updates on award nominations, lawsuits and band break-ups, newly announced concert dates, and record company news (sales, analysis, new product development, and mergers.)

If you're looking for more "traditional news," you'll have to search—but not completely in vain. Mostly embedded within the "Correspondents" section of the news page are interviews with newsmakers (a recent posting featured an in-depth interview with former U.N. chief weapons inspector Hans Blix) and some commentary and reporting about current events (such as the devastation of Hurricane Katrina or national election results).

But overwhelmingly, this "news" site moves to the beat of contemporary music, not mainstream news.

Why You Should Visit

MTV.com is an exemplar of truth in advertising. It provides what it promises: the music industry, delivered to your computer screen, with adjustable volume. Musical culture is the generational glue that binds young people to the rest of our society: politics, education, technology, and even philosophy (the "Think" section offers implicit commentary on socially significant issues). MTV's Web site offers dispatches from the battlefront of the American youth movement. (And a shout-out to the site for aggressively seeking to register new voters through its "Rock the Vote" initiative.)

The site also offers breaking entertainment news—usually having to do with concert promotion or announcements of new CD releases. There's not a great deal of depth in the news reporting, but that's perhaps appropriate for a medium that has succeeded largely on the strength of the three-minute pop song set to an infectious backbeat and propelled by highly forgettable rhyming lyrics.

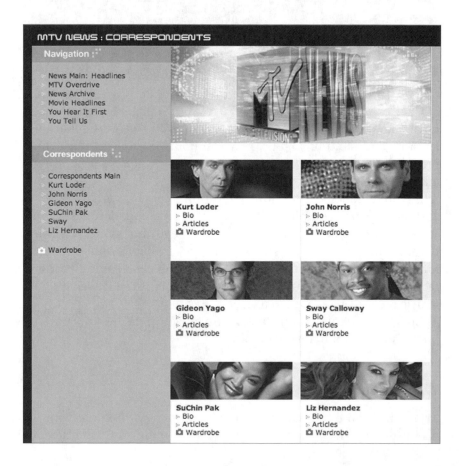

Keep This in Mind

MTV thrives because the music industry thrives. A cynic could say that MTV.com is just an adjunct to the music industry, a 24-hour-a-day commercial for the latest CDs and DVDs. In truth, much of what passes for content on MTV.com is not markedly different from the "pop-up" ads that offer chances to hear the latest single or see a movie trailer.

Still, the Web site provides a basic service for those whose lives move to the soundtrack of contemporary music. You want information about your favorite pop star? MTV.com will overwhelm you with interviews, archived news articles, biography, concert dates, and a discography.

Off the Record

The concept of simply showing music videos, which made MTV an almost-instant phenomenon when it was launched in August 1981, was first developed by none other than Mike Nesmith, the guitarist for the American mop-top TV celebs The Monkees.[1]

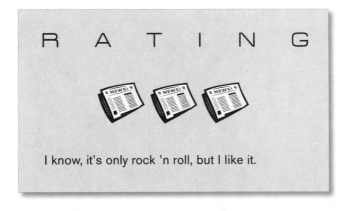

I know, it's only rock 'n roll, but I like it.

Endnote

1. See www.nndb.com/people for the article on Mike Nesmith and his contributions to MTV.

47

The Nation
www.thenation.com

Overview

In an age when the "nation's newspaper" (*USA Today*) resorts daily to a colorful front page to attract readers, *The Nation*'s commitment to the potential power of the written word is noteworthy. And while that approach, which began in 1865, continues to differentiate the liberal political journal from other rack-filling publications, *The Nation*'s similar style online fails to exploit the tools offered in cyberspace, burying it on the crowded newsstand of the Web.

What You'll Find There

Visitors hunting for a genuine multimedia encounter won't find any game meat at TheNation.com. Except for weekly RadioNation podcasts, *The Nation*'s Web site is void of much of the available technology and lacks many visual design elements like photos and graphics (though the site has recently launched—with the help of YouTube—a section called "Video Nation," which consists largely of writers talking about topical issues, brief interviews with political figures, and speeches sponsored by *The Nation*).

A stunning design and interactive multimedia features are not the only things missing from the site; those on the lookout for objective reporting certainly won't find TheNation.com doling out praise for the Bush administration, or any other "elephants" for that matter. But this is not the "We Report, You Decide" style of bias. With its prominently placed "national progressive calendar," *The Nation* never leaves any room for ambiguity about its convictions.

Much of its editorial content is equally, unabashedly subjective, from a blog written by the publisher/editor saying "[I]t won't be long before Leavenworth has enough Republican congressmen for a quorum" to an article declaring that Bush's occupation of Iraq "has created

conditions just as bad—if not worse—than Saddam Hussein's ruthless regime."

Of the Web site's dozen sections, only one is labeled "Politics." But all, including "Books & Arts," "Blogs," "Columns," "The Right," "The World," "Features," "Ideas & Culture," and "Web Only," could easily be titled "Politics." Yet, *The Nation* is beholden to neither major political party, but rather remains loyal to a set of ideas and principles.

Visitors to TheNation.com will occasionally be impeded by the black "Sub" tag attached to articles available only to print subscribers. But for those only interested in reading the online edition, the articles are usually not stale when they do become available to all, which might not be the case on Web sites dealing in breaking news.

Why You Should Visit

The Nation online lacks the bells and whistles accessible on the Web, but it is neatly organized and easily navigated. Advertising is scarce and that certainly doesn't go unnoticed in this world of pop-ups. The content is posted weekly, prior to arriving in print, and updated regularly. The writers bring information to the forefront that would otherwise remain obscure—such as a report detailing an alleged Bush proposal to bomb *Al Jazeera*—and it does so with wit, intellect, and sometimes sarcasm. The weekly rants of Calvin Trillin (aka The Deadline Poet) are concise, entertaining, and illuminating. Two other Web site features—"Newsfeed," which links the reader to "important articles from around the Web," and "Sites We Like," a list of the "best sites on the Web"—let you take a day trip through the virtual landscape of the left. But before you leave TheNation.com, make sure to read what "The Editors" have to say.

Keep This in Mind

Victor Navasky, whom the *New York Times* recently called "one of the reigning voices of the intellectual left for the last three decades," handed over the reins of publisher to *The Nation*'s editor Katrina vanden Heuvel. As editor, vanden Heuvel became a familiar face on the cable news punditry circuit, helping along her magazine's resurgence by filling the void left by Democrats when television producers wanted guests with anti-Bush opinions, according to Navasky. While the editor and other writers of *The Nation* gained rare exposure through the mainstream broadcast media, it has used the Internet to preach to more of the entire congregation, not just to the choir. In

---

DEADLINE POET | *posted August 31, 2006 (September 18, 2006 issue)*

The Choice on Iraq

CALVIN TRILLIN

The choice this fall's about Iraq, Bush says.
He's right, but here's how Democrats should spin it:
To figure out the end of this grand mess,
Why keep the very clunks that got us in it?

June 2004, *The Nation* partnered with CBSNews.com, as did the *National Review Online, American Prospect*, and the *Weekly Standard*. The convergence both broadened the swath of opinion read by CBSNews.com users and provided *The Nation*'s opinion-makers with a much broader audience.

Off the Record

Throughout its 140-year history, *The Nation* has struggled to survive, never exactly considered a moneymaker. But when George W. Bush switched his primary address to 1600 Pennsylvania Avenue in 2001, *The Nation* doubled its circulation to 187,000. During the first two years of his first term, Bush obviously aided, albeit indirectly, more than just big business: *The Nation*, a niche publication usually supported by private donations, started turning a profit for the first time in 2003.

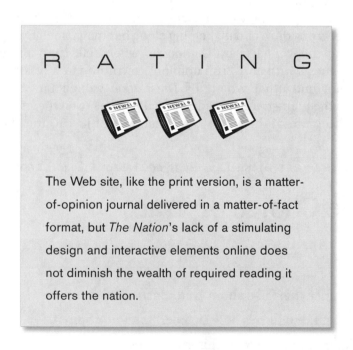

RATING

The Web site, like the print version, is a matter-of-opinion journal delivered in a matter-of-fact format, but *The Nation*'s lack of a stimulating design and interactive elements online does not diminish the wealth of required reading it offers the nation.

48

National Aeronautics and Space Administration (NASA)

www.nasa.gov

Overview

There are lots of Web sites you can visit to learn what's happening in the world, but where do you go to get the news of *other* worlds?

Yes, other planetary systems, galaxies, and even the expanding universe itself sometimes make the news. If you're feeling lost amid the vast penumbra of stars and the daunting void of the firmament, and you don't know the Big Bang from a Big Gulp, there is a place to get your bearings in the cosmos of the Internet: NASA.gov.

Most everyone has an image of the National Aeronautics and Space Administration (NASA), depending largely on one's age. Some will remember the early black-and-white television broadcasts of the *Apollo* missions in the 1960s. Others will recall the moon landing, the first launch of the space shuttle, or the *Columbia* shuttle disaster. Younger humanoids will perhaps recall the stunning images sent back from Mars by the space agency's dual robotic rovers.

NASA has always been front-page news, but visitors to its site might be pleasantly surprised to find so much other useful information at their fingertips.

What You'll Find There

People think of astronauts when they think of NASA, but the manned space program makes up only a small part of the space agency's vast roster of projects. The Web page reflects this, offering viewers a glimpse behind the scenes into a number of critically important NASA projects, from satellite imagery used to assess global warming

to charting asteroids and other space junk that might be hurtling toward earth.

The top third of the home page is divided between a graphic promoting NASA's latest high-profile projects (such as "Project Constellation," its long-range plan to build a space station on the moon) and a menu of links "For Kids," "For Educators," "For Researchers," and "For Industry." Each of those links takes you to a series of Web pages designed for these niche readers, alerting them to items of interest. The kids' page is especially well designed, featuring interactive games, quizzes, virtual tours, and young reader-friendly information about space. The pages for researchers are, understandably, more technical in nature but still accessible to the lay reader.

Across the top of the page run icons for "Breaking News," "Missions," "About NASA," and "Work for NASA." The news stories are clearly written, eschewing scientific jargon, and well illustrated with multiple links and sidebar stories. The "Missions" section provides information about past and present missions, including timelines and extensive video and audio coverage of recent shuttle flights. "About NASA" takes the reader through the growth of the space agency from its founding by an act of Congress in 1958.

The bottom two-thirds of the home page is divided into three parts: "Life on Earth," "Humans in Space," and "Exploring the Universe," each of which takes you to pages offering information on everything from NASA's research into wind power to real-time charting of comets for night-sky watchers.

All the stories and features are extremely well organized and written for the general reader, providing the right balance between technical information and easily digested prose. Many of the pages feature stunning images from NASA's network of satellites and, of course, the Hubble Telescope.

Why You Should Visit

In survey after survey, average Americans continue to demonstrate a lack of knowledge about basic scientific matters, and the gap is growing between what most American students know about science and their counterparts in other countries. "America is losing its dominance in innovation," one expert noted recently. "The country's once-tight lock on the world's best science and technology talent is loosening as top foreign students have new opportunities in their own country. And America's students are not filling the vacuum."[1]

No one ever feels compelled to visit a site merely for their own good, but in this case, NASA's user-friendly pages make the process of re-education painless. The information covered is unarguably important and deserves a look. To be glib, what could matter more than the fate of the universe?

Keep This in Mind

NASA has earned quite a few critics, in both the scientific and political communities, over the past decade. The space agency has been criticized for everything from its lax quality control to its over-reliance on the space shuttle. More recently, the agency's high-profile announcement that it is aiming to put people back on the moon—as a prelude to sending humans further into space to explore Mars— generated lots of criticism. One prominent academic critic blurted "What for?" when learning of the moon and Mars missions.[2] Given its multibillion-dollar price tag, many Washington sources say the project has little chance of being completed.

Off the Record

NASA's first space shuttle, *Enterprise*, was supposed to be named *Constitution*, but a write-in campaign by *Star Trek* fans persuaded NASA officials to name the shuttle after the starship *Enterprise*, featured on the popular sci-fi television show.

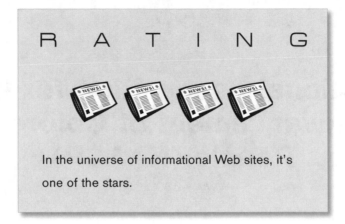

RATING

In the universe of informational Web sites, it's one of the stars.

Endnotes

1. From an "OnPoint" radio program broadcast, produced by WBUR, Boston Public Radio, Dec. 3, 2004. Transcript available through www.wbur.org.
2. Kelly Young, "Critics say NASA moon plan too costly," *New Scientist*, Sept. 20, 2005 (www.newscientist.com).

49

National Association for the Advancement of Colored People (NAACP)

www.naacp.org

Overview

The battle to end racism and the struggle for equality in the U.S. has been a long, slow, and often arduous fight. Since its founding in 1909, the National Association for the Advancement of Colored People (NAACP)—the oldest civil rights group in America—has manned the frontlines. From small, subtle triumphs to momentous Supreme Court victories, the NAACP succeeded in its mission more often than not.

In the early years, its heroic leaders and members and legendary actions could fill a history textbook: from organizing nationwide protests against the D.W. Griffith film *Birth of a Nation* to its special counsel Thurgood Marshall arguing the unconstitutionality of school segregation before the Supreme Court and winning the landmark case *Brown v. Board of Education*, from its efforts to end lynchings to NAACP member and volunteer Rosa Parks refusing to give up her seat on a segregated bus in Alabama. During the 1990s, however, the organization spent more time dealing with internal scandals than fulfilling its mission, and the NAACP has still not recovered from the damage that was done to its image and reputation.

But the war against injustice and inequality in this country rages on, from the voting booth to the courthouse to the workplace, and the NAACP now has another weapon in the fight for progress: a Web site—a vital forum it uses to appeal to new members and contributors, issue clarion calls, post "news," and detail its agenda on a wide-ranging scope of social ills.

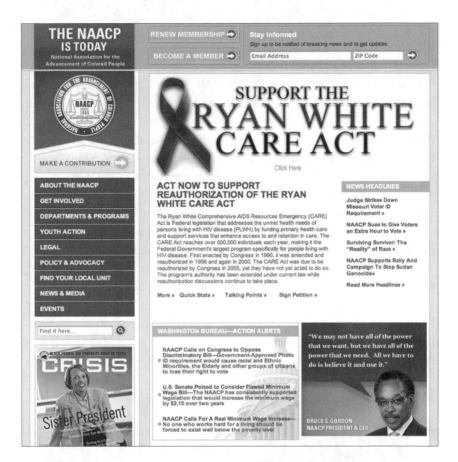

What You'll Find There

The main feature of the NAACP.org home page usually involves a call to action—from registering voters to urging Congress to pass certain legislation (i.e., in the fall of 2006, the dominant headline implored users to sign a petition for federal legislators to reauthorize the Ryan White Comprehensive AIDS Resources Emergency Act). Users can also read the organization's press releases. Links to several of its most recent releases appear on the first screen of the home page under the heading "News Headlines." While many appear to be written in a style no different than stories in a daily newspaper, remember that these are not news articles in the traditional sense but rather press releases authored by its staff. Nonetheless, they are still worth reading, since they cover some interesting and varying topics (for a full list of releases, click the "Read More Headlines" link): "Judge Strikes Down Missouri Voter ID Requirement," "NAACP, NAHB Release Groundbreaking Report on Housing," "Surviving Survivor: The 'Reality' of Race," and "NAACP Urges NCAA To Extend & Expand Ban in South Carolina." In the middle of the home page, the NAACP again solicits the help of visitors to the site. Under the banner "Washington Bureau—Action Alerts," several headlines about legislative bills it either opposes or supports link to pages that outline "The Issue," "The Action We Need To Take" (i.e., contact your representative with a list of ways to do so), "The Message," and a downloadable letter users can sign and send to their congressperson.

Running down the left side of the page is a menu of links: "About the NAACP," where users can learn about its remarkable history; "Get Involved," whether it's by donating money, becoming a member, or pledging to "Arrive with Five" other people at the polls on Election Day; "Departments & Programs," which includes links to a variety of subsections (from its "Prison Project" to "Religious Affairs") and separate sites (such as the "Hollywood Bureau" link to the NAACP Image Awards site); "Youth Action," featuring initiatives for a new generation

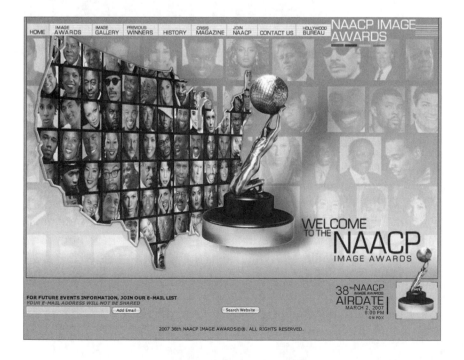

of civil rights leaders; "Legal," which highlights this department's "History & Achievements" and provides an active "Docket" of its civil rights cases; and "Policy & Advocacy," drawing attention to matters ranging from education and criminal justice to civic engagement and international affairs.

Why You Should Visit

Race is still very much an issue in the U.S. and the world, and the media, politicians, and the general public are rarely brave enough to confront it. The NAACP does—in thoughtful and provocative ways rather than through easy, sensational means. For those who have suffered the woes of second-class status because of skin color or ethnicity, NAACP.org offers empowerment. For those who haven't, it provides education.

Keep This in Mind

While its history is admirable, more recent activity at the NAACP is not. A year and a half after being appointed as executive director in 1993, Benjamin Chavis "resigned after a deal became public to pay more than $300,000 in NAACP funds to a former female aide threatening a sexual harassment claim."[1] The internal problems of the NAACP would not end there. A 1999 memo detailing allegations of sexual mistreatment of female employees and inappropriate favoritism by then-president Kweisi Mfume was kept secret and basically ignored for five years. When the media finally uncovered the internal investigations, the NAACP—described as a "terribly sexist organization"—found itself yet again hindered by an all-but-ruined reputation.[2]

Off the Record

After declining invitations to speak at the NAACP's annual convention each year during his first term, President George W. Bush earned the dubious distinction of becoming the first U.S. president not to do so while in office since Herbert Hoover.[3] In July 2006, Bush finally attended and addressed the convention.[4]

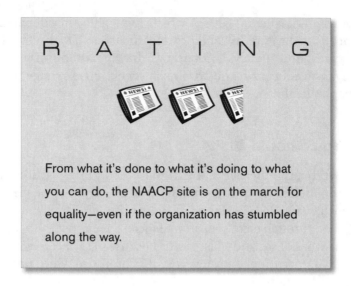

R A T I N G

From what it's done to what it's doing to what you can do, the NAACP site is on the march for equality—even if the organization has stumbled along the way.

Endnotes

1. Kelly Brewington, et al., "Pattern of abuse claims at NAACP kept quiet: Mfume, supporters deny impropriety at office," *Baltimore Sun*, May 8, 2005.

2. Ibid.

3. Murray Dubin, "President declines NAACP's invitation again," *Philadelphia Inquirer*, July 8, 2004.

4. "Bush invokes civil rights in NAACP speech: President says he wants Republican Party to improve African-American ties," Associated Press, July 20, 2006.

50

National Enquirer

www.nationalenquirer.com

Overview

The *National Enquirer* can boast about something that most publications can only dream of: Everybody knows who they are. That's good. Also bad.

Good, because the *National Enquirer*'s campaign to establish itself as the go-to publication for a particular type of journalism has allowed it to build a base of subscribers that make it one of the most widely read publications in the country, with almost 1 million faithful weekly readers.

Bad, because when many people hear the words "*National Enquirer*," they immediately think of other words like "scandal," "irresponsible," and "tabloid."

But the story is more complex than that. The *National Enquirer* has done some real reporting and, over the past couple of years, has emerged as a genuine story breaker. Yet it has continued to pursue stories that deal almost exclusively with the world of celebrity gossip and pop culture ephemera. And its Web site distills this publication—which expends journalistic earnestness on vapid cultural flotsam—into a concoction that is even more frothy and frivolous than its parent publication.

What You'll Find There

Reading the *National Enquirer*'s site is like standing behind the velvet ropes at the Oscars and catching fleeting glimpses of celebrities as they race by, looking well-coifed and waving amiably (or looking irritated by the paparazzi and brusquely turning away). Either way, you see a little, you get excited, and then it's all over.

There are lots of stories listed on the home page—almost all having a celebrity tie-in and usually celebrated with a splashy photo (one

recent story carried the almost-surreal headline "Yanni Arrested for Alleged Domestic Battery").

Click on any of the many stories that appear under the "More News" banner, and you'll get a short, staff-written article—usually very short. None of the stories on the Web site provides much depth or context. Even for celebrity journalism, most of the articles are irritatingly brief.

Many articles carried on the Web site deal with salacious aspects of the celebrity world: drunkenness, adultery, eating disorders, spousal abuse, and the like. The overall impact of reading one after another of these stories is at first numbing, then nauseating. But there's more: The stories under "Crime/Investigation" feature criminals, well-known and unknown, whose exploits have placed them in the public eye; the "Ask Dr. Erika" links will take you to breezy medical advice columns dealing with everything from frigidity and fertility to child-rearing and calorie counting.

Columnist Mike Walker posts several stories on the site, adding more gossip and salacious rumor to a page already groaning under the weight of innuendo and voyeuristic titillation.

Why You Should Visit

Because enquiring minds want to know (to quote their famous former advertising slogan). The *Enquirer* is our national early warning
system for the next celebrity upheaval waiting to convulse the cable
TV talk-fests and fill the pages of knock-off gossip tabloids. Now that
celebrity watching has become the national pastime, publications
like the *Enquirer* provide a compass to the whirligig of pop culture
trends.

And, as more serious journalism continues to be ushered to the
rear of mainstream media vehicles, the *National Enquirer* is often
cited as the source of a breaking celebrity story by more credible news
outlets.

Keep This in Mind

Reading the *Enquirer* will give you inside details about your favorite
celebrity, but you won't get much to think about after you've logged
off. In what could be a useful addition to the Web site, the *Enquirer*
encourages readers to participate in forums to discuss stories on the
site, but the comments reflect the same level of engagement as the
original reports: short and fawning.

Yet, the *National Enquirer* knows its audience and its subject
matter. So long as there is a large segment of the population salivat-
ing for celebrity news and gossip, the *Enquirer* is likely to continue
to prosper.

Off the Record

After the *Enquirer* lost a high-profile libel case against Carol Burnett in
1981 (the magazine erroneously reported that she had been seen drunk
in public with Henry Kissinger), the publication changed its reporting
methods and implemented a rigorous system of fact-checking. It now

has the reputation of being thoroughly accurate—though still obsessed with cheesy celebrity misdeeds.

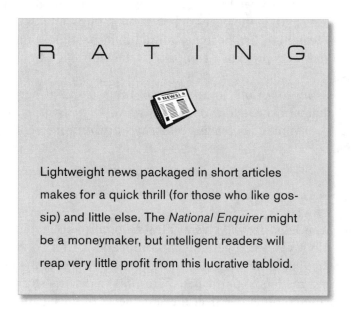

R A T I N G

Lightweight news packaged in short articles makes for a quick thrill (for those who like gossip) and little else. The *National Enquirer* might be a moneymaker, but intelligent readers will reap very little profit from this lucrative tabloid.

51

National Geographic
www.nationalgeographic.com

Overview

Long before Animal Planet or the Discovery and History channels, long before global warming and "green" initiatives became front-page news, and long before endangered species had a list, 33 men founded a society "to increase and diffuse geographic knowledge while promoting the conservation of the world's cultural, historical, and natural resources."[1] In 1888, only nine months after forming, the society (once headed by Alexander Graham Bell) published its official journal, for which it is now known throughout the world. And *National Geographic*, through remarkable photography and exploratory (and sometimes dangerous) reporting from all corners of the globe, has inestimably helped readers know the world, from its animals and habitats to its people and cultures to its history and geography.

Although the magazine remains its prize possession (there are editions in 31 languages), the National Geographic Society—a financial backer for thousands of scientific research and global exploration projects and a fierce supporter of education and conservation—also publishes four other niche periodicals and thousands of books. It also produces documentaries like the Academy Award-winning *March of the Penguins* and broadcasts original programming on its own cable/satellite channel. Through those media assets and its expansive Web site—largely an outlet for National Geographic News—the National Geographic Society reaches about 280 million people a month in locales as diverse as the areas it covers. And as that number rises, so do the survival chances of the planet and all those who inhabit it—if awareness ever translates into action.

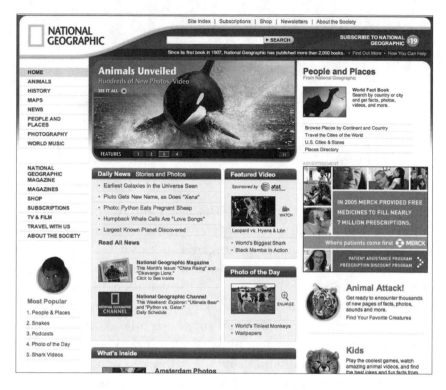

What You'll Find There

Unsurprisingly, striking images dominate the main screen of the NationalGeographic.com home page. At the top middle of the page, a slideshow-type display—graphics or photos embedded with headlines, subheads, and links to read more—rotates through the site's top four to five features. Running down the left side of the page are links to the front pages of its various sections—"Animals," "History," "Maps," "News," "People and Places," "Photography," and "World Music"—as well as links to its magazines and store. Below the prominent, visually appealing teasers, five additional headlines/links are provided under the heading "Daily News: Stories and Photos."

On the "News Front Page," you will find a list of about eight National Geographic News headlines, each of which are accompanied by a story summary and small photo (the top story has a slightly larger photo and headline). At the top left, users can link to news organized in more specific subsections: "Animals & Nature," "Archaeology & Paleontology," "Environment," "Health," "History &

Culture," "Offbeat," "Science & Space," and "Travel & Adventure." At the top right are four "Editor's Picks," the day's "Best News Photo," and "Video in the News." The news stories have a style more similar to the ones that appear in daily newspapers, albeit often very different subject matter (i.e., "Humpback Whale Calls Are Love Songs, Biologists Suggests," "Alien 'ID Chart' to Aid Search for Extraterrestrial Life," and "Nepalese Porters May Be World's Most Efficient Haulers"), rather than the long-form journalism typical of *National Geographic* magazine. But users are provided with links to several "Related"

National Geographic News articles and multimedia, along with "Sources and Related Web Sites" for each story.

Why You Should Visit

Logging on to NationalGeographic.com is like visiting the Museum of Natural History, only it's updated daily and delivered to your desktop. You'll leave feeling a whole lot smarter. If your globetrotter fantasies of remote destinations and exotic adventures and worldly knowledge have gone unfulfilled, NationalGeographic.com is a virtual odyssey like no other. Even though the world is said to be getting smaller, there is still much to learn about Planet Earth—from its varied landscape to its diverse people and the universe in which it resides. And as both continue to evolve, the National Geographic Society continues to teach.

Keep This in Mind

Each of the five National Geographic Society magazines—*National Geographic, National Geographic Traveler, National Geographic Adventure, National Geographic Explorer*, and *National Geographic Kids*—maintain what are essentially separate sites within the NationalGeographic.com domain. Unsurprisingly, all are visual masterpieces with loads of content to discover.

On the home page of its flagship publication, *National Geographic*, users will find graphic links to features (each occupying its own section of the site) from the current month's print edition. Clicking on any of the links will, at first glance, result in disappointment for those expecting the full story. Instead, the site offers only "a taste of what awaits you in print from this compelling excerpt." But users can still satisfy their appetite, thanks to a healthy menu of online-only offerings that accompany each feature: a "Photo Gallery" of captivating images and the technical details behind them; notes from reporters and photographers "On Assignment"; a chance to "Learn More" about the subject through related links, bibliography, and previous *National Geographic* coverage; and maps, forums, audio slideshows, and videos. Even with all that, users might feel because the entire article is not available, they've missed the main course.

Off the Record

While on assignment in Sudan for *National Geographic* in August 2006, Paul Salopek, a two-time Pulitzer winner who also writes for the *Chicago Tribune*, was arrested and charged with espionage by the Sudanese government. Both publications, along with the likes of Jimmy Carter, Bono, and other prominent figures, led the appeal for his release; after a meeting between New Mexico Gov. Bill Richardson and Sudanese President Omar al-Bashir, Salopek was freed from a Darfur jail, where he had spent 34 days.

Endnote

1. From the National Geographic Society's mission statement, which is posted on the NationalGeographic.com home page.

52

National Public Radio (NPR)

www.npr.org

Overview

There was a time when Americans gathered around radios to learn the news of the day. With the advent of television, and its subsequent development, that reliance on radio news broadcasts dramatically diminished. But radio survived—only to face further threats in the future when droves of listeners ditched the traditional dial in favor of new technologies such as MP3 players and subscription-based satellite radio services. Nonetheless, National Public Radio (NPR), founded in 1970 as an outgrowth of the Public Broadcasting Act of 1967, continues to attract an ample audience, which has expanded exponentially through the years: from 2 million weekly listeners in the early 1980s to more than 26 million today. NPR attributes that growth to its news service—a refreshing rarity on airwaves often strewn with minute-long updates and shout fests.

NPR, an "independent, private, nonprofit" organization, does not own any radio stations; it produces and distributes programming to more than 800 local member stations throughout the country. Funded largely by member dues, corporate sponsorships, and occasional donations (in 2003, the estate of the late widow of McDonald's founder Ray Kroc bequeathed more than $225 million), NPR excels by offering listeners an eclectic mélange of programming, from breaking news to classical music to special oral history projects. And for those who expect heavy audio content from its online counterpart as they would video from a cable news network Web site, NPR.org delivers a ton. Thanks to NPR.org, listening to great radio journalism is no longer a forgotten pastime or an activity reserved for commuters driving to and from the office.

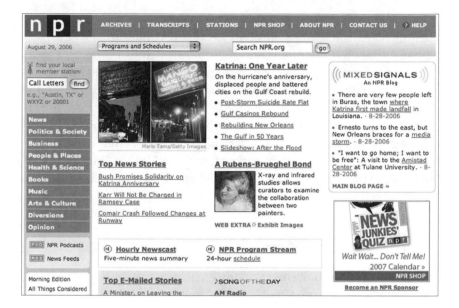

What You'll Find There

Users who log on to NPR.org probably won't be immediately wowed, but they'll soon realize why the site won five 2006 Webby Awards for its broad range and use of technology. Unlike so many other news sites, NPR.org relies solely on content produced by NPR. The site, however, is no less rich for its unwillingness to cull content from wire services (though there is a small "Latest Headlines" box in the far right column of the home page with breaking news "From the Associated Press"). In fact, that self-sufficiency is what makes the NPR.org experience so unique.

The site's home page design makes navigation simple, most of which can be done from the narrow strip down the left side of the page. You can access the front pages of various sections—"News," "Politics & Society," "Business," "People & Places," "Health & Science," "Books," "Music," "Arts & Culture," "Diversions," and "Opinion"—and NPR.org's program-specific pages, including those for its two most popular shows, *Morning Edition* and *All Things Considered*. A link to the "NPR Podcasts" directory, which allows you to search for and subscribe (at no cost) to any of its more than 300 podcasts "by Topic," "by Title," or "by Provider" (several are produced by local member stations but can still be found here), is located in this menu as well.

The home page is anchored by a major news package (a photo, a headline/link, and a story summary) at the top middle of the page, followed by links to three other "Top News Stories" and another to a spotlighted feature. Next, users will find audio links to "Hourly Newscast" and to currently airing programs, a small section listing "Top E-Mailed Stories" and "Editor's Picks," and more than a dozen other current features (each with a headline/link, thumbnail photo, story summary, and Web extras—audio slideshows, videos, and sidebars). From the right column of the home page, users can access the NPR blog "MixedSignals" and special projects, often taking an engaging oral history format, such as award-winners "This I Believe" and "StoryCorps."

Why You Should Visit

NPR is consistently ranked as the most trusted news source in America, and its audience has proven to be better informed than consumers of all other print and television media. For those who would rather not have their news watered down, NPR.org is their kind of cocktail. Nearly every story is presented in audio format (click the "Listen" link between the headline and byline on story pages); most of these radio reports are accompanied by Web extras while print-style articles complement some. NPR's mission is "to create a more informed public." This Web site, where smart correspondents and commentators make smart listeners, is a major reason why NPR achieves that goal every day.

Keep This in Mind

In order to fully enjoy NPR.org, much of which consists of content first broadcast on radio, some users will need to install the proper software on your computer to open and play audio files. Although most computers are already equipped with the required software, there's no cause for alarm if your system is not. Simply visit the Web sites of

RealPlayer or Windows Media Player to access free, and usually quick, downloads. Or, if you're an inexperienced computer or Web user, click the "Help" link in the top right corner of the NPR.org home page.

Off the Record

Between September 1998 and May 1999, three members of the U.S. Army's Psychological Operations unit (PSYOP), roamed NPR's head-quarters in Washington D.C. as interns, supposedly unbeknownst to the news organization's top brass (a situation that also occurred at CNN from June 1999 to March 2000). Once the PSYOP personnel were discovered, the relationship was deemed "inappropriate," ending the internships. While NPR maintained that the interns performed only marginal duties that did not affect news coverage and the military insisted it only wanted "training from media professionals," some media critics wondered if the news operations had unwittingly become targets of some covert operation.[1]

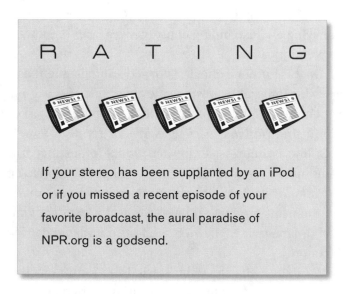

R A T I N G

If your stereo has been supplanted by an iPod
or if you missed a recent episode of your
favorite broadcast, the aural paradise of
NPR.org is a godsend.

Endnote

1. J. Max Robins, "US Army PSY-OPS personnel assigned to CNN, NPR," *TV Guide*, April 15, 2000 (www.unknownnews.net /2000-1.html).

53

National Review

www.nationalreview.com

Overview

Once upon a time, conservatism wasn't the ascendant political ideology. It did not jibe with the occupants of the White House, Congress, the intelligencia, or Main Street. Conservativism was, in those good old days, a minor annoyance to the liberal majority. For those born under the Reagan–Bush (I and II) conservative revival, such a time might be hard to imagine.

What changed? Well, that depends on the social theorist you happen to ask. But almost everyone—left, right, and center—agrees that the journal of political thought, *National Review*, has played a central role in reviving and expanding conservatives' grip on power in contemporary America.

And now, this former iconoclast-turned-establishment darling has embraced the Internet to promulgate its brand of make-no-apologies-for-being-right philosophy. Whether the pitbull, market-driven principle fueling *National Review* excites or repulses you, National Review Online is impressive. In fact, unlike other magazines that sometimes merely transfer their print-based publication to an online format, *National Review*'s online presence has plenty that can't be found in the print product and also omits a great deal that's sandwiched in the magazine. The Web site is also updated daily with lots of fresh content.

Surely William F. Buckley, who started the journal in 1955 when conservatism was as desultory as a Humphrey liberal is today, could not have imagined the day when a cybernetic spin-off of *National Review* would register 1 million hits a day.

A million … that's a lot—even to a conservative.

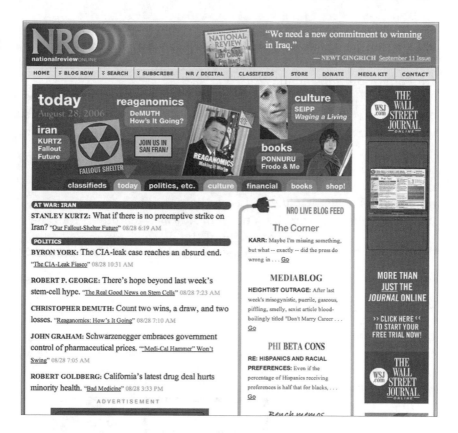

What You'll Find There

Because *National Review* has always been a journal of analysis and commentary rather than a traditional news magazine, that's the approach the Web site takes—lots of analysis and commentary. *National Review* is famous for its columnists, from former contributors like Joan Didion, Robert Bork, and George F. Will to current writers Dinesh D'Souza, Larry Kudlow, and, of course, William F. Buckley.

These commentators are sprinkled throughout the site under a somewhat unusual but easily navigated page built on a sort of tier system, with icons for each section above brief, teasing paragraphs. Topics range from "At War" (which introduces commentary from the U.S. perspective, as well as Middle Eastern and European views) to such standard categories as "The White House," "Economy," "Culture," "Books," and lots of other occasional titles.

The page also includes links for any of the previous week's postings (day by day), as well as a menu of that day's important commentaries and editorials from publications including the *Washington Post*, the *Wall Street Journal*, and the *New York Post*.

Perhaps the principal advantage of the online version of the *National Review* is its extensive use of blogs. A dozen of the journal's writers maintain robust and regularly updated blogs, tackling with typical ferocity the large issues of the day, from immigration and Supreme Court decisions to the errant political gossip column.

And perhaps surprisingly for such a serious-minded publication, the National Review Online addresses lighter public preoccupations, including television, movies, and books. It also features a thorough business section, updated throughout the day, covering the fluctuations of domestic and world financial markets.

Why You Should Visit

If you've tired of the talk-radio style bombast that earmarks much of the conservative message, this is your site. *National Review* yields to no publication, including those sometimes-eye-glazing, think tank-issued special reports, in its depth and cogency. This is the thinking person's guide to the conservative way of life. How refreshing to find an online site that has enough confidence in its readers to follow lengthy and complex arguments that might just happen to be longer than one computer screen. Those who oppose conservatism will find, usually, a thoughtful articulation of the subject being discussed.

YOUR WEEKLY UPDATE FROM THE NRO EDITORS: U.N. Shenanigans; Col. Graham; Oriana Fallaci, R.I.P; Arnold & the Dems; & more. Go.

Keep This in Mind

National Review is not above taking a shot at liberals. As with many other conservative media, the publication can't seem to resist the occasional tweak at the expense of the Clintons or, when they're feeling really frisky, Franklin Roosevelt.

Off the Record

Buckley and pal Willi Schlamm, a former communist, spent two years trying to raise the $300,000 necessary to publish *National Review*. The first issue in 1955 carried the Buckley-authored statement about this new journal: "It stands athwart history, yelling Stop, at a time when no other is inclined to do so, or to have much patience with those who so urge it."[1]

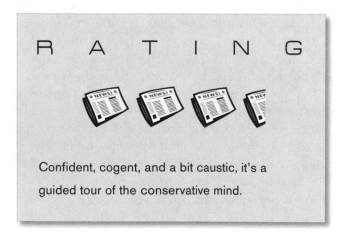

RATING

Confident, cogent, and a bit caustic, it's a guided tour of the conservative mind.

Endnotes

1. William F. Buckley, "Publisher's Statement," available at www.nationalreview.com/flashback/buckley200406290949.asp.

54

National Rifle Association (NRA)

www.nra.org

Overview

Few issues in contemporary society generate as much controversy and passion as gun control. Dead center in the crosshairs of this debate is one of the most vocal and aggressive groups on the political landscape: the National Rifle Association (NRA). With a membership that is known as much for targeting electoral districts as for targeting bulls-eyes, the NRA—because of its size and ferocity—regularly becomes news. Not surprisingly, the image-conscious group also provides extensive "news" coverage on its Web site, NRA.org, and a companion Web site, NRAHQ.org ("HQ" for "headquarters").

Though not a traditional, mainstream news site with an interest in appearing to be objective, the NRA's Web page is nonetheless essential reading for anyone who wishes to understand some of the issues central to the ongoing debate about the place of firearms in American society (there's a separate Web page and association for U.K. residents[1]). Since gun control as an explosive political issue isn't going away any time soon, Web surfers who may want to know what makes gun owners tick—and gets them ticked off—should pay NRA.org a visit.

What You'll Find There

Visitors to the site will find what, at first, looks like the home page of many other news organizations, with the page sporting a banner that reads "NRA Top News Stories." Headlines are provided for the site's featured stories, as well as stories that feature "NRA in the Media." These headlines are all linked to longer versions of the stories, which are written by NRA staffers with a decidedly pro-gun slant. Most of

the articles focus on pending gun-control legislation or on exposing the threat to gun ownership by groups as diverse as the Humane Society and the United Nations.

The site also offers an abundance of articles, historical documents, court cases, and essays about the Constitution in its "Second Amendment Center," as well as a link to NRANews.com, which is not as much a news site as "a free-speech roundtable of political conversation and live, late-breaking news about your Second Amendment freedoms."

In the "Programs" section, you will uncover dozens of subsections that link to NRA pet projects, such as "Eddie Eagle," a gun safety education program at various elementary schools across the country; "Hunting News," which includes everything from ads for NRA's "Great American Hunters Tour" to recipes for game preparation, such as "British Columbian Caribou Mountain Breakfast (Moose Liver, Bacon and Eggs with Onions)"; and "Women's Programs," which features the kind of headlines hunters—and people who just don't get hunting— find irresistible: "Ladies Make Memories, Take Venison During NRA Women on Target Hunt."

Why You Should Visit

The NRA is a force in American political culture, like it or not. Millions, apparently, like it; millions also do not. Even hardened critics of the NRA, however, must admit that the group—and its Web site—is well organized, thorough, dynamic, and attentively updated. If there is anything happening in the country that even touches on Second Amendment freedoms, the NRA site is all over it. Political junkies know full well the power of the NRA to make or break a local, congressional, or senatorial candidate. As former President Bill Clinton noted in his autobiography, "The NRA was an unforgiving master: One strike and you're out."[2] The site, with its updates and its action alerts, is the best way to take the pulse of this critically important organization.

Keep This in Mind

Little on the site represents an even-handed discussion of gun-related issues. The NRA is, after all, an advocacy group, not a news organization. The site is stuffed with information—much of it is technically accurate, but all of it is subject to wildly different interpretations.

SAFETY PROGRAMS
EDDIE EAGLE

What is The Eddie Eagle GunSafe® Program?

The Eddie Eagle GunSafe® Program teaches children in pre-K through third grade four important steps to take if they find a gun. These steps are presented by the program's mascot, Eddie Eagle®, in an easy-to-remember format consisting of the following simple rules:

If you see a gun:

STOP!
Don't Touch.
Leave the Area.
Tell an Adult.

Readers in search of objectivity can find lots of other Web sites that are diametrically opposed to the views expressed on NRA.org. Few of those sites, however, are as passionate, focused, and just plain thick as the NRA's site.

Off the Record

The presidency of the NRA has attracted the interest of lots of notable people. One of its first presidents was former U.S. President Ulysses S. Grant and one of its most recent presidents was the actor Charlton Heston. Even the noted liberal activist/filmmaker Michael Moore—a lifetime NRA member—has publicly stated his interest in the group's highest office (though he's also said that his first act, if elected, would be to abolish the organization[3]).

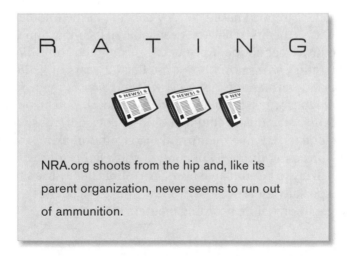

RATING

NRA.org shoots from the hip and, like its parent organization, never seems to run out of ammunition.

Endnotes

1. www.nra.org.uk
2. Bill Clinton, *My life*, New York: Knopf, 2004, p. 629.
3. For more on Michael Moore's thoughts about the NRA, consult the archives available at michaelmoore.com.

55

New York Daily News

www.nydailynews.com

Overview

There are moments in the history of journalism that clearly stand out as landmarks—Johannes Gutenberg's 15th-century invention of the printing press the tallest of all. The founding of the New York *Daily News* in 1919 ranks high on that long list of notable achievements. To those who read the 50-cent tabloid on their daily subway or bus commute in the New York City metropolitan area, accustomed to its bold headlines and sensational tendencies, this statement might cause more bewilderment than a guitar-strapped naked cowboy dancing in the middle of Times Square. But as the first daily American tabloid, its impact on the newspaper industry cannot be overstated. Not only did the *Daily News*— owned by the *Chicago Tribune* for the first 72 years of its life and by Mortimer Zuckerman (of *U.S. News & World Report* renown) since— popularize the format, but it also spawned a new brand of journalism.

The *Daily News* online edition has not followed in those once pioneering footsteps. While there's nothing groundbreaking about it—a design, consisting primarily of content shoveled from the print version, not likely to be emulated by many Webmasters—the site is functional, especially for anyone who doesn't have the chance to grab the morning edition before boarding the train.

What You'll Find There

The *Daily News* promotes itself as "New York's Hometown Connection," and visitors to its Web site will see why. On the home page and throughout the rest of the site, coverage of the Big Apple and surrounding areas is typically given priority.

The home page's template is simultaneously simplistic and hectic. "The Covers"—the front (and back) line in the fierce battle with crosstown tabloid rival, the *New York Post*, to win readers—immediately

draw attention. Directly above these front (news) and back (sports) page images, a navigation bar spans the three-column page, providing these clear options: "News & Views," "Sports," "Entertainment," "Biz/Money," "Boroughs," and "City Life." Rolling the cursor over these main sections reveals drop-down menus of shortcuts to more specific subsections.

The majority of the home page's original content is posted in the middle, and widest, column, where a large photo entices users to click on it to read the full (but brief) story. The next news package includes a headline—in a bold font nearly the size of the newspaper's name at the top of the page—that usually matches the one from the front cover of that day's print edition. As users scroll down the page, they'll find more than a dozen additional headlines (accompanied by story summaries and "Full Story" links) culled from a variety of sections, from breaking news and crime to sports and gossip. The site makes sure to let readers know when it has landed an "exclusive"—slapping the word in bright red font before the story summary.

On the "News & Views" front page, flanking the main column to the left, a narrow strip contains a bulleted list of about two-dozen "Breaking News" headlines, nearly all of which link to Associated Press stories. Local stories also take precedence here. Back on the home page, users will also find links to specialty publications along with a "Daily Dish" of gossip and some "Odd!" stories from across the county. The strip bordering the right side of the page looks a lot like newspaper classifieds. While Web-only content is rare, sports hounds get thrown a treat: "TheBigBlogs" sniff out all the goings-on of the city's major teams.

Why You Should Visit

While it's the largest city in the U.S. and one of the most important in the world, New York City is an enigma to many people, even to many American citizens. So, in that sense, everyone can benefit from logging on to NYDailyNews.com. But reading newspapers should not only be informative, it should also be fun. And this site is definitely that, from entertaining gossip columns to insightful sports coverage to irreverent headlines. Itself the subject of a Bravo television series in 2006, the *Daily News* brings its audience daily episodes of the reality show that is New York.

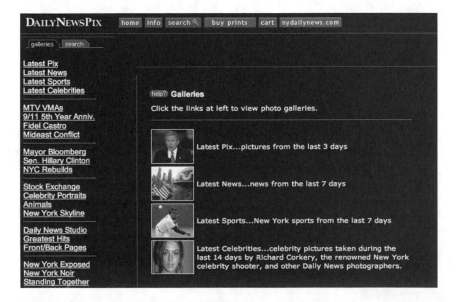

Keep This in Mind

The *Daily News* described itself as "New York's Picture Newspaper" from 1920 to 1991. While this slogan has since been replaced with another motto on the newspaper's front-page title banner, a camera icon has always been and continues to be used in the middle of the *Daily News* nameplate—both in print and online. It has maintained the tradition for good reason: The *Daily News* is still very much a "picture paper," and its site is loaded with photography. The *Daily News* operates what it calls "the world's largest online searchable image database"—the newspaper's online photo archive at DailyNewsPix.com, which is updated daily and where you can browse the extensive library for free or purchase prints for a fee. From historic collections to the latest snapshots, this online archive is a treasure trove of photojournalism.

Off the Record

For more than 60 years, until moving in the mid-1990s, *the Daily News* resided in a rather recognizable Manhattan skyscraper on 42nd Street near Second Avenue. Referred to as The News Building, it was home to the *Daily Planet* in *Superman: The Movie* and its first sequel. The lobby of the 37-story building, built when the *Daily News* had the highest circulation of any newspaper in the country, features a giant rotating globe—also a reminder of Clark Kent's *Planet*.

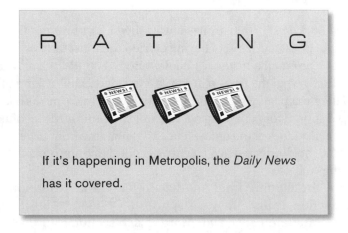

RATING

If it's happening in Metropolis, the *Daily News* has it covered.

56

New York Post
www.nypost.com

Overview

Once upon a time, newspapers were classified according to their physical size, either as a "broadsheet" (long, rectangular pages) or a "tabloid" (short, almost squarish pages). Soon, these labels came to designate a style of journalism, with broadsheets considered more traditional and sober and tabloids more sensational and gossipy. And even though the digital revolution has obliterated such physical distinctions for Internet users, the *New York Post* remains a prime example of American tabloid journalism, complete with screaming front pages, pun-filled headlines, rumor-mongering, and unabashed political slant. To the journalistic connoisseur, the *New York Post* is jug wine.

Yet, in a news landscape that sees declining circulation and revenues each year among the more "respectable" newspapers, the *New York Post*'s intoxicating brew of frivolity, urban brashness, and 15 minutes of infamy appears to be just what many news consumers are looking for.

What You'll Find There

The *New York Post*'s strength has always been its irreverent front page (which can boast, perhaps, of having carried the most tasteless headline in mainstream media history: "Headless Body Found In Topless Bar"[1]). That's exactly what the *Post* online gives its readers: a full-color reproduction of the front page, which morphs every few seconds into its back page (always a sports story), flashing not one but two pun-filled and often jaw-dropping headlines at the online reader. Though the front page is miniaturized, the bold, outsized headlines easily dominate any other text on the rest of the Web site.

Above the flipping front-and-back diorama are the more traditional section icons: "News," "Sports," "Opinion," "Business/Real Estate," "Entertainment," and "More." Each section is further broken

up into categories such as "More Local Stories" (extensively covered), "More National Stories" (adequate), and "More International Stories" (woefully lacking in depth or context—almost as if the *Post* is merely covering world events to prove it's a real newspaper).

The thoroughbred in the lineup is, without a doubt, the sports section. In the print and especially the online version (which features breaking sports news, updated scores of games in progress, and links to all the teams of the major sports leagues), the mix of meat-and-potatoes sports reporting and highly entertaining columnists (with a decidedly New York bias) makes the *Post* online a great one-stop shop for both local and national sports cruisers.

Why You Should Visit

For the same reason some people visit New York City you may be interested in visiting the site: There's really no other news source quite like the *New York Post*. It's famous for its sardonic humor, sneering headlines—and its Citizen Kane-like owner, Rupert Murdoch. The *Post* is also a useful bellwether newspaper; trends that are often started there sometimes leech into other, more "respectable" mainstream newspapers. For instance, the *Post* long ago abandoned standard English spelling in its headlines for words like "Prez" (for president) and "Pervs" (for sex offenders). The editors also don't seem to lose much sleep over their abandonment of objectivity, with headlines and subheads usually tipping off the reader to the *Post*'s conservative leanings. And the *Post*'s reliance on gossip and celebrity news helped engender such publications as *People* and the *National Enquirer.* (The Web site even boasts of having "the world's most famous gossip column," called PageSix, though even in the print edition it never actually *runs* on page six.)

Keep This in Mind

Today's online version of the *Post* is just the latest incarnation in a life span that dates to 1801, when it was founded by Alexander Hamilton. The *Post* has gone though a remarkable number of ownership and editorial changes that make it a kind of unofficial gazetteer of the U.S. Though staunchly conservative in its present form, it was once edited by the passionate abolitionist William Cullen Bryant and was later managed by Oswald Garrison Villard, a founding member of the NAACP and the ACLU (though it's a safe bet most *Post* readers today are blissfully unaware of the paper's radical history). It became a tabloid during the Depression, was purchased by Australian press baron Murdoch in 1977, sold shortly thereafter because of U.S. restrictions on foreign media ownership, and later repurchased by Murdoch's News Corp. in 1993 after the media mogul became a U.S. citizen.

But for all its storied history, the *Post* continues to break new ground with its audience-pleasing mix of dumbed-down front pages, breathless metro reporting, and kitchen-table conservatism.

Off the Record

Rupert Murdoch, according to an oft-repeated anecdote, once asked the chairman of the high-end retail store Bloomingdale's why he never purchased ads in the *New York Post*. "Because, dear Rupert," he replied, "your readers are my shoplifters."[2]

Endnotes

1. This headline is legendary and has been cited in many books and articles. For additional commentary, see "Faces in the news," Oct. 2, 2002 at Forbes.com.
2. This anecdote is retold in *The Post's New York: Celebrating 200 years of New York City as seen through the pages and pictures of the* New York Post, by the staff of the *New York Post* (New York: Collins, 2001).

57

New York Times

www.nytimes.com

Overview

Good journalism has never been about the technology. The Internet is just another step in the inevitable evolution of the means of story-telling. From the invention of movable type, through the telegraph, radio, network television, and cable broadcasts, one component has always emerged as indispensable to great journalism: the words themselves.

So if the best words make the best journalism, then the best journalistic Web sites are the ones that feature the best writers. No amount of technological legerdemain can mask a poorly reported, written, or edited piece. In a word, words *matter*. And in the crowded and noisy buzz of the World Wide Web, they matter more than ever.

Which brings us to the best-written newspaper anywhere, in any medium: the *New York Times*. Detractors can roll their eyes if they wish—just as its defenders can pretend to ignore some fairly serious ethical and reporting lapses in recent years—but there's no disputing the consistent world-class quality of the *Times*. There are the familiar names, the prizewinners, and high-profile writers, but you're just as likely to encounter a moving and richly written story buried deeply within some section by a writer you've never heard of. And almost all of these writers (with notable and painful exceptions) are available on the *Times*' Web site.

What You'll Find There

The online version of the *New York Times* offers a page that attempts to showcase all of the *Times*' important stories, columns, and special features, without being too crowded. The site mostly succeeds. The first thing you'll notice is the top story, with a headline and a sentence or two from the story's lead paragraph. The *Times* has never gone for

big headlines, and the Web site follows that rule. The articles that are listed under the main story feature even smaller heads.

There's a photo on the main page, but the *Times* is fairly restrained in its use of graphic images. Small thumbnail pix accompany story boxes teasing features from the Sunday magazine or a special section within the paper. There are also small photo boxes in the middle of the second screen, promoting stories and reviews from the paper's arts critics, as well as content available only to subscribers of "TimesSelect," a subscription-based roster of content including the op-ed columnists (Maureen Dowd, Thomas Friedman, and Frank Rich, for starters), "Talking Points" (issues being tracked by the editorial board), and an archive of stories dating back to 1851. Were it not that all of the other content of the paper is available—and can be easily located using an extensive index just below the main page—the loss of the op-ed columnists would be a body blow to the experience of reading the *Times* online. (Individual readers will have to decide if the loss of these benchmark commentators justifies the fairly modest monthly fee to subscribe to the service.)

Running down the left side of the main page, in exceedingly modest-sized type, is a roster of additional content available online, from blogs to an "NYC Guide," as well as columns from the paper's ombudsman, information about downloading podcasts, features from the upcoming Sunday magazine, and a full list of recent corrections.

At the bottom of the news pages you can find a list of the "most popular" stories, based on how many of them have been e-mailed to other people by *Times* readers.

In every one of the stories posted on the site, *Times* editors have embedded lots of useful links to related stories and helpful background information. For instance, in a recent review of a new *Superman* movie, readers were also directed to an interview with the director, the original Vincent Canby review of the first *Superman* movie, and a run-down of the career of *Superman* actor Christopher Reeve.

For an introduction to blogs, visit the Blogs 101 page.

DealBook
Daily news on mergers & acquisitions, I.P.O.'s, venture capital and more. Edited by Andrew Ross Sorkin.

Diner's Journal
Frank Bruni, restaurant critic for The Times, reports on restaurant news and trends, the life of a critic and more.

The Empire Zone
Several reporters track statewide elections in New York this year.

First Look
Talk with our editors and developers about new features and services that we're developing for NYTimes.com.

Pogue's Posts
Quick hits from the desk of technology columnist David Pogue.

The Pour
Eric Asimov, chief wine critic for The Times, discusses the pleasure, culture and business of wine, beer and spirits.

The Public Editor's Journal
Byron Calame, the readers' representative, responds to complaints and comments from the public and monitors the paper's journalistic practices.

Screens
Virginia Heffernan, Times TV critic, on Web video and media convergence.

U.S. Open '06
Michael Kimmelman and other Times writers provide updates, insights, scenes and live coverage of selected matches from the U.S. Open tennis tournament.

The Walk-Through
Writers for The Times offer residential real estate news, trends and tidbits.

The online edition also offers e-mail alerts so you can be kept informed of any stories that might address your personal inventory of interests.

Why You Should Visit

Aside from its intrinsic qualities (great writing, generally impressive reporting, full transcripts of presidential press conferences, and complete Supreme Court decisions), there's an extrinsic value: People talk about the stuff that's in the *New York Times*. Politicians, sports stars, and leaders in every field often react to the stories in the *Times*. So read it and stay atop the curve.

Keep This in Mind

Like any journalistic operation, the *New York Times* has made its share of blunders—sometimes huge ones. Allowing reporter Jayson Blair to invent and distort news over a period of months while he operated unchecked brought a requisite measure of deserved contempt from the journalistic community—and gave the *Times*' critics a field day. And the paper's credulous reporting of the Bush administration's claim of weapons of mass destruction in Iraq was shameful. Some people have even found the paper to be treasonous: On June 28, 2006, the House of Representatives passed a motion condemning the paper for reporting the details of a government program aimed at tracking secret financial dealings among terrorist operatives, and one congressman called for an investigation into whether the paper had violated the Espionage Act.

Off the Record

The *New York Times*' chief correspondent in Moscow during the 1930s was a reporter named Walter Duranty. His work earned the paper a Pulitzer Prize, but many historians and journalists have now concluded that Duranty was an active communist propagandist who purposely downplayed Stalinist atrocities. The *Times* has never disavowed his work.[1]

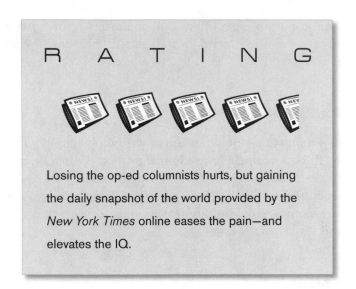

Losing the op-ed columnists hurts, but gaining the daily snapshot of the world provided by the *New York Times* online eases the pain—and elevates the IQ.

Endnote

1.   Andrew Stuttaford, "Prize specimen," www.nationalreview.com/stuttaford.

58

New Yorker
www.newyorker.com

Overview

The *New Yorker* is arguably the greatest magazine in the world. Its covers are works of art that lure readers to open the treasure chest and discover the jewels within its pages. Throughout its history, spanning more than 80 years, the *New Yorker* has published some of the best, and most important, literature of the 20th and 21st centuries. And by no means is that literature restricted to fiction and poetry, although those forms have long been a staple of this publication. It is the literature of narrative nonfiction and long-form journalism—from in-depth profiles to original investigations—that truly distinguishes the *New Yorker* from the rest of today's periodical press, much of which is either fixated on reducing word counts or obsessed with celebrity.

Under the editorship of David Remnick, a former *Washington Post* reporter and then a writer for the publication he has presided over since 1998, the *New Yorker* has thrived, making it once again the gold standard of explanatory reporting and investigative journalism. But because the *New Yorker* is more concerned with telling important stories through the traditional means of great writing rather than using attention-grabbing photos and graphics, its Web presence is limited and lacks visual sophistication.

What You'll Find There

The *New Yorker*'s print and online editions are strikingly similar—so much so that even the fonts are mostly the same. Ads, many of which are in-house promotions to attract readers to its online store or entice them to subscribe to the magazine, line the top and right side of the *New Yorker*'s home page, where several stories from the current print edition are featured—each under the name of the section in which it

appears, with a headline (doubling as the link to the complete story), a subhead or blurb, and byline. On the left side of the home page in traditional *New Yorker* font is a vertical navigation menu, where users will find links to its various classic sections: "Goings On About Town," "The Talk of the Town," "Fact," "Fiction," "The Critics," "Shouts & Murmurs," and "Cartoons."

At NewYorker.com, there is a reward for those who choose to visit the site in addition to reading the magazine, and it comes in the form of "Online-Only" content. Limited but useful, the online exclusives typically include an interview with a writer about an article currently in the magazine. Video interviews and audio slideshows, nonexistent here not long ago, have been slowly integrated into this section since 2006 when the magazine hired its first Web editor.

Why You Should Visit

The roster of past contributors to the *New Yorker* reads like a writers' hall of fame (it used an entire issue in August 1946 to publish John Hersey's *Hiroshima* and serialized Truman Capote's *In Cold Blood* in

1965 before it was published in book form a year later), and most of its current contributors would all be locks for future induction if such a place existed.

While the *New Yorker*'s Web site has lagged behind other media sources in harnessing the power of the Internet, it at least recognizes when the site should be utilized, like in 2004 when it published Seymour Hersh's Abu Ghraib prison abuse scoop online two days before the magazine hit the newsstands.

Keep This in Mind

In Fall 2005, the *New Yorker* issued a set of eight DVD-ROMs containing every cover and page of every issue from its first in February 1925 to its 80th anniversary edition in 2005. That's 4,109 issues—a half-million pages accessible from your home computer in a format identical to the published print version. *The Complete New Yorker,* with a price similar to the yearly magazine subscription rate and with

annual updates available, compensates its tech-savvy readers for the shortcomings of its Web site.

Off the Record

In 2004, the *New Yorker*—considered liberal but nonpartisan—endorsed a presidential candidate for the first time in its 80-year history. Remnick, along with other editors at the magazine, blasted Bush's record as "one of failure, arrogance, and ... incompetence" and expounded its support for Democrat John Kerry in a 4,500-word editorial that was simply headlined "The Choice" (without consulting the *New Yorker*'s owner). Remnick plans to continue the endorsements, saying he had only one regret about breaking the institution's long tradition of silence on presidential elections: "In retrospect, I wish we had convinced more people."

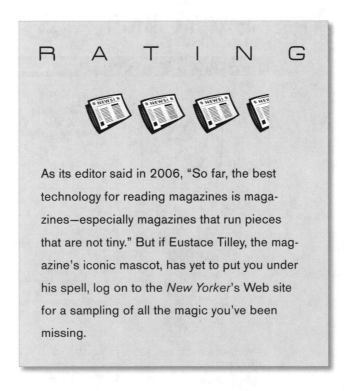

R A T I N G

As its editor said in 2006, "So far, the best technology for reading magazines is magazines—especially magazines that run pieces that are not tiny." But if Eustace Tilley, the magazine's iconic mascot, has yet to put you under his spell, log on to the *New Yorker*'s Web site for a sampling of all the magic you've been missing.

59

Newsweek
www.newsweek.com

Overview

Of all mainstream news organizations, newsweeklies face the toughest challenge when it comes to utilizing the Web, which offers immediacy and timeliness in a manner no other medium can match. Although major newspapers and broadcast outlets are still very much in the process of attempting to realize the full potential of the Internet, the transition from daily to instantaneous journalism is not as drastic as the fundamental shift in both philosophy and practice required by newsweeklies online. *Newsweek*—while not alone among similar magazines in its failure to fully exploit available technology—is a prime example of the difficulties faced when trying to make the weekly news format appeal to an audience conditioned to expect the news now.

Founded in 1933 by a former editor at *Time* (which debuted 10 years earlier and has rarely squandered the circulation lead in the years since the new competition arrived on newsstands) and bought by the Washington Post Co. in 1961, the magazine first appeared online in 1994 but not as Newsweek.com on the World Wide Web until four years later. Now nearly a decade old, *Newsweek*'s Internet sibling is still struggling to find its way on the information superhighway, despite making a slough of strategic (partnering with MSNBC), smart (posting what it calls "Web Exclusives"), and superficial (slapping the words "Daily Edition" in its title banner) moves since 2000.

What You'll Find There

For a magazine that loves large headlines and even larger photos and graphics, the Newsweek.com home page is surprisingly bland and filled with tiny, nearly unreadable headlines. At the top of the page's left column, users will find a relatively small photo teasing the "Top Story," which can range, in a matter of minutes, from a shrewd column

255

about U.S. foreign policy by Fareed Zakaria (editor of *Newsweek International* familiar to viewers of ABC's *This Week*), to a feature about a hard-to-beat video game with an unrecognizable byline, to an article dissecting an upcoming campaign strategy by chief political correspondent Howard Fineman. To the right of the changing lead story are two headlines from "Today's Columnists" (with dime-sized photos of the corresponding writer); several links to "Web Exclusives"; and links to the site's "NewsMinutes" videoclips, which frequently combine Associated Press footage with voiceovers by *Newsweek* correspondents and editors.

Spanning both columns are links to other standard site features, from a daily newspaper-produced editorial cartoon to a celebrity photo gallery where users can vote on their favorite photo (the results are published in the next print edition). Here users can also take a quick look, and that's all it takes, at an unusual blog called "The Daily CW" ("CW" is short for "Conventional Wisdom") that presents *Newsweek*'s concise opinion about a hot issue; an entry consists of the date (i.e., "Sept. 13, 2006"), a subject (i.e., "Iraq war"), a red arrow used in much the same way movie critics are known to use thumbs (i.e., pointing downward), and a succinct explanation (i.e., "Sixty tortured and shot bodies found dumped around Baghdad. Suicide bombings increasing in Afghanistan. Are you watching the news, Dick Cheney?").

The rest of the home page is set up in a two-column format, with the week's headlines organized by date down the left side and special sections, a podcast called "Newsweek on Air," and links to content for

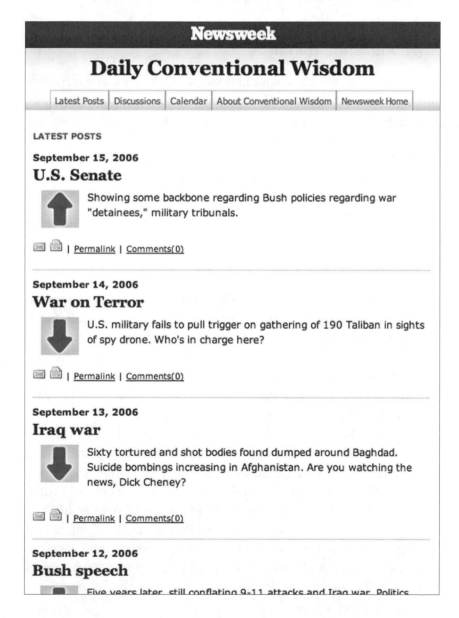

Newsweek

Daily Conventional Wisdom

| Latest Posts | Discussions | Calendar | About Conventional Wisdom | Newsweek Home |

LATEST POSTS

September 15, 2006
U.S. Senate

Showing some backbone regarding Bush policies regarding war "detainees," military tribunals.

| Permalink | Comments(0)

September 14, 2006
War on Terror

U.S. military fails to pull trigger on gathering of 190 Taliban in sights of spy drone. Who's in charge here?

| Permalink | Comments(0)

September 13, 2006
Iraq war

Sixty tortured and shot bodies found dumped around Baghdad. Suicide bombings increasing in Afghanistan. Are you watching the news, Dick Cheney?

| Permalink | Comments(0)

September 12, 2006
Bush speech

Five years later, still conflating 9-11 attacks and Iraq war. Politics

the international print edition in the right column. In a narrow strip running down the far-left side of the page, an image of the current cover of the U.S. print edition serves as a link to the cover story, and a menu lists the site's sections: "Periscope," "National News," "War in Iraq," "Enterprise," "Education," "Entertainment," "The Boomer Files," and "Columnists," among others (22 links in all).

Why You Should Visit

Newsweek is one of three major national newsweeklies, and it continues to wield power and influence. And for those of you who aren't pulling a copy out of the mailbox every week, checking in with the Web version on occasion isn't a bad idea. With access to the U.S. and international print editions, along with the online-only content, you'll be able to read stories that cover a broad range of issues (mostly through commentary and analysis), providing passable amounts of depth and context.

Keep This in Mind

If you're looking for the latest headlines at the beginning of the work-day, Newsweek.com probably won't suffice—but its host will. From the *Newsweek* site (which is technically called *Newsweek.com on MSNBC*), you'll find its saving grace—an extensive menu located on the far left of the home page below the list of Newsweek.com sections of links (in bold text) that connect to the MSNBC site and the Web pages of NBC News' programs including *Meet the Press*.

While its "Daily Edition" description disappoints due to its lack of fresh content, Newsweek.com's tagline "Our Voices. Your Voices. Every Day" suits the site well. Columnists are ubiquitous; *Newsweek* even offers readers a chance to be one. Through its interesting "My Turn" feature, which is unique among mainstream media outlets, *Newsweek* publishes 900-word essays by its readers. But if you have a story to tell, the chances of seeing it in the magazine or on the site are slim. Each month 600 entries are submitted; it publishes two each week—one online and one in print.

Off the Record

Glad to know whose opinion you're reading in your newsweekly of choice? Thank *Newsweek*, which only a few years after its first issue instituted signed, or bylined, columns—one way it has tried over the years to differentiate itself from rival *Time* and other competitors.

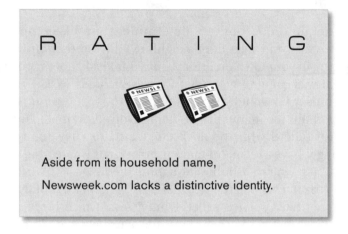

RATING

Aside from its household name,
Newsweek.com lacks a distinctive identity.

60

OhmyNews

english.ohmynews.com

Overview

Here's a quick question to determine your likely opinion of OhmyNews: If your next door neighbor told you that an event was happening in your town on Friday, but your local paper reported that the event was going to be on Saturday, which day would you go? In other words, who would you trust more?

OK, perhaps too many variables are involved. Your neighbor might be a local official who should be expected to know, or your local paper might have a record of making errors in the dates of events. But generally, it's a fair question: Who's more credible?

That's the question at the heart of a fairly new and rapidly expanding Internet news service called OhmyNews, which began in South Korea (and is still based there), but has since expanded its coverage from regional Korean news to global reports, covering everything from natural disasters to the World Cup soccer tournament. But what makes OhmyNews different is that almost all of the content is written by "correspondents"—that's their word for readers who submit news.

OhmyNews is another in the growing legion of Web sites that seeks to enlist "citizen journalists"—its international news service uses about 1,000, and in Korea, the site has relied on tens of thousands— to report the news. Although the service also claims that it maintains a staff of editors to fact-check and work with "correspondents," many of the stories have the flavor of being hastily written by Internet foot soldiers on the ground, close to the events being reported, with jarring subjectivity and often a lack of context.

What You'll Find There

OhmyNews has a great looking home page showcasing lots of different stories from lots of different regions of the globe, covering everything

from serious issues like genocide and the war in Iraq to international festivals and sporting events. The range of stories covered is truly impressive. The site features about a dozen "major" stories, each blurbed with a thumbnail photo or graphic. The reporter's name appears in parentheses after the blurb (about 30 of the service's correspondents are "featured reporters," or consistent contributors who've done enough work for the site to earn the status of a "regular").

Other nonbreaking stories, features, and photo essays are listed on the page under banners like "Global Lens," "Hot Seat," and "Citizen Journalism." These stories are also authored by OhmyNews contributors, and the range of writing skills and reporting detail differs widely. Most of the stories are competently presented, though, in some cases, there's little or no attempt to present information objectively. A lot of the reporting on the site is more akin to the kind of blogging that's spreading like wildfire on the Internet, rather than traditional news reporting—not always a bad thing, but sometimes quite bad.

The site's philosophy is best summed up by this statement on the Web page from the site's president and CEO, Oh Yeon-ho: "Our motto is 'Every one can be a reporter.'" Some readers will find that statement liberating and democratizing, while others might shudder at the implicit abandonment of traditional journalistic protocols.

For the mainstream news junkie, the site also provides links to some major wire stories by the *International Herald-Tribune* and the Associated Press.

Why You Should Visit

This site is indicative of the potential that many Internet gurus have been predicting since the dawn of the digital information age. Once a local South Korean phenomenon, OhmyNews expanded into Japan, and then throughout Asia, and now, just four years after its founding,

it's well established throughout Europe and the U.S. There's no stopping it now—though one hopes there will be time to assess what's lost as well as what's gained by enlisting so many readers with little or no formal training or news judgment. Such arguments can be labeled as elitist, but one reader's "snobbery" is another reader's "standards."

Keep This in Mind

Everyone has a perspective on the events unfolding around them, and the "citizen journalism" movement has opened up the formerly cloistered world of news gatekeeping. While this is cause for cautious optimism—and while OhmyNews claims to vet each story for libel and quality control—readers need to be aware that anyone can be a correspondent. Is proximity to an event—and a computer—really the only qualification a journalist needs?

Off the Record

To its great credit, OhmyNews does pay its correspondents a small fee (about $20) for their contributions to the Web site. In the world of "citizen journalism," such remuneration is almost unheard of.

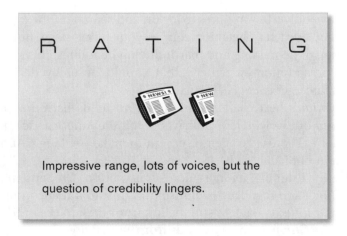

RATING

Impressive range, lots of voices, but the question of credibility lingers.

61

The Onion
www.theonion.com

Overview

When Tim Keck and Christopher Johnson, while students at the University of Wisconsin-Madison, dreamed up the idea to poke fun—and in some cases throw jabs—at the political establishment and the institution of mainstream media nearly two decades ago, did they realize their independent Midwestern tabloid would eventually develop into a worldwide phenomenon? Probably not.

But since the first print edition in 1988, *The Onion* has met and exceeded the most fanciful of expectations. In large part, the success of this experiment in humor, parody, and satire can be attributed to the launch of *The Onion*'s Web site in 1996, attracting a more national and global audience than it ever could via its ink-on-the-fingertips version.

What You'll Find There

If you have only a few minutes to log on and search for the top stories of the day, don't set TheOnion.com as your home page. But, after a long week of depressing and fear-inducing headlines, this site is the perfect prescription—a remedy that should be enjoyed in lieu of another late-night *Seinfeld* rerun.

The Onion's best characteristic is its no-holds-barred approach. Here, everyone—right, left, Hollywood, middle America, rich, poor—is fair game. There is no agenda, except to make you laugh. And more often than not it succeeds.

Take, for example, its most notorious edition. On September 26, 2001, *The Onion* managed to infuse humor into a tragic moment in history. Despite its readers still reeling from the attacks of 9/11, the staff of *The Onion* did not shy away from what it does best: imparting its satirical prose, echoing what many were thinking, and, in some strange way, capturing the surreal events forever. The headlines from

its "special" coverage of the attacks say it all: "Hugging Up 76,000 Percent"; "U.S. Vows to Defeat Whoever It Is We're At War With"; "American Life Turns into Bad Jerry Bruckheimer Movie"; "Hijackers Surprised to Find Selves in Hell: 'We Expected Eternal Paradise for This,' Say Suicide Bombers"; "God Angrily Clarifies 'Don't Kill' Rule"; "Bush Sr. Apologizes to Son for Funding Bin Laden in '80s."

But it doesn't take a momentous occasion for *The Onion* to thrive. It does so on a weekly basis. Even during a slow news cycle, *The Onion* still manages to induce laughter: "Bush Vows to Eliminate U.S. Dependence on Oil By 4920"; "Police Search of Backpack Yields Explosive Bestseller"; and "Longtime Married Couple Subjected to Excruciating 'Romantic Weekend Getaway'."

This easily navigated site looks much like a "real" news site: the headline, photo, and lead paragraph of the top story take a prominent spot on the page; a menu of sections—"Sports," "Local," "National," "International," "Politics," "Business," etc.—spans the top of the page; photographs, accompanied by a one-sentence blurb, link to other "Recent News"; and "In Brief" headlines tease laugh-out-loud, paragraph-length snippets. Then there are the "Opinion" columns, horoscopes, and the "STATSHOT"—a parody of a *USA Today* feature.

Why You Should Visit

Don't check this site out for factual information, only for laughs. The design is clean, the creativity is evident, and the writing is smart (a scroll through its headlines certainly serves as proof). Because TheOnion.com, like its print companion, is only updated weekly, it is a site that can be, and should be, browsed leisurely. There's not even a need to check in with TheOnion.com daily—unless, of course, you just can't resist.

Keep This in Mind

No matter how real they might sound, the headlines and stories that appear on TheOnion.com are fictitious. Don't forget this small but significant fact: It is all undoubtedly false, made up, not true. While this might seem like a bizarre warning, many have fallen victim to "America's Finest News Source"—somehow unaware of its satirical disposition. In an era of the cliché, one—"Don't believe everything you read"—seems to have been forgotten.

While *The Onion*'s content is far from factual, these embarrassing and preposterous gaffes actually occurred: The *Beijing Evening News* (the Chinese capital's largest circulation newspaper) reprinted on its international news page in June 2002 translated sections of an article from *The Onion* that reported Congress's displeasure with the Capitol building in Washington D.C., even quoting politicians who threatened to leave for a new home in Memphis or Charlotte if a "new, state-of-the-art building" was not constructed. The article, which mocked professional sports teams' demands for new stadiums, included an architectural rendering of a retractable-dome capitol, which the Beijing newspaper republished without credit.[1]

Foreign newspapers unfamiliar with the ways of *The Onion*, however, are not alone. A controversial minister used an article ("'98 Homosexual-recruitment drive nearing goal") as supporting material to his outlandish claim on his "God Hates Fags" Web site; a columnist used quotes—fabricated remarks—from an article to back her claims that Harry Potter books draft children into satanic cults; MSNBC's Deborah Norville reported that 58 percent of exercise in America is accomplished on television—yes, once again, this misleading information was lifted from none other than that oh-so-reliable source known as *The Onion*.[2]

Off the Record

The Onion's 9/11 edition nearly claimed for its staff of self-proclaimed slackers the most prestigious and sought-after award in journalism. This, as much as it might sound like one of those zany headlines on its site, is no joke. *Philadelphia Daily News* editor Zachary Stalberg said his fellow Pulitzer Prize judges "were blown away" by *The Onion*'s coverage of the Sept. 11 attacks.

R A T I N G

Peeling through the layers of *The Onion*'s Web site will make you cry—mostly out of laughter. Though sometimes because these far-fetched but authentic-looking reports seem all too similar to the wacky current affairs of the "real" world.

Endnotes

1. Henry Chu, "Reeled in by a spoof, Chinese daily shrugs off its capitol error," *Los Angeles Times*, June 7, 2002.

2. See the Wikipedia article on *The Onion* and link to these examples from "*The Onion* taken seriously" section.

62

People
www.people.com

Overview

If all indications are accurate and we do indeed live in a celebrity-obsessed culture, *People* is the magazine of record. The weekly publication, an offshoot of *Time*'s "People" page, first hit newsstands in March 1974 with a mission of "getting back to the people who are causing the news and who are caught up in it, or deserve to be in it." That early vision has morphed during the past 30 years into something quite different.

While people can debate whether *People* is evolving or devolving as it ages, there's no denying its ability to cater to the hunger of readers. By mid-2006, *People*'s circulation neared 4 million. One of Time Warner's only gold mines, *People* generated more than $1 billion in revenue last year. During the past several years, People.com has garnered more attention—first from the company itself, then from Web browsers. By posting scoops, breaking news, and frequent updates, People.com doubled the number of visitors to the site in 2005. Thanks to the site's revamped approach, celebrity hounds no longer have to wait until their next trip to the grocery store to find out who's dating who, who's dumping who, and who's having whose baby.

The print magazine tries, however halfheartedly, to balance coverage (editors claim human interest stories are as common as celebrity content), but People.com has no such desire, even tagging it as "The #1 Celebrity Site on the Web." If they're not red-carpet elite, it's not People.com's beat.

What You'll Find There

People.com is simply but colorfully designed. A large vertical photo takes center stage on the home page and usually serves, along with the headline and blurb that run below it, as a teaser to the site's

"Photos" section, which consists of more than a dozen slideshows on topics ranging from celebrity vacations to movie premiers to fashion faux pas, or its "Style Watch" section. Back on the home page you'll find "The News Now" easy to spot—in large, bright-pink text. There, three stories—a bold headline, a subhead, and a "Read It" link—are positioned prominently, along with a small photo of each subject, at the top of the left column. Don't be surprised if you stumble upon headlines such as these after logging on: "Pam Anderson & Kid Rock to Divorce," "Author Helen Fielding Has a Baby Girl," and "Britney Spears: Being Single Is Awesome." Then click "Read It"—and weep. One thing you can be sure you won't encounter is a great journalist. The "news" here, despite the bylines, reads like postings of e-mails the writers received from celebrities' assistants. The "News" page—accessible by clicking a story link on the left side of the home page or by using the menu across the top—lists the site's "Top 5" stories down the left side, and the headlines sound much the same as the ones mentioned earlier.

If you want an interactive experience, the possibilities at People.com are limited: a "Photo Poll" or two where you scroll through an image gallery and decide which is "Beyoncé's Best Look?" There's also occasional audio slideshows and some video content. For "Insider" information, click on the link in the navigation bar, and the special features section will deliver trademark *People* content—the most beautiful people on the planet (i.e., Hollywood), celebrity weddings, the hippest fads, the latest births, and, of course, everything that could ever be written about *American Idol*. And for those who enjoy that guilty-pleasure moment right before unloading the items from your shopping cart and placing them on the conveyor belt, the "Magazine" page lets you catch a glimpse of the issue "on newsstands now."

Why You Should Visit

Find yourself fantasizing about leaning against a metal barrier while all the Hollywood types strut past you on the way into the theater showing the world premiere? Avoid the airfare costs; just fly to the nearest computer and pull up People.com. For those who need to know the latest about the lives of superstars but would rather not plow through a thoughtful, well-reported, and well-written profile of those influential personalities, People.com should be bookmarked.

Keep This in Mind

In recent years, *People* has used its Web site to break "news" (if Paris Hilton's engagement can be considered such) rather than sitting on an exclusive until next week's print edition. Unlike many magazines, *People* believes early online scoops will propel newsstands sales, not cause them to crash.

People, in print and online, differentiates itself from many of the checkout-line rags by refusing to publish

30-Second Polls: What's on Your Mind?
Is Angelina your Wonder Woman? Would you work for Donald Trump? Tell us – and look for results in PEOPLE
READ IT ▸

Caught in the Act!
See where the stars (Mary-Kate! Charlize!) have been seen and heard
READ IT ▸

The Week's Best Celeb Quotes
Kevin's happy accident, plus more from Meredith Vieira, Paris Hilton and other stars
READ IT ▸

uncorroborated gossip, or so its editors claim; although the "Insider" page on People.com is considered its "Gossip & Features" section, the publication appears distinctly more restrained than much of its competition when deciding what's appropriate to print. That position produces a double-edged effect: Celebs are often pitching exclusives to *People* instead of the magazine endlessly chasing stars; critics might be tempted to rename the magazine *Publicist*.

Off the Record

People reportedly paid $4.1 million in 2006 for Brangelina baby pics. The magazine has refuted the figure, but it declined to reveal the "correct" fee it spent for the photos of Shiloh, the daughter of Brad Pitt and Angelina Jolie. The multimillion-dollar investment resulted in *People*'s Web site setting a one-day traffic record of 26.5-million page views.[1]

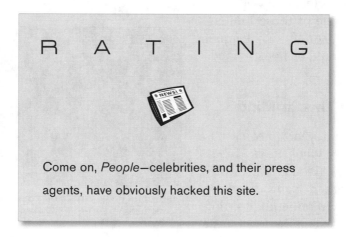

R A T I N G

Come on, *People*—celebrities, and their press agents, have obviously hacked this site.

Endnote

1. Jill Goldsmith, "People who need *People*: Sucking up to celebs builds mag as TW money machine," *Variety*, July 9, 2006

63

Poynter Institute
www.poynter.org

Overview

There are as many different kinds of journalism being practiced on the Web as there are Web sites. But don't let such a multiplicity of approaches fool you. There are still standards that ought to govern journalists everywhere, whether they work for a traditional "mainstream" news site or a cutting-edge, youth-oriented blog. But who serves as the arbiter of what is acceptable in the news business, of helping working writers calibrate the changing ethical landscape of public discourse?

That would be the Poynter Institute, a quasi-think tank that addresses all the topical concerns roiling the journalistic waters every news cycle. Poynter's Web site is invaluable—not only for the professional news set but also (and perhaps, mostly) for the consumer of news who wants to understand how the media goes about its business.

In a world where news is available through a dizzying array of vehicles (from the blessedly simple broadsheet to iPods and cellular phones), Poynter is an oasis of stability and incontrovertibly clear information. To understand the world, you've got to follow the news. To understand the news, go to Poynter.org.

What You'll Find There

Poynter's site is crammed with dozens of stories that all take as their jumping-off point the state of the news business. Stories about newspaper circulation trends, ethical scandals, and media-company mergers butt up against columns that explore the future of interactive media, Q&As with modern media barons, and blogs kept by working journalists.

But what you see on the home page is only a small part of the Poynter story. The site serves as a kind of unofficial repository of thought about the media in our society. There are hundreds of articles in its archive that address all the significant upheavals in journalism, from the Jayson Blair scandal at the *New York Times* (and many lesser media indiscretions that never make the national news) to the changing readership habits of the average news consumer.

For those who want to swim in the deep end of the news stream, Poynter.org maintains an archive of critical (though arcane) data about circulation, readership, and even psychological and neurological studies of media-related topics (eye-tracking studies that trace the pupil's reaction to different colors on a Web page, for example).

There are dozens of columns updated regularly by working writers, editors, and photographers who report on the daily joys and struggles of putting out the news. Readers who appreciate behind-the-scenes perspectives can luxuriate for hours in Poynter's immense, veil-lifting Web site.

Why You Should Visit

Spending just a little time each day with Poynter.org will help you get more out of all the other sites you visit for news and information. Poynter frequently writes about what's making news in the online publishing world, offering critiques of some of the best-known and most widely used Web sites. In addition, Poynter hosts periodic conferences where journalists gather to discuss the news trade, with transcripts, speeches, and Q&As from the sessions often posted on the Web site.

Though their names are hardly household words, Poynter's Web site is home to some of the most important media ethicists, professors, and publishing consultants in the business. Reading Poynter regularly replicates the experience of attending a master class with the best editorial minds in the country.

Poynter provides an invaluable service that seems, at times, in danger of disappearing from American cultural life: dispassionate critiques of the media, absent any predetermined right-wing or left-wing slant. If serious journalism continues to be subsumed by the current wave of infotainment washing over the masses, it won't be Poynter's fault.

Keep This in Mind

The focus of the site—and much of Poynter's work—is aimed at the professional journalist. The articles and columns are often filled with the jargon of the news trade, and there's a lot of "insider" references that might be lost on the lay reader. Yet none of the pieces is written in the typical eye-glazing academic style that often complicates an

ASNE / POYNTER
ETHICS TOOL
DECISIONS ON DEADLINE

issue rather than clarifying it. If you can make sense of a well-edited, comprehensive newspaper, you can make sense of Poynter's Web site.

As the news business continues to splinter and as readers (and journalists) continue to grope for a usable notion of what's worth reading (or reporting), a site like Poynter becomes ever more valuable.

Off the Record

The Poynter Institute not only provides a Web site full of valuable resources for professional journalists, but also maintains a robust roster of in-person training sessions, educational programs, and workshops—in everything from broadcasting to ethics. The courses are hosted throughout the country by some of the most accomplished journalists and cover the spectrum, from high school journalism to newsroom management.

RATING

Journalism's task is to watch society; Poynter's job is to watch journalism.

64

Prevention

www.prevention.com

Overview

Americans' obsession with health issues has become epidemic. Most bookstores have separate sections for diet, fitness and exercise, and general well-being, while the number of Web sites that provide health-related information has expanded exponentially. Reports from once-obscure science journals now find their way onto the front pages of most American newspapers, with seemingly every local network news show feeling obligated to showcase an MD with the requisite "medical minute." We can't get enough of the news about our own bodies.

Which is to say, *Prevention*'s time has come.

Once a predictably staid staple of doctors' offices and library magazine racks, *Prevention* magazine—and now Prevention.com—has become one of the benchmarks of popular health information, dispensing prescriptions for fit living to a nation obsessed with reading about healthy living (whether people are as determined to actually get healthy as they are to *read* about getting healthy is another matter).

So Prevention.com is well-positioned to exploit this medical mania. The site has a lot of information and covers lots of topics, but Prevention.com is not the end-all, be-all of medical Web sites. Nor should it be the last step in your quest to achieve total wellness.

What You'll Find There

The site is well organized, bright, and easily navigated. The home page offers a main health story aimed at middle-aged people (usually), illustrated by a fit-looking female model (usually), and offering a brief sentence that will lead you into the short (usually) article just by clicking on the headline.

There's technically not much "news" on the Web site, as most news purists would define it—mostly features about health, with titles such

as "Success Story: My Family Helped Me Lose 76 Pounds," "Walk Your Way to Better Health," and "Thirty Days of Heart-Smart Tips."

These features—about a half-dozen on the home page—are apparently aimed primarily at a female readership (a recent review of the Web site revealed that every photo that accompanied a story featured a smiling, physically fit, 40-something, white, well-dressed female).

Running down the left side of the page is a roster of "Easy To Follow Guides" aimed at promoting wellness; "Take Control of Your Cholesterol" is a good example of the kinds of items found here.

There's a refreshing lack of ads on the page, which features only one nonobtrusive ad soliciting subscriptions to the magazine itself. The rest of the page is filled with links to archived articles in one of six categories: "Health," "Fitness," "Food & Nutrition," "Weight Loss," "Beauty," and "Home & Family." Any of these links will take you to a page that lists recent headlines about that aspect of fitness and a searchable archive of past stories from the magazine. The articles are useful, though short—and in some cases, quite under-reported in terms of medical information.

Why You Should Visit

For many readers, health is a topic of interest but one that they don't know much about. Prevention.com is a good entry-level site for the health-conscious reader who doesn't want—or need—an abundance of information. The articles are written in a breezy, feature-style manner with a generally upbeat tone and plenty of "bulleted" lists of what to do (or avoid doing) to improve your health. The reader-friendly prose eliminates the jargon that creeps into many medical reports.

Keep This in Mind

If you are seeking information about a serious health issue, Prevention.com is probably not the place to go. The articles aim as much at boosterism as they do at informing readers about a medical topic. And the title—*Prevention*—is really quite apt, as the site offers lots of pre-emptive suggestions but little information about how to deal with a variety of serious illnesses.

There's also an abundance of stories that offer only one side of a medical situation. It sometimes feels like many of the stories' conclusions were pre-determined before the writer began working on the article. A final quibble: For articles about complex medical issues, the stories are pretty short—some only two or three paragraphs. The site makes no pretense about being a clearinghouse of complete medical

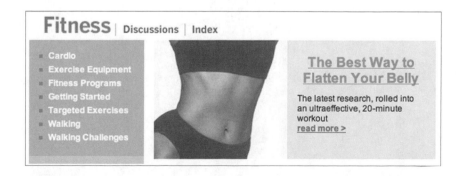

Fitness | Discussions | Index

- Cardio
- Exercise Equipment
- Fitness Programs
- Getting Started
- Targeted Exercises
- Walking
- Walking Challenges

The Best Way to Flatten Your Belly

The latest research, rolled into an ultraeffective, 20-minute workout
read more >

information, but the abbreviated length of most stories suggests no real attempt to explore the issues beyond a surface presentation.

Off the Record

Prevention is owned by Rodale Press, which in addition to publishing magazines and Web sites, is the largest independent book publisher in the U.S. Rodale is the publisher of the massively popular book, *The South Beach Diet*.

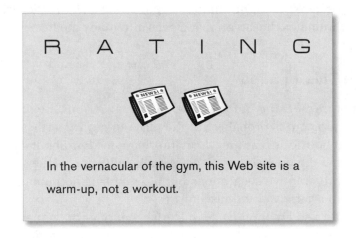

RATING

In the vernacular of the gym, this Web site is a warm-up, not a workout.

65

The Progressive

www.progressive.org

Overview

Sometimes, you can tell everything you need to know about a Web site by its name. In the case of *The Progressive*'s site, the online version of the nearly century-old magazine, you get the expected—with a bonus.

The expected involves a publication aimed at fomenting social progress: economic, racial, environmental, and, of course, political. When *The Progressive* launched its first issue in 1909, founder (and senator) Robert LaFollette Sr. stated his intention of "winning back for the people the complete power over government—national, state, and municipal—which has been lost to them." The content of the magazine and the site bears witness to that continuing mission.

Here's the bonus: *The Progressive*, unlike many other publications aimed at reforming the world and correcting its flaws, is not a strident, angry forum but rather a thoughtful and sober publication. Its contributors have included such progressive intellects as Clarence Darrow, Martin Luther King Jr., George Orwell, and Edward Said, with some of today's best and most probing commentators—from Ruth Conniff to Howard Zinn—regularly contributing to the publication.

Add to this roster of worthies a number of "Web exclusives" for online readers, and you've got a site that merits regular scrutiny.

What You'll Find There

The first thing one notices about the site's main page is how stuffed with content it appears to be. Under a small, olive-colored banner begins the parade of articles, essays, columns, breaking news, timelines, and "backgrounders."

The page begins with stories written expressly for the online site. These pieces usually involve analysis of some major news event, such as a Supreme Court decision, a foreign policy quagmire, or some clash between free speech advocates and the less tolerant components of our society. Most of these stories have a pronounced "progressive" slant, rather than an objective approach to the story. One of the nice touches is that the editor of the publication, Harvard-educated Matthew Rothschild, often writes these pieces, rather than simply donning an eyeshade and providing the "vision" for the publication. Like most of *The Progressive*'s staff of contributors, Rothschild is a great writer.

The page also features a "McCarthyism Watch," which sounds a bit alarmist, but in fact contains thoroughly reported instances of the government appearing to overstep its bounds. There's an archive of stories in this section, with headlines such as "Pentagon Boots Reporters off Guantanamo" and "Muslim Family Terrorized in Georgia."

A separate section heralding "Featured Articles" includes longer pieces and interviews with people who have a front-row seat for the clash of ideologies that sometimes splits our society. These interview subjects include Seymour Hersh, Kurt Vonnegut, Studs Terkel, and Helen Thomas.

Running along the length of the left side of the page is a menu of links that leads directly to some of the publication's better-known writers, as well as links to past issues and articles and an extensive blog called "Blogressive." The blog features lots of interesting and "lighter" stories, but is a bit disappointing in its brevity. The main point of the blog seems to be to generate reader comment rather than genuinely explore issues in the more casual arena of the blogosphere.

Why You Should Visit

There's an awful lot of anger among the punditry all along the political spectrum. And while the writers for *The Progressive* pull no punches, the restraint and intelligence with which they approach the issues makes reading the site a rewarding experience—quite the opposite of so much talk radio-style ranting.

The Progressive has also earned several honors that testify to its commitment to thoughtfulness and thoroughness, including the George Polk Award for Magazine Reporting and *The Utne* Independent Press Award for Political Coverage.

Keep This in Mind

The Progressive lacks the clout and cache of some of its louder and more prominent left-of-center comrades. You don't find many "calls to action" on the site, nor are you assailed on every page with a petition drive or e-mail campaign. *The Progressive* seems to believe deeply that "knowledge is power"—and then leaves you to decide what to do with the information you've just acquired.

McCarthyism Watch

Matthew Rothschild has been with *The Progressive* since 1983. He keeps a running tally of civil liberties infringements in his "McCarthyism Watch." In the January 2002 issue he writes about *The New McCarthyism*.

Off the Record

The Progressive was one of the first national voices to rally against the scourge of McCarthyism in the 1950s, and its continuing commitment to explore infringements of the First Amendment makes the site a highly recommended stop for free speech advocates.

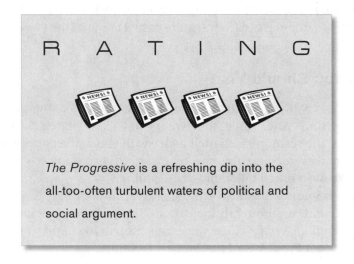

R A T I N G

The Progressive is a refreshing dip into the all-too-often turbulent waters of political and social argument.

66

Public Broadcasting Service (PBS)

www.pbs.org

Overview

To those generally unacquainted with PBS, the acronym usually invokes thoughts of telethons and "educational" (read: boring) programming. But to its loyal base of fans, the television network, which was founded two years after the passage of the Public Broadcasting Act of 1967, serves as a sanctuary from the ratings-driven and frequently vacuous programming aired on commercial networks. From investigative series and nightly newscasts to documentaries profiling important figures and shows exploring science, nature, and the arts, watching PBS is one free and easy (not to mention entertaining) way of boosting your IQ.

The same can be said of logging on to its Web site, PBS.org, which contains the individual, companion sites for "more than 1,300 PBS programs and specials" and "more than 175,000 pages of content." That's good: The site likely has news and information of interest and appeal to just about everyone. And bad: It's not always the easiest task for visitors to find what they're looking for.

What You'll Find There

In the middle column on the home page, you will find five of PBS.org's leading features—each teased with a small photo, headline/link, and brief description—under the "Explore Features" banner. These usually link to one of the site's main sections: "Arts & Drama," "History," "Home & Hobbies," "Life & Culture," "News & Views," and "Science & Nature." You can access the front pages of these sections through the drop-down menu at the top right of the home page. Each section front contains three "Featured Sites" and

links located at the top of the page to between four and nine subsections. Running down the left side of these pages are links to the sites of ongoing PBS series.

The "News & Views" page contains links to more focused topics: "Business & Finance," "Health," "Military," "Opinion & Analysis," "World," "Government & Politics," "Law & Order," "Newsmakers," and "Special Issues." It also links to the home pages of various PBS news programs: *FrontLine* (investigative documentaries), *Now* (analysis of and perspectives on current events), *Washington Week* (journalists discuss the news), and *NewsHour with Jim Lehrer* (nightly newscast).

The "Online NewsHour," as the section is called, should be the destination for anyone looking for daily headlines. The site provides—in mostly audio and video formats (along with transcripts)—the latest news from the most recent airing of the program, from a "News Summary: A synopsis of the top stories of the day" to exclusive interviews with "Newsmakers" to "In-depth Coverage" of hot-button issues. You can also browse the Online NewsHour "by region" or "by topic" (look for the small links just below the title banner), which opens areas of the show's site that otherwise would go unnoticed.

Why You Should Visit

Because that's only the beginning of what you'll find there. The individual sites of *NOVA*, *Nature*, and other PBS staples alone could occupy browsers for hours. Journalist Mark Glaser's "MediaShift" blog, which focuses on developments in digital media, is worth

bookmarking. PBS.org is an amusement park of information—you'll want to experience every ride, but it may take a few trips before conquering them all. It's also worth noting that most of the content here involves audio and video; so if you'd rather read a story than see or hear one, this might turn into a frustrating visit. And in some cases, the frustration might mount when what appears to be content turns out only to be a preview of an upcoming program or a trailer-like vignette aimed at getting you to buy a DVD. But even despite these flaws, there's enough inside the PBS.org megasite for you to explore —day after day, week after week.

Keep This in Mind

All modern media outlets seem to be attacked for being either too liberal or too conservative. PBS maintains balance: It gets criticized by both sides. The right often cites it when referring to the "liberal media." The left finds its corporate sponsorships objectionable. PBS, according to the legislative act that spawned it, is mandated to present "objectivity and balance" in what it airs. And although PBS receives a minority of its funding from the government, interference is prohibited. In 2005, PBS hired its first-ever ombudsman—Michael Getler, who held the same title at the *Washington Post* for the previous five years (it's traditionally been a newspaper gig)—to serve as an "independent internal critic ... seeking to ensure that PBS upholds its own standards of editorial integrity." He writes a regular online column, which can usually be linked to from the bottom right of the home page.

Off the Record

PBS does not have its own news department or production division per se. Programming is instead produced by one of its member stations. Of the approximately 350 member stations, those in Boston, Washington D.C., New York, and Miami (and a few others) create the most content, which is then distributed by PBS nationwide to local member stations.

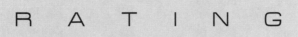

It might not be the best site for a quick look at the latest news updates. But if you're looking for just about any other type of information, PBS.org will probably have it—as long as you have time to search around a bit.

67

Republican National Committee

www.gop.com

Overview

Love it or hate it, the political system in the U.S. is dominated by two parties. And, for the past several years, the power has been mostly in the hands of the Republican Party—leaving their counterparts, the Democrats, as the "loyal opposition."

So what have the Republicans done with all their power? Mostly, they use it to gloat, if the Web site of the party's national committee is to be believed.

American politics has always been a hardball sport, and neither major party is about to take the gloves off now. So while we shouldn't be surprised to see the Republicans use their bully pulpit to, well, bully their political opponents, it is a bit dispiriting to think that those in a position to improve people's lives seem mostly interested in scoring political points.

Want to know more about the Republicans who are making decisions every day on your behalf? Check out GOP.com. See what they believe. Then make up your own mind whether to be disturbed or reassured.

What You'll Find There

The site features lots of articles attacking the Democrats. The home page at GOP.com features a large photo or icon, often of an angry-faced Democratic leader, and several "news" stories bearing the headline "The REAL Dem Agenda." Next to this photo box is a sidebar labeled "Action Center," which allows viewers to do everything from sign a birthday card for the President to link their Web site to the RNC's site. You can also use the "Action Center" to register to vote,

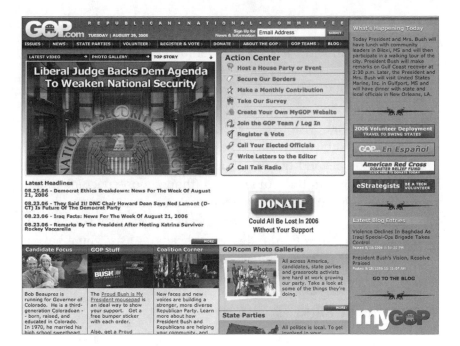

contact your elected officials, and even get the phone numbers of popular conservative talk-radio shows.

Along the middle of the page are several feature stories about up-and-coming political stars in the Republican Party, profiles of prominent Republican officials, and a map of state and local Republican organizations for people who wish to get more involved closer to home.

In tiny type along the top of the page run links for "Issues," "Volunteer," "Donations," and "About the GOP." Clicking on these links leads to information and usually an e-mail prompt to contact an official in your area. And—this being a participatory democracy—there are blogs by Republican operatives bashing the Democrats and inviting other Republicans to add their voices to the chorus of GOP (Grand Old Party) lovers. There are also other blogs challenging the attacks on the Republican administration, with headlines like "Bush Administration's Environmental Decisions Praised."

For the truly plugged-in, an updated "What's Happening Today" box lists all of the landmark Republican events scheduled that day, from major party fundraisers to the President's foreign-travel agenda.

Why You Should Visit

Thomas Jefferson said, "The price of Democracy is eternal vigilance." So be vigilant. The current GOP is one of the most effective political operations in the history of our republic. Elected representatives from local school boards up to the Oval Office have sworn allegiance to its principles and vision.

If you don't know what the Republicans stand for—and if you're willing to look beyond the screaming headlines about the devilish Democrats—you can find some useful (though non-specific) guidelines about the party's ideology and intentions. For like-minded people, GOP.com will satisfy your Republican cravings. And if you already find yourself in opposition to the Republicans, at least you'll have a better idea why you're rooting against them.

Keep This in Mind

The news on the site is not news in the standard sense of objectively reported stories. In addition, the information about "issues" presented on the site is not in the vein of public service, but rather propaganda. Finally, and perhaps most disappointingly, the Web site offers little in the way of complexity or context when it discusses what the Republican Party is about. Bland platitudes and sophomoric campaign slogans fill most of the articles and essays. This is, alas, what political discourse has come to mean in the early 21st century.

Off the Record

The Republican Party's symbol, the elephant, was created by *Harper's Weekly* cartoonist Thomas Nast in 1874. The cartoon featured a Democrat jackass trying to frighten a Republican elephant. Though neither image was particularly flattering, they resonated with the reading public and have become iconic since that first appearance.

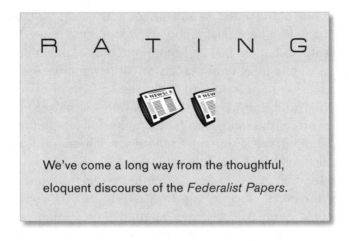

68

Reuters

www.reuters.com

Overview

Reuters is one of the oldest news services in the world—dating back to the time before even telegraph wires carried the news. For more than a century, Reuters has had the reputation of being one of the leading providers of general news from all parts of the globe. Even today, Reuters continues to lead in the dissemination of news from around the world. But as a glance at its Web site makes very clear, Reuters has recently changed its fundamental focus, shifting from its traditional reporting to one much more specialized—and lucrative. In short, Reuters decided to follow the money.

"More than 90 percent of our revenue derives from our financial services business," according to the "About Us" section on Reuters.com. "Some 330,000 financial market professionals working in the equities, fixed income, foreign exchange, money, commodities and energy markets around the world use Reuters products."

So while the "Reuters" name continues to accompany dispatches about the war in Iraq or earthquakes, floods, and other natural disasters that make news, the company has rededicated itself to serve the titans of commerce, and its Web site reflects this in its emphasis on finance and its wealth of investor-related tools and technology.

What You'll Find There

The site usually leads with a major breaking news story but fills the rest of the home page with mostly business-related copy. The "Business" icon is the first to appear on the page and usually introduces a story of interest to the investment community (often a result of that day's stock trading). Next to this headline and blurb are smaller headlines teasing other stories from the business world.

The next major section, "Investing," is closely related. Under this icon are lots of stories about picking the next hot stock and evaluating corporate earnings reports for insights about potential profitability, as well as separate "Comment and Analysis" by Reuters columnists who follow the ups and downs. There are lots of graphics showing the daily fluctuations of the stock markets from major financial capitals and a search engine that allows you to type in a stock and call up its performance chart.

All of this information is free, though Reuters has made a major thrust in the last few years to sell many of its information services to the investment community—services tailored specifically to traders and investment professionals. Still, an awful lot of free information is available for the professional—or even the casual—trader to glean from the Reuters site.

When you get to the second screen of the Reuters site, you'll find the more traditional icons: "News," "Politics," "Technology," and even "Science," "Health," and "Entertainment." Clicking on any of these (which look a little lonely without any photos or graphics) brings you to a menu of regularly updated stories by Reuters correspondents. Not unexpectedly, the stories are generally well reported and reflect a traditional mainstream balance—though also the brevity that is common to much wire service reporting. There is not much depth here beyond the financial stuff.

And what would a major news Web site be without blogs or streaming video? Reuters obliges, with news and business blogs as well as brief videos filed by reporters around the world.

Why You Should Visit

The site is worth visiting for something old, something new. Reuters represents a solid tradition of newsgathering that stretches back to the 1840s. Reuters has credibility and reach—two often overlooked but indispensable qualities in the digital age. The "new" aspect is the focus on commerce and the world of finance. Many of the stories Reuters covers in depth have to do with things like pension plans, interest rates, and international trade—all matters that are worth paying attention to.

Keep This in Mind

If money is your game and you're a serious investor, you probably already know that Reuters is only one of a fiercely competitive group of financial news providers. Reuters would have you believe it is the best,

though entrenched financial services companies like Bloomberg and Dow Jones would certainly chafe at that characterization.

Off the Record

Although Reuters espouses neutrality and fairness in its reporting, it has recently come under attack from some conservative critics in the U.S. who oppose the service's avoidance of the word "terrorist" in its news accounts. According to a Reuters internal memo, "One man's terrorist is another man's freedom fighter, and Reuters upholds the principle that we do not use the word 'terrorist'."[1]

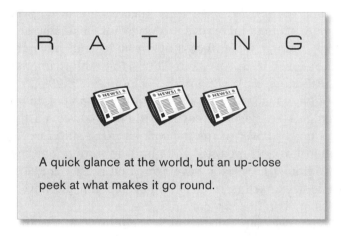

A quick glance at the world, but an up-close peek at what makes it go round.

Endnote

1. R. Hollander, "Questionable integrity," www.nationalreview.com/comment/hollander20031020085.

69

Rolling Stone

www.rollingstone.com

Overview

Rolling Stone, founded in San Francisco in 1967 by Jann Wenner and music critic Ralph J. Gleason, remains the most influential music magazine published today. As one record company executive put it, "The *Rolling Stone* cover is the most coveted piece of real estate in the music industry." And the magazine, which is published biweekly, has had its share of memorable covers. Along with the unchanged *Rolling Stone* logo, unforgettable photos of music legends have graced the magazine's oversized cover. In 2005, the American Society of Magazine Editors (ASME) named the January 22, 1981, edition of *Rolling Stone*, which featured a nude John Lennon curled up next to Yoko Ono, the top magazine cover of the past 40 years. Lennon also appeared on the cover of the magazine's first edition in November 1967, when text accompanied the photo in a more newspaper-like design. Although musicians have appeared most frequently, movie stars, cartoon characters, models, and even politicians have had their mugs plastered on the pop-culture bible.

While its Web site has yet to become such an institution, RollingStone.com rocks on occasion—providing some suggestions as to what you and everyone else should be listening to.

What You'll Find There

The home page of RollingStone.com leads with its latest story, usually from its "Rock & Roll Daily" blog, at the top left of the page (headline, summary, and photo). Browsers will also find a few other features— usually a video clip, blog entry, or music review—displayed less prominently in the middle of the page. To the right, the cover of "The Current Issue" is followed by several links to articles from that edition. Another dozen or so headlines from its so-called "News" section

and its blog stack the left side of the second screen of the home page. The "Editor's Picks," which includes the top five videos and songs, is featured next. The right side of the page offers the "Reviews" section, which seems somewhat downplayed despite the fact that the magazine is perhaps best-known (and most read) for its album reviews. The site's "Reviews" section is divided into three categories: CDs, Movies, and DVDs.

The file folder-like tabs at the top of the home page, just below the standard banner ad at the top of the site (one of its only ads), provide a user-friendly way to navigate the site. Roll the cursor over the "Artists," "News," "Reviews," "Photos," "Videos," "Politics," "Community," and "Listen" tabs, and each reveal color-coordinated subsection menus.

The best way to explore the site, however, is by using its search tool, which allows users to select "ALL," "Artist," "Album," or "Song" from the drop-down menu before entering their keywords.

Why You Should Visit

In recent years, what was once a niche market has exploded. The publication of magazines dedicated to coverage of the music industry has

surged to the point of saturation. But while *Spin*, *Vibe*, *Source*, *Blender*, and *Uncut*, along with a surplus of music-oriented Web sites, vie for the same audience, *Rolling Stone*'s content, which is more wide ranging than its competition, make it the go-to source for those interested in any and all genres of music.

While the site lacks the technological innovation and visual appeal you might expect from a publication geared toward a primarily younger audience, it does meet the expectation of usefulness—through the ability for visitors to search by artist, album, or song and find dependable news and reviews. Its critics are often harsh, rarely rewarding albums the coveted five stars.

Thanks to its history and tradition, the magazine enjoys an unrivalled status. As *Billboard*, a competing magazine, once reported, "*Rolling Stone* became much more than a magazine; it is now a cultural institution." Scrolling through its archive of covers (in the "Covers" subsection of the navigation menu's "Photos" tab) is like taking a stroll through the history of American pop culture.

Keep This in Mind

Jann Wenner, *Rolling Stone*'s founder, is still its editor and publisher. Although the magazine has always been identified almost solely with music, it has had its eye on the political scene for several decades, starting with Hunter S. Thompson's gonzo journalism in the early 1970s. It continues to provide in-depth political coverage. While *Rolling Stone* was formed amidst the hippie movement, it adheres to traditional journalistic standards—although some critics might argue that its political stories originate from a progressive proclivity. In 2006, *Rolling Stone* was nominated for an ASME National Magazine Award for reporting, along with the venerable institutions of the *New Yorker*, *Atlantic Monthly*, and *Harper's Magazine*. It won that award three times in the past, including in 2004.

Off the Record

The legendary Thompson is not the only superstar wordsmith to start at *Rolling Stone*. Cameron Crowe's *Almost Famous*, an award-winning film starring Kate Hudson in 2000, is a semi-autobiographical account of Crowe's days as a teenage journalist for *Rolling Stone*.

William Miller, the young writer in the movie, frequently seeks advice from Lester Bangs (played by Philip Seymour Hoffman), who also began his career at *Rolling Stone* and is often credited as one of the most influential voices in rock music criticism. In the movie, Miller eventually publishes a *Rolling Stone* cover story about his time on the road with the band Stillwater. In its December 6, 1973 edition, *Rolling Stone* published a cover story on the Allman Brothers Band written by a 16-year-old Crowe.

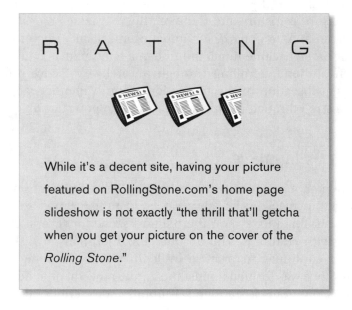

RATING

While it's a decent site, having your picture featured on RollingStone.com's home page slideshow is not exactly "the thrill that'll getcha when you get your picture on the cover of the *Rolling Stone*."

70

Rotten Tomatoes

www.rottentomatoes.com

Overview

The two trends in the past decade that have, arguably, exhibited the greatest influence on society in general—and certainly among those under 40—are the rise of the Internet and the growth of movies as a primary cultural preoccupation. Once upon a time, movies were a diversion, something that you took a break from everyday life to see. Now, for many, movies have become the biggest events in their lives. Fans of certain movie franchises, such as *Star Wars*, wait on line days, even weeks, for tickets. The media covers film openings as they once covered political conventions—complete with pundits, spin doctors, and video retrospectives.

And fueling this national obsession with all things cinematic is, of course, the Internet—24-hour-a-day access to the stars and scenes from our favorite movies, delivered to laptops and desks all around the globe.

Has anyone had the foresight to yoke these two massive social movements together, marrying the cinematic and the digital? Yes, indeed. And they're having fun doing it at RottenTomatoes.com.

What You'll Find There

The site's primary focus is on critical reaction to the movies. Rotten Tomatoes serves as a vast clearinghouse for established opinion makers and wannabe critics in the world of cinema, from well-known reviewers like Roger Ebert to totally unknown bloggers who merely have strong—sometimes *really* strong—opinions.

The home page offers a list of recent movies and a searchable archive, with the aim of providing an overview of a film's critical reception (resulting in either a "certified fresh" designation or the label "rotten," based on the calculated consensus of the critics). The

ratings are excerpted for a quick and easy read, with the full reviews often available just by clicking. The site is graphically attractive with clear headings and a menu of icons for other services running down either side of the home page.

Those sidebar menu items lead to thoughtful, innovative, and useful information, from updated showtimes for movies in your local area to ratings of "hot rentals" and trailers for upcoming movies. The site also offers heavily trafficked message boards and forums for the discussion of all things cinematic, from "The Best Woody Allen Movies" to "Favorite Soundtracks."

If you're not sure what movie you'd like to see, simply click on the "tomato picker" icon and enter an actor, director, or genre, and you'll be given a broad range of recommendations. And because movies make news, there is a lot of news related to the movie industry, from blockbuster deals for upcoming productions to exposés of stars' private lives—all conveniently linked and available at other Web sites with one click.

Of course, since movies and money go hand in hand, an extensive online gift shop lets movie buffs order everything from DVD boxed sets to movie posters and memorabilia.

Why You Should Visit

Want to hold your own when the conversation at your workplace, school, or YMCA pilates group turns to movies? This Web site will make you feel like an expert on the movies. And because it's designed with the movie lover in mind, the site has a casual and upbeat style, eschewing academic-style writing and including quirky reviewers from unknown or little-known publications.

Keep This in Mind

Movies are entertainment, sure. But should they really command as much time and attention as they do? Is it possible—as some sociologists theorize—that all this movie watching is turning our minds to mush? And should we really be trying to find new and better ways to celebrate the ubiquitous culture of entertainment?

That's largely a personal choice, of course. Reading all those reviews of *The Texas Chainsaw Massacre* won't make you any smarter, but for our money, it's probably better to have access to all that opinion than

be stuck following like sheep the handful of frequently quoted movie gurus who used to set the cinematic agenda for us.

Off the Record

As is becoming increasingly clear, one person with a good idea can make a great impact in the digital age. Rotten Tomatoes was created by movie buff Senh Duong 15 years ago as a place to find out what critics outside of your local area (and, hence, unavailable to you) thought about movies. Today, more than 5 million readers a month visit RottenTomatoes.com to scope out more than 125,000 movie titles from the site's rapidly growing database of reviews.

R A T I N G

In a world saturated with pop culture, Rotten Tomatoes keeps it reel.

71

Rush Limbaugh
www.rushlimbaugh.com

Overview

The conservative commentator Rush Limbaugh shouldn't be thought of as just a talk-radio host. He's more of a national litmus test. Many people on the right admire—and even worship—Limbaugh's pull-no-punches brashness, his messianic zeal on behalf of conservatism, and his tart social observations. To the political left and its corps of true believers, Limbaugh symbolizes everything that's wrong with the political process today: He's loud, confrontational, and often (they claim) misleading, bending facts to suit his iron-clad political notions.

For those who are unfamiliar with Limbaugh's daily sermonizing on his national radio show—which many people credit for reviving AM radio from its moribund existence in the early 1980s—his Web site is a perfect reflection of the Rush Limbaugh experience: opinionated to the point of ideological purity, shamelessly self-promotional (his photo appears no less than half a dozen times on the home page!), and stuffed with anti-liberal commentary presented as "news."

There's no denying the popularity of Limbaugh to millions of faithful listeners and readers (known semi-affectionately as "ditto heads"), but his Web site shouldn't be considered anything more than a sales tool to extend the reach of his empire.

What You'll Find There

At RushLimbaugh.com, you'll find Rush, Rush, and more Rush. There's probably more content crammed onto his home page than any other site on the Web, yet it's all about Rush: his take on the news, his commentary on social issues, ads for his newsletter and radio programs, transcripts of his radio shows, and merchandise from his store.

   At the top of the home page under photos of Rush in both a suit and tie (brandishing his beloved cigar) and in a leather jacket, readers will find the first "news" section under the icon "America's Anchorman," where Limbaugh waxes philosophical about topical issues such as immigration, gun control, or global warming. (Limbaugh has said that any concern about the ozone layer is "balderdash, poppycock," the product of "environmental wackos" and "dunderheaded alarmists."[1]) These commentaries are not so much explorations of an issue (as one might expect from similarly ideologically driven columnists such as George Will or William F. Buckley), but rather verbal shouting sprees, beholden more to preordained conclusions than the weight of objective fact.

   Throughout the page, one can find lots of other news headlines emblematic of Rush's intractable hatred of the left and his abiding belief in the infallibility of conservatism, such as "Bush Admission a Sign of Victory, Not Defeat" or "Only the Rich Pay Taxes!" Such conservative myopia is what has given Limbaugh his popularity among die-hard red-staters, as well as moderates who have grown frustrated at large-scale governmental inefficiency and bureaucratic bungling.

The majority of space on the Web site's home page is devoted to ads for Rush's various product lines and for advertisers who share Rush's embrace of conservatism in all its feisty declamations.

Why You Should Visit

If you haven't been paying attention to the conservative talk-radio revolution in the past decade, you've missed one of the most important stories in the history of media. In the church of AM radio punditry, Limbaugh is the Pope. And his Web site is as close as you can come to replicating the experience of listening to conservative talk radio without actually listening to conservative talk radio. The influence Limbaugh has in shaping the national political conversation is extreme.

Keep This in Mind

Limbaugh's pulpit—and his Web site should be seen as an extension of his conservative ministry—is viewed by the political punditry as critical in swaying voter opinion. From his steady drumbeating of the Monica Lewinsky scandal and his call for impeachment to his mockery of Hillary Clinton as a "femi-Nazi," Limbaugh's influence among a segment of the voting population is impressive and undeniable.

Off the Record

Although Limbaugh is no stranger to controversy, he would presumably have been content to have avoided his most recent headline-making scandal. In 2006, he turned himself in to authorities on the charge of illegally acquiring prescriptions for painkilling drugs. In an agreement with prosecutors, Limbaugh agreed to two and a half years of drug treatment and counseling, and a $30,000 fine to pay for the expense of the State of Florida's investigation of the matter.

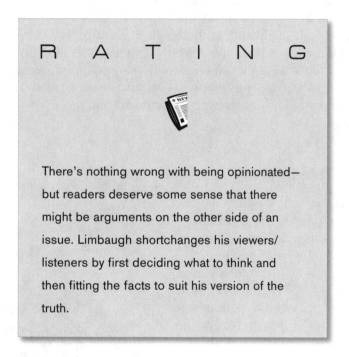

R A T I N G

There's nothing wrong with being opinionated—but readers deserve some sense that there might be arguments on the other side of an issue. Limbaugh shortchanges his viewers/listeners by first deciding what to think and then fitting the facts to suit his version of the truth.

Endnote

1. From the Web site of Fairness and Accuracy in Reporting, based on Limbaugh's broadcast of March 8, 1992.

72

Salon

www.salon.com

Overview

Once in a while, you encounter a Web site with a name that is perfectly emblematic of what the site offers. Such is the case with Salon.com, which seeks to be an online "salon," fomenting those kinds of discussions one would have in such a place: casual, informed, eclectic considerations of a variety of subjects. The hipness quotient is fairly high, but even the uninitiated can pass through this salon and feel plugged in.

Salon.com is also a good example of the difficulty many news and information Web sites have had finding a successful business model. Since its founding in 1995, the site has experimented with various fee-for-content approaches, settling on its current hybrid approach to online commerce: offering a "premium" membership (which comes complete with subscriptions to various print magazines—how's that for a counter-intuitive use of the Internet?) and free content for everybody else, though you must first watch a brief ad for that day's particular sponsor before gaining access to the site.

Overall, Salon.com acquaints you with some of the ideas and trends that are shaping our culture.

What You'll Find There

Salon.com's emphasis is on politics and current events but not on breaking news. The site offers the online equivalent of a smart but clearly opinionated local barbershop, with its gregarious commentators each throwing in their two cents. Salon.com's slate of writers and columnists pick apart the happenings on the national and world stage and refract them through a mostly (though not exclusively) liberal lens. The most impressive feature of Salon.com's home page is its eclectic quality: The page is as likely to feature an analysis of the

Mideast peace situation as an offbeat sports or entertainment story or a think piece analyzing some about-to-break-on-the-shore cultural wave.

After the main story on the page—often a first-person account or some quirky news-essay (a recent main feature explored the travails of some poor fellow who took photos of his kids skinny-dipping on a camping trip and then found himself accused of child pornography)—there's also a handful of current events analyses and commentary and a "Blog Report" that showcases regularly updated blogs on just about any topic that might be discussed by adults who commute, vote, eat, exercise, raise children, or watch reality TV shows.

The rest of the page is a hodgepodge in the best possible sense. Columns about how the Democrats can retake the White House sit cheek-by-jowl with reviews of independent movie festivals, child-rearing debates, book reviews, and interviews with fringe musicians, dancers, or artists. In fact, Salon.com has a ton of unclassifiable arts coverage. It seems that its writers are given free reign to cover what they want when they want. This makes for an energetic, engaging arts section with no clear theme but lots of fun stuff to read (and an opportunity to record your own thoughts in one of the site's many heavily trafficked message boards).

Why You Should Visit

More and more, what's *happening* on the news pages seems to be less important to people trying to keep up than what it all *means*. And Salon.com's editors aren't shy about telling you what they think it all means. Two of its marquee columnists, Joe Conason and Sidney Blumenthal, are worth reading regularly for their iconoclastic take on the country's creeping conservatism. And any site that posts the occasional Garrison Keillor essay or Tom Tomorrow cartoon is certainly worth visiting.

Keep This in Mind

Salon.com is an idea in search of a purpose. The site is filled with great articles, but it's similar to one of those resale shops you stumble upon while on vacation: It's great fun to browse through while you're

there, but you might not make a special trip to get there. There are sites with much more—and better—breaking news; there are sites with more pointed and enlightening commentary; there are movie review, book review, and entertainment sites that offer a broader range of coverage. The same goes for sports, politics, technology, and health. Salon.com has all of that, but whether you choose to become a regular visitor depends on whether you find something in this site—its blogs, columnists, reviewers, or message boards—that speaks to you. The barbershop metaphor also applies here: If you like the chatter and the ambiance of the place, you're likely to return (even if you don't need a haircut).

Off the Record

Salon.com's prospects were, once upon a golden time (now known as "the Internet bubble"), much better than they seem now. Although the site has passed its 10th anniversary and is still publishing, its stock price has fallen from a high of about $15 to about 25 cents a share, and its staff has been pared to about one-third of what it was during the go-go cyber days of the late-1990s.

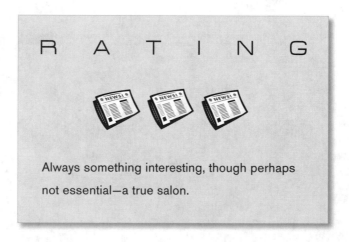

R A T I N G

Always something interesting, though perhaps not essential—a true salon.

73

San Francisco Chronicle

www.sfgate.com

Overview

Since 1865, the residents of the San Francisco Bay area have been able to peruse one of the more celebrated and important newspapers in America: the *San Francisco Chronicle*. Drawing on a tradition of Pulitzer-winning reporters and provocative national columnists—as well as a reputation for hard-hitting metro muckraking—the *San Francisco Chronicle* has moved into the online arena, preserving much of what makes the paper great but also embracing the increasingly popular trend in journalism to turn news on the Web into a friendly, frothy mix of local "what's happening" digests and lighter, reader-friendly features.

The print edition of the *Chronicle*—a paper owned by the Hearst media monolith—boasts a daily circulation of more than a half-million readers. The paper's Web site acknowledges that widespread popularity with some features that seem more in sync with populism than journalistic inquiry.

Still, as newspapers continue to grope with ways to serve their long-time readers while attracting younger Web surfers, compromises are necessary. The *Chronicle's* Web presence clearly acknowledges those tradeoffs.

What You'll Find There

At www.sfchron.com, the newspaper's official site, you'll find almost nothing. That's really just an on-ramp for the paper's de facto Web site, www.sfgate.com. (The "sfchron" site provides a bare minimum about how to contact the paper's offices, how to subscribe, and an icon to get to SFGate.com, where the real action is.) At SFGate.com, readers can find most of the stories that appear in the print edition, with the exception of syndicated material, some freelance articles, and magazine inserts like *Parade*.

Readers can also find other things on the site that *aren't* in the *San Francisco Chronicle*: blogs (about a dozen, dealing with everything from politics to celebrity), chat boards, podcasts, ads for community events, updated traffic and weather, and the day in pictures.

There are, to be sure, examples of quality journalism and reporting from the *Chronicle* on SFGate.com. Stories from that day's morning edition are flagged on the first third of the Web page with a brief description of each and a menu of icons for sidebar stories. There is also a box for the latest Associated Press headlines, and the Web page stays updated in typical news site fashion. The *Chronicle* continues to boast of a highly regarded sports section, as it provides thorough coverage of the Bay area sports scene with depth and candor (and it should be remembered that the *Chronicle* broke the news of baseball superstar Barry Bonds' steroid use, a piece of reportage that found its way into a best-selling book called *Game of Shadows*).

The look of the home page for SFGate.com seems, however, to mimic a chamber-of-commerce brochure about the greatness of the Bay area rather than a newspaper Web site. Ads for casinos and car dealerships share space in the area that news people call "above the fold." (The *Chronicle* shouldn't be criticized for doing what many other newspapers are doing, which is turning their Web pages into a mix of ads, local boosterism, and some news—but the trend is troubling nonetheless.)

Why You Should Visit

The *San Francisco Chronicle* has a rich and storied tradition in American journalism, and its continued significance was signaled by its purchase in 2000 by Hearst Media Corp. The paper has smartly embraced the suburban migration in Northern California, and its popularity makes it an important opinion shaper and a bellwether of West Coast thinking.

In an increasingly politically polarized nation, the *Chronicle* offers the opportunity to eavesdrop on the conversation in an important part of the country. And its Web site is fun and user-friendly, offering all kinds of information, especially to locals or those who might be planning to visit the area.

Keep This in Mind

Once renowned for its international coverage, the paper has lately come under some criticism for focusing more on local events and less

---

Opinion   IDEAS   INSIGHT   COMMENTARY

Chronicle Editorials

An alternative universe
TALK ABOUT doublespeak. President Bush insisted this week that "the United States does not torture. It's against our laws and it's against our values." In the same speech on Wednesday, he announced he would be asking...

Op-Ed Columns

Debra J. Saunders
Bring it on?
TWO FACTORS will work against Republicans trying to retain control of the House of Representatives and the U.S. Senate on Nov. 7 -- and they both have to do with the downside of being the party in power in Washington....

on substantive world and national reporting. The paper has also increased its coverage of the local entertainment scene in an apparent attempt to out-do the growing number of publications, such as the *Oakland News* and the *San Jose Mercury News*, also homing in on the advertising dollars in the Bay Area.

Off the Record

The *San Francisco Chronicle* has enjoyed a long-time rivalry with its crosstown nemesis, the *San Francisco Examiner*, once a Hearst paper (the young William Randolph took it over in 1887 at age 23, a scenario "borrowed" by Orson Welles in his classic *Citizen Kane*) and now owned by billionaire Philip Anschutz. The *Examiner* has recently gone from broadsheet to tabloid format, and its once-considerable place in journalism has diminished considerably.[1]

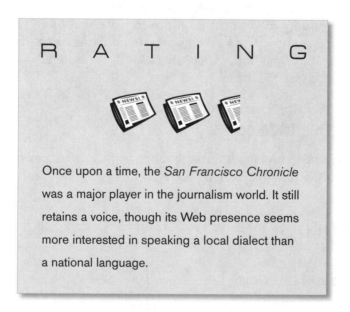

R A T I N G

Once upon a time, the *San Francisco Chronicle* was a major player in the journalism world. It still retains a voice, though its Web presence seems more interested in speaking a local dialect than a national language.

Endnote

1. From the Wikipedia (wikipedia.org) article on the *San Francisco Examiner*.

74

Slate

www.slate.com

Overview

This online magazine of news and opinion is one of the great success stories of the information age. After a high-profile launch in the mid-1990s—and not a few public stumbles (including a headline-grabbing editor change) as it groped its way toward viability—Slate has become one of the most revered (and copied) sites on the Web.

What makes Slate so popular? The answer probably has something to do with Slate's ability to be hip while remaining thoroughly grounded in a journalistic ethos. Slate has done in a few years what many newspapers have been trying to do for decades: make news cool.

What You'll Find There

Slate's users are greeted every morning by a mix of articles that take the news everybody's talking about and then tell you *why* everybody's talking about these things. The stories are usually well researched and well written (Slate employs some of the best writers in journalism today, in any medium), but they also have a "knowing" quality that creates the sense that the reader is "in" on what's really going on. Spend 20 undisturbed minutes on Slate, and you'll be able to hold your own at any workplace water cooler.

The site is chock full of icons and attention grabbers, but the design caters to people who still love newspapers and magazines, so it's easy to navigate and clear what awaits your next click. The articles are thorough enough to provide more context than you would normally get in a metro daily but still short enough that you can get what you need before your latte cools. (This was not always the case. Slate's early reviewers bashed the site soundly for its lengthy articles; as one critic put it, "If I wanted to read long printed articles, I would be better off with the *New Yorker*."[1])

Slate also provides a compelling and much-needed "Election Scorecard" for campaigns of national importance. Rather than simply take its own poll, Slate compiles and crunches the results of dozens of different "tracking polls" that have come to dominate the media's modus operandi of election coverage. What readers get is an up-to-the-moment snapshot of a candidate's momentum. The Election Scorecard captures both the science and the drama of modern campaigns.

Why You Should Visit

Many news-related Web sites suffer from a bad case of "me-first-itis." They front load their sites with what's happening *now* and leave little room for background, context, or alternative perspectives. Slate offers a handy remedy for this in its daily dissection of what's making news—nationally and globally. The site critiques the front pages of major newspapers around the globe and assesses what's getting play and what's getting buried. While talk-radio blathers about mainstream media bias, Slate actually shows you who's promoting what angle and who's skewing the news. (Visitors to the site, however, should be aware that many of Slate's writers and editors have been culled from the ranks of the "progressive" [read: political left] media pool, from outlets such as the *Village Voice*, *Mother Jones*, and *The Nation*.)

Keep This in Mind

Being hip is good, but knowing that you're hip can grow tiresome. Slate's corps of culturally plugged-in scribes knows the score, but sometimes these reporters seem more interested in showing how savvy they are than just giving you the story. Almost every article comes with a heavy serving of not only cutting-edge opinion but also a certain coy, cosmopolitan smugness. Spending too much time on Slate can create the kind of backlash one feels when stuck at a dinner party full of really glib, cultured guests who have all seen the latest Wim Wenders film but would never—never!—go to a NASCAR race or buy a can of Cheez Wiz.

Off the Record

Despite its progressive roster of writers and its commitment to cover stories affecting all communities, Slate's readers are overwhelmingly male and economically well-heeled. According to the most recent Nielsen/NetRatings statistics (as reported in the *New York Sun)*, Slate male readers outnumber female readers 64 percent to 36 percent with almost one-third of the readership reporting an annual income of more than $100,000.

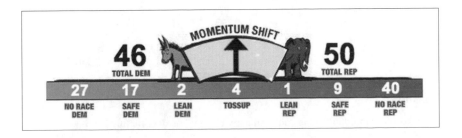

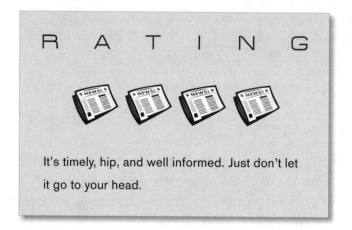

R A T I N G

It's timely, hip, and well informed. Just don't let it go to your head.

Endnote

1. Jakob Nielson, "Slate Magazine: An early review," useit.com, July 1996.

75

The Smoking Gun
www.thesmokinggun.com

Overview

In Spring 1997, as the Internet's potential lured everyone with an idea for a site into its Web, two former colleagues at the *Village Voice* concocted a unique dot-com concept that possessed both remarkable promise and considerable risk. The Smoking Gun (TSG), however, has continually hit its target throughout the last 10 years—and has the ammunition to last another few decades.

Bill Bastone, TSG's editor who founded the site with Daniel Green, said he never thought about who exactly would visit the site; it "was just a vehicle we were going to use to disseminate documents we thought were interesting ... I thought if I found something funny, kooky and stupid, there's a good chance someone else might think the same."[1]

Known in the early days solely for its amusing, or depressing (depending on your point of view), postings of arrest mug shots of celebrities, TSG is so much more—a beacon of investigative journalism (often scooping mainstream media, albeit on things perhaps not quite worthy of Woodward-and-Bernstein status) and a model of cyberspace success. By 2000, TSG was purchased by cable network Court TV. And then, with a staff double its previous count (Bastone hired two muckrakers to join himself and Green), working in a converted Court TV mailroom, they took phone calls from law enforcement sources, shuffled through public document after public document, and made a ton of Freedom of Information requests.

What You'll Find There

You're welcomed to the site by an unorthodox home page that consists of a dominant graphic—a file folder. After just a few clicks, The Smoking Gun's "gotcha."

You could start by clicking on today's "Featured Document," which could be anything from an explosive exclusive that debunks a purported "memoir" to a lawsuit over a celebrity sex videotape. Or flip through the TSG files that contain a decade's worth of entertaining stories by clicking on the "Archive" section, which is organized by year. Then head "Backstage" to scroll through the "riders"—the requests, or demands, for "necessary" concert comforts—of the biggest names in music.

But no trip to the mishap and misbehavior museum is complete without a stroll through the gallery of mug shots, neatly hung by category, which include the Mona Lisas of "Sports" legends, infamous "Killers," "Hollywood" stars, "Gangsters" who need only a one-name introduction, "Music" industry giants, and even "B-List" celebrities.

Why You Should Visit

In addition to its unreal-but-real content, TSG is relatively ad-free and extremely navigable. But one of the top reasons to play with TSG is merely its existence. Without the Internet—and the medium's deep, if not endless, news hole—there is no TSG. Where else could one publish much of the 1,903-page grand jury testimony from the Michael

Jackson case? While the shoe-leather reporting is nice, TSG consistently beats the big boys by posting its new knowledge immediately. Simply put, there are not many people doing what TSG is doing.

In a world where the line between news and entertainment is as blurred as Nick Nolte's vision during a DUI stop, TSG discharges it all, from the dirt on Dubya to the most recent arrest of a hot-for-student teacher, from a 23-page British dossier detailing the torture tactics of Saddam to reports of NFL cheerleaders in a toilet tussle. Perhaps TSG is best known for its 2006 exposé "A Million Little Lies: Exposing James Frey's Fiction Addiction," which catapulted the site into the national media spotlight and even caused the book's biggest fan, Oprah Winfrey, to disavow Frey's work.

Keep This in Mind

On the "About" page, TSG guarantees "everything here is 100% authentic." To date, that guarantee has been upheld—mainly because TSG relies on court files, lawsuits, arrest reports, FOI requests, and well-placed government and law enforcement sources. In more than a decade, the site has never been sued. Legal threats are far less uncommon. But those are posted too. When Victoria's Secret execs insisted the site remove the posting of its ironically conservative dress code for employees, the site's boss, who covered the Mob

for the *Voice* for 10 years, resisted: "I've been threatened by members of the Genovese crime family … and chased by people with shovels. The bra merchant doesn't mean much to me."[2]

Off the Record

In 2000, TSG caught fire, and the site's popularity soared, when Fox stopped asking *Who Wants to Marry a Multimillionaire?* after TSG revealed that the reality show's multimillionaire had more than large bills in his luggage—namely a restraining order issued after he was accused of hitting his ex-girlfriend. Three years later, 3 million people (a 10-fold increase) visited the site each month. In early 2003, TSG received 20 million page views in a less than two days when it blasted another round at Fox and reality TV, reporting that a *Joe Millionaire* finalist once appeared in bondage and fetish flicks.

Way more entertaining than reading your local newspaper's police blotter.

Endnotes

1. César G. Soriano, "The Smoking Gun joins high-caliber media: Dirt-digging Web site hits TV, radio, books, mags," *USA Today*, Aug. 18, 2003.

2. Jim Romenesko, "The smaller news that was," Poynter Online (www.poynter.org/ dg.lts/id.3776/content.content_view.htm), Dec. 29, 2000.

76

Sports Illustrated
sportsillustrated.cnn.com

Overview

Long before sports became the lingua franca of water cooler conversations on Monday morning, an upstart publication called *Sports Illustrated* decided there was a market for people who wanted thoughtful, in-depth coverage of their favorite sports teams and athletes.

Since that time—a half-century ago—the market for sports has changed, and so has that once-bold and probing publication. Among the many changes in the way sports is covered and disseminated is the proliferation of sports-focused Web sites. And of course, *Sports Illustrated*'s Web site seeks to build on the reputation of its parent publication—though in today's sports marketplace, both heir and progeny come up a bit short.

Keeping up with the ever-changing international sports circus is more than a full-time job, and different Web sites choose to do it differently. In some areas, *Sports Illustrated*'s site hits a home run; in others, the team never makes it onto the field.

What You'll Find There

The home page of the Web site is bustling with color and text, though on closer inspection, there is not as much content there as it first seems. The site features a large, nearly quarter-screen photo of some late-breaking sporting event, with a related story advertised in the center column of the home page. There might also be a related blog entry from one of *Sports Illustrated*'s staffers and a sidebar story related to the main story.

A banner announcing "Top Stories" brings readers to any one of about a half-dozen pieces about major sports news events of the previous 24 hours (and, for readers seeking more news or greater comprehensive coverage, there is a handy icon for CNN.com, an affiliated

news site in the Time Warner empire). The stories are satisfactory and provide the basics, though they tend to be shorter than an average newspaper article and also generally lack any unusual angles or insights. The roster of stories is pro-forma; the biggies are there but presented without much difference from what one would get on a nightly sports report on TV.

Along the bottom of the page are three colorful boxes advertising other features of the page: "SI on Campus," "Scorecard Daily," and "Fantasy Plus." These components do present different views of the world of sport but not necessarily better or more interesting ones. "SI on Campus" traffics in college sports but doesn't seem particularly urgent or compelling. Stories about college stars rumored to be considering entering the pro draft or a recent piece about which pro venue was best for NCAA games seem a bit forced—like a low-percentage three-pointer as the shot clock dissolves. "Scorecard Daily" is a look behind the scenes of the major sport of the season but again involves lots of rumor and speculation. "Fantasy Plus" provides additional information about athletes who might be involved in the swap-market that comprises the challenge of fantasy league play.

A banner across the top of the page features icons for the major sports, as well as "SI Kids.com," "Video," "High School," and, of course, the ever-popular "Swimsuit." The rest of the home page is filled with ads for sporting goods, poker Web sites, dating services, and subscriptions to the magazine.

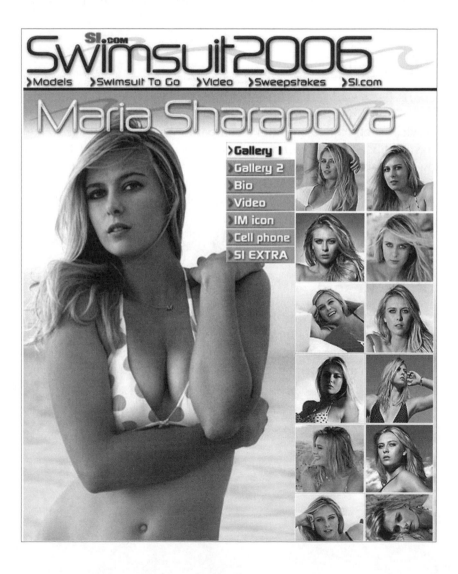

Why You Should Visit

Sports Illustrated, the magazine, no longer commands the respect in the journalistic field—or even the sports field—that it once had. The magazine has shrunk and has moved away from its award-winning (and hard-hitting) explorations of scandals, issues, and trends that made it a must-read during its heyday in the 1960s and 1970s. But it still has a few heavy hitters—analysts like Peter King—who remain important voices in the world of sport. And the magazine still breaks stories from time to time—stories that leech into the mainstream sports media.

Keep This in Mind

Sports Illustrated sort of invented the world of national sports journalism, making their recent decline somewhat ironic. Other sports services such as ESPN (with its companion magazine and Web site) have eclipsed *Sports Illustrated* in many aspects that *SI* formerly owned. Some critics have noted that *Sports Illustrated*'s fall from grace coincided with its focus on sports celebrities and its plethora of "commemorative issues." Even the swimsuit issue—a perennial best-seller—represents (to purists) an abdication of the magazine's former mission: to be the thinking person's guide to the world of sport.[1]

Off the Record

Sports Illustrated would have been called, simply, *Sport*—the name preferred by magazine magnate Henry Luce, who started the magazine—but another publication owned that name and refused to part with it (even after Luce offered $200,000 for the rights to the name).

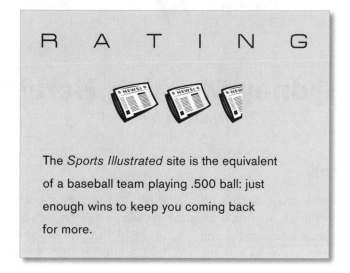

RATING

The *Sports Illustrated* site is the equivalent of a baseball team playing .500 ball: just enough wins to keep you coming back for more.

Endnote

1. See Michael MacCambridge's *The franchise: A history of* Sports Illustrated Magazine, published by Hyperion Press, 2004.

77

Sydney Morning Herald
www.smh.com.au

Overview

For Internet users far from the Land of Oz, the thought of regularly signing on to an Australian newspaper site is as foreign as the monstrously large island at the edge of the world. But if your knowledge of the country/continent is limited to hackneyed and stereotypical imagery (koalas and kangaroos, Crocodile Dundee and the Crocodile Hunter, Foster's beer and Outback Steakhouse), then a Web excursion to the home of the 2000 Summer Olympic Games is in order.

Based in Australia's oldest city, the *Sydney Morning Herald* is Australia's oldest newspaper. And it's come a long way since 1831, when it began as a weekly, printing 750 copies of its four-page first issue. Nine years later, the newspaper became a daily and has since continued to mature as an Australian institution. The *Sydney Morning Herald*'s first Internet venture occurred in April 1995, when it developed a site to post content from its "Computers & Communications" section. More than a decade later, those primitive online origins have evolved into a modern spectacle that puts the capabilities of information technology and the power of the Web on full display.

What You'll Find There

Those who log on to the home page of www.smh.com.au—divided into two unequal vertical sections—will find a large, colorful vertical photo at the top middle of the screen just below the title banner and site's navigation menu, which presents the expected headings: "News," "Entertainment," "Business," "Sport," "Travel," "Tech," and "Sections." Rolling the cursor over each of these headings reveals drop-down menus listing several subsections. The aforementioned photo, which usually teases an entertainment, celebrity (an increasing

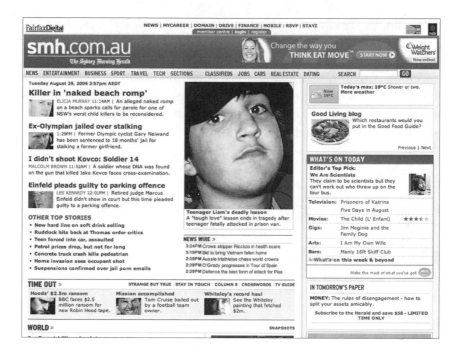

number of Hollywood stars have Australian roots), or quirky feature, is accompanied by a small headline/link to the full story and another link to related multimedia. To its left are four headlines that link to the site's top stories—a mix of international and national news—and usually include a byline, a one-sentence summary, and sometimes a thumbnail photo. The top-story package also includes three to four smaller headlines that link to sidebar stories and other related content. Below the dominant photograph, you will find the site's breaking news service, "News Wire," and headlines/links to five of the most recent news reports.

The rest of the left two-thirds of the page is neatly carved up into eight sections: "Time Out," which includes entertaining "Strange But True" stories; "World," where you can scroll through the daily "Snapshots" photo gallery; "National" with daily news about Australia and more in-depth "News Specials"; "Opinion," where an index of the site's two-dozen blogs—some of the best on the Web—is available; "Business"; "Technology"; "Entertainment"; and "Sport."

The right third of the page consists of several other site features. You can access a variety of reviews, including television, film, DVDs,

CDs, books, restaurants, bars, and arts. Other sections, such as "Travel," "Personal Finance," "Health & Fitness," and "Home & Lifestyle," and companion sites—real estate (domain.com.au), automobiles (drive.com.au), and jobs (mycareer.com.au)—are spotlighted as well. The front pages of the site's numerous sections retain a design very similar to that of the home page, while subsections vary only slightly in format.

News blogs

Talking Pictures

NEW: Stunning slideshows, insightful images, and the story from behind the lens... explore the world of *Herald* photographers.

The Anvil

Most of us will spend most of our lives working. It's an endless game and now it seems all the rules are being changed. The *Herald*'s Workplace Reporter, Nick O'Malley, looks at everything from office politics to industrial relations.

Rocco Bloggo

Sydney Morning Herald artist Rocco Fazzari takes you behind his illustrations and into the newsroom.

FOI

The headquarters for the Herald's FOI editor, Matthew Moore. In theory, Freedom of Information laws allow journalists and the public to scrutinise the operation of all levels of government. But the reality is often quite different.

Frankenstein

A weekly brainstrust debating issues from dream analysis to rewriting the national anthem. The most creative comments each week feature in the Out There column on the back page of Monday's *Herald*. Edited by Dylan Welch.

News blog

This is where we house our discussions on the news of the day. It's wide-ranging and there are plenty of contributors on plenty of topics.

Life and leisure blogs

All Men Are Liars

NEW: He's the *other* Sam in the City. Sam de Brito has spent a decade writing for newspapers, film and TV dramatising life's quiet truths. Now he expounds on the business of being a bloke.

Sam and the City

Dating: Chat about love, sex, romance, flirting, chasing and cheating with the Herald's dating blogger, Samantha Brett.

The Daily Truth

Comment: Author and journalist Jack Marx rummages around in the world of current and not-so-current affairs, matters of cultural import and issues of no social consequence at all, strange thoughts, fringe theories and utterances commonly left unuttered.

Lost in transit

Travel: The latest musings and travel tips from Rob Woodburn, one of Australia's most experienced travel writers.

Radar

Pop culture: If you're after consensus you've come to the wrong place. This is current affairs Radar-style, courtesy of Dominic Knight and friends. Radar is the Herald's Wednesday work and lifestyle liftout.

Why You Should Visit

The *Sydney Morning Herald* is Australian for online news. Calling this site comprehensive would not even come close to aptly describing the amount of content you will find here. And yet there's never a sense of being bombarded, overwhelmed, or unable to successfully navigate the site with ease. Indeed, it is balance that enables www.smh.com.au to flourish rather than flounder—a balance between dense content and clean design, between serious and superficial news, between staff-produced and wire-service (*New York Times*, Associated Press, Australian Associated Press) content, and between traditional journalism and engaging blogs. The site manages to be many things at once: creative yet simple, informative yet entertaining, exhaustive yet accessible. After one visit, you'll be lured back down under again and again.

Keep This in Mind

This is certainly not the only Australian newspaper site on the Web. Despite its respected status within the industry, the *Sydney Morning Herald* is not the most-read newspaper in Australia—or, for that matter, in Sydney, the country's most populated city. The *Daily Telegraph*, a tabloid owned by Rupert Murdoch's News Corp. that tends to take a more sensational approach, has a weekday circulation nearly double that of its broadsheet competitor in Sydney. The *Herald Sun*, Murdoch's Melbourne tabloid, enjoys even better numbers. Both the *Daily Telegraph* and the *Herald Sun*—along with the country's only "national" newspaper, the *Australian*, which has a lower circulation than all of the aforementioned—have a fairly robust Internet presence through News Network (www.news.com.au).

Off the Record

For the first 113 years of its existence, the *Sydney Morning Herald* did not print news on the front page. Long after it became the norm for most other newspapers, it finally—and only after much deliberation—replaced the public announcements, notices, and ads that perpetually owned the prime real estate with news articles on April 15, 1944.

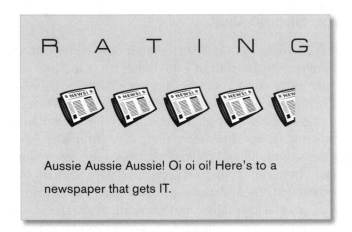

RATING

Aussie Aussie Aussie! Oi oi oi! Here's to a newspaper that gets IT.

78

Time

www.time.com

Overview

We live in an age when solicitations for subscriptions to weekly magazines arrive, with annoying regularity, in the mail, via telemarketers' unwanted phone solicitations, through e-mail, even falling out of the magazines themselves.

But there used to be only *one* weekly news magazine for the entire country, once upon a *Time*.

When Henry Luce and Briton Hadden started *Time* magazine in 1923, they had a monopoly on the soon-to-emerge news magazine market. Since its founding, *Time* has not only remained a profitable and prominent title on the racks that now groan under the weight of competing weeklies but also a brand name in the journalism world, the Cadillac of newsweeklies.

Opinions abound about whether this once groundbreaking weekly remains a must-read or merely a thin distillation of its former, robust self. That debate can also be extended to the Web site, which contains much of what makes *Time* so popular and much that fuels its detractors' fusillades.

What You'll Find There

Like its print forebear, the *Time* Web site contains lots of everything, from the news features that are carried in the magazine to all manner of "popular journalism": Washington gossip, movie reviews, trends in health, science stories, and traditional feature stories on people in the news.

The site's home page provides a comprehensive array of stories that span all conceivable readership interests, from international stories to lighter-than-air entertainment featurettes. The main story on the home page is, generally, tied to the cover story of that week's issue

(however, certain "special reports" are available online only to subscribers of the print edition). The icons "U.S.," "World," "Business &
Technology," "Entertainment," "Health & Science," and "Specials"
pretty much cover all the bases.

   And yet, that's precisely the problem with the Web site. For all its
comprehensiveness, *Time* lacks a clear focus. No story seems to be
more important than any other story. Whether it's civil war in the
Sudan or the dietary impact of saturated fats, each story is madden-
ingly similar in length (and much too short for any real insight), and
most are authored in the same user-friendly journalistic patter. Moving
from one story to the next, one gets a sense of the same voice, the same
sense of middling urgency, the same "here's another good thing to
know about" gentle hectoring. Even their columnists, such as Joe Klein,
aren't likely to tell you something you can't read somewhere else.

   If you're looking for great literary journalism, *Time* isn't the place to
go. Nor if you're looking for cutting-edge opinions. Nor even the best
news reporting on domestic and international news. *Time's* Web site
is to journalism what Sears is to oil paintings—a big selection that's

impressive-seeming if viewed in the right light. But all those pretty pictures don't turn a department store into an art gallery.

Why You Should Visit

Because *Time* still starts conversations. It's as close as we have to a still-relevant national news source. People and topics on the cover of the print product set the agenda for talk-radio programs and network

news affiliates. And its annual "Person of the Year" remains an attention-getter, with pundits, pollsters, and local anchors milking the suspense (and then dissecting the decision) in their typically excessive way.

And for all of its "middle-of-the-road" approach to covering the news, there's probably something noble about trying to be all things to all people in this day and age of fragmentation. Those who prefer their journalism a little harder-edged or who expect a magazine Web site to run "magazine-length" pieces (meaning more than one and a half screens of text) will be disappointed by *Time*'s site. But if you're a really busy person and you just want to keep up, there are worse places to go than *Time*.

Keep This in Mind

Time has been seen by some of its critics as drifting away in recent years from the repertoire of traditional "news" and heading toward lighter, reader-friendly features on celebrity and pop culture. That might be where the readers are—and *Time* certainly wouldn't be the first publication to chase readers' dwindling attention spans. However, its failure to offset such a move with more meaty, thoughtful, and lengthy analytical news stories makes the practice journalistically damnable. (One of the great, unfulfilled promises of the Internet age is the "infinite news hole"—the room to run stories that would never fit on the printed page.)

Off the Record

Time has only published one official editorial in its entire history. In 1974, the editors called for the resignation of Richard Nixon.

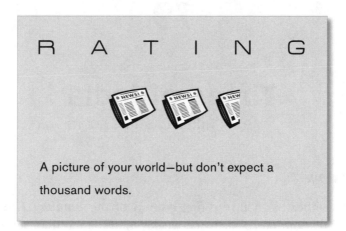

R A T I N G

A picture of your world—but don't expect a thousand words.

79

Times of India

timesofindia.indiatimes.com

Overview

On November 3, 1838, the first edition of the *Bombay Times and Journal of Commerce*—a twice-weekly newspaper that served the British inhabitants of western India and the city's business community—was published. Little more than a decade later, the paper morphed into a full-fledged daily—the first of many major changes that would aid in its continual growth. Another decade passed before the *Bombay Times* merged with two other city papers to form the *Times of India*. Its new masthead encapsulated a new mission, broadening coverage to include all of India rather than one city or one segment of the population. Another 85 years passed before the newspaper came under Indian ownership, nearly coinciding with Indian independence in 1947. In a span of about 10 years beginning in 1950, the company—still operating under the name Bennett Coleman and Co. Ltd., which was formed in 1892—added a Delhi edition (headed by its first Indian editor), *Filmfare* (now India's largest English-language film magazine), *Femina* (currently the country's largest women's magazine), and *Economic Times* (the world's second-largest financial daily newspaper behind only the *Wall Street Journal*).

In 1996, the newspaper reached a circulation of 1 million; only four years later, its circulation doubled. In 2006, *The Times of India* sold more than 2.5 million copies a day, and its readership regularly topped 7 million.

What You'll Find There

The *Times of India*'s Web site is accessible directly or through IndiaTimes.com, which has served as a portal to the Times Group (the newspaper's corporate parent) online products since 1999.

The design of its home page is simple but not compelling, offering no enticing elements to pull users deeper into the site. It typically leads with a stand-alone photograph of a Hollywood or Bollywood celebrity. Below the photo is the boldfaced headline of the day's top story—usually unrelated to the image. A list of several smaller headlines that serve as links to their respective reports in a section labeled "Top of the Hour" fills the remaining top portion of the home page. Also accessible from the home page is a section containing "Breaking News by the Second," as the site calls it, along with blogs, the newspaper's columnists, and other top stories—many of which are culled from wire services (a mix of the familiar acronym of the Associated Press with the less recognizable initials of the Press Trust of India; the site also heavily depends on Reuters and its own service, the Times News Network).

What it lacks in visual quality, the *Times of India*'s Web site makes up for with quantity. From local, regional, national, and international news to entertainment, sports, business, and lifestyles (items that usually send users back to IndiaTimes.com), the site is full of choices, evidenced by the lengthy menu that runs down the left column of the home page.

Why You Should Visit

Traveling to the Web site of the *Times of India* can feel a bit like traveling to the country itself. But any confusion or clutter is offset by the incalculable insight offered at the site into the politics, people, culture, and customs of Indian society. Plus, English is the only language spoken here, although a slight difference in the style of writing as compared to the American press is somewhat noticeable—much less flair, much more terse. And while it might not be a daily trip for most users scouring the Internet for the day's news, the *Times of India* site should be scheduled on the itinerary as often as possible.

Keep This in Mind

Despite its position as the leading newspaper in India and as the most-read daily in the world, the credibility of the *Times of India* has suffered a slough of setbacks in recent years. In 2003, the Times Group sustained an ethical blow when a business reporter for the *Economic Times* was arrested for allegedly trying to extort large sums of money from a financial services company to quash a negative piece about that company's boss.[1]

But more damaging to the *Times of India*'s historically stellar reputation is its parent company's business-trumps-journalism edict. Critics have condemned the organization for "breaching the 'walls' that separate advertising, management and editorial," saying management meddles excessively with editorial policy and too often shifts its staff among the disparate departments. Worse yet, the company began "selling news" in 2003, resulting in "gushing endorsements of flop movies, fashion and lifestyle products and the promotion of hotels and restaurants that enter into a payment agreement."[2]

Cities

DELHI
Zones for security? ✐
Manoj Mitta

Now, there may soon be special security zones across India to combat terror threats, insurgency and organised crime.
[10 Sep, 2006 0003hrs IST]

- AHMEDABAD   - BANGALORE
- CHANDIGARH   - DELHI
- HYDERABAD   - KOLKATA
- LUCKNOW   - MUMBAI
- PATNA   - PUNE
- THIRUVANANTHAPURAM

Off the Record

R. K. Laxman, a cartoonist for the *Times of India* during the last half of the 20th century, created the celebrated character known simply as "The Common Man" early in his career at the newspaper. "The Common Man" (representing the average Indian) appeared in the paper daily in Laxman's one-panel comic strip called *You Said It*, which functioned much like an editorial cartoon that often tweaked the political establishment. The character served as the sole observer of what was taking place in the cartoon. "I would say he symbolizes the mute millions of India, or perhaps the whole world, a silent spectator of marching time," Laxman once said. "The Common Man" is so revered that a 10-foot bronze statute of the character stands in the city of Pune and is so synonymous with the *Times of India* that the figure appeared on a stamp issued by the Indian Postal Service in 1988 to commemorate the newspaper's 150th anniversary.

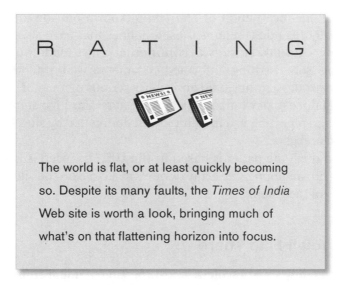

The world is flat, or at least quickly becoming so. Despite its many faults, the *Times of India* Web site is worth a look, bringing much of what's on that flattening horizon into focus.

Endnotes

1. Reported by Sucheta Delal, a freelance journalist who previously worked as a top reporter at the *Times of India*, in a piece headlined "Selling news or buying silence?" on March 5, 2003, available at www.rediff.com/money/2003/mar/05dalal.htm.
2. Ibid.

80

The Times of London
www.timesonline.co.uk

Overview

Internet media moguls who are perpetually wondering how to keep on top of the next new thing can probably empathize with the ownership of *The Times* of London. After all, this paper has been trying to set the curve in global journalism for more than 220 years. That kind of longevity, almost unheard of among media companies of the Western world, has helped *The Times* establish its reputation as a credible voice in the media world—from the Age of Enlightenment to the digital age.

The online incarnation of *The Times* (known outside the U.K. as *The Times* of London) retains those qualities that have always made the paper-and-ink edition a continental must-read: world-class reporting, sober writing, informed commentary, and depth. If this Web site exudes a rather staid and overly serious demeanor, consider it a small price to pay for a publication that retains high standards of editing and reporting in a medium often dominated by sites boasting of speed and glitz.

And though the paper is based in the U.K., its reach is genuinely global, with an impressive array of news available on the site from all quarters of the globe.

What You'll Find There

Under an oddly arresting black-and-lime Times Online banner, you'll find the major stories of the day, topped by a breaking story that is often approached from several angles: main news story, related sidebars, maps and graphics, photo gallery, streaming video, and blogs. The rest of the first screen offers global news, as well as "Your World View"—a series of stories posted by readers about their global travel experiences (complete with interactive maps and facts about local

346

geography). There's an additional extensive collection of columnists and editorials further into the site.

The Times Online also covers the expected beats ("Sport," "Business," and "Entertainment") with multiple links for dozens of stories, columns, and reviews under each of those headings. A games and puzzles section should satisfy all the cryptographers and sudoku players. There's also a news section giving you breaking news from all compass points, and a "Related Reports" section that provides everything from lengthy personal interviews with political and cultural figures to analyses of popular trends.

There are robustly attended message boards on most of the topics in the news and entire separate sections on lighter areas such as "Property," "Driving," and "Food & Drink," with articles, essays, photo galleries, and insightful commentary for each. Perhaps one of its most useful features is the "Our Papers" section—full-color representations of a week's worth of front pages from *The Times*. Clicking on any of those reveals a list of headlines from that day's newspaper (and clicking on the headlines brings the full stories to the screen).

Briefly put, there is nothing brief about this site. If you've got the time, you'll emerge from its labyrinthine richness with a much better understanding of the world, as articulated by a busy corps of British scribes.

Why You Should Visit

With more news sites relying on big headlines, colorful screen shots, and titillating news, it's getting harder to find what many readers still desperately seek: a thinking-person's news site that covers the world and doesn't "dumb down" stories or cater to our basest whims. *The Times*—which some media watchers think has fallen a few pegs since media mogul Rupert Murdoch took it over in the early 1980s—is still an important, authoritative voice. Going digital

has not compromised its two-century commitment to quality; instead, it seems to have enabled the staff to tell important stories in even more ways.

Keep This in Mind

A Web site derived from a *very* British newspaper shouldn't be faulted for being very British itself. So expect British spellings, lots of references to internal British politics and cultural history, typically thorough coverage of issues of local concern to U.K. residents, and a lineup of European columnists who often have a very different take on world events than their colleagues in other parts of the world— especially in America. If you can't afford an actual trip across the pond, then you can at least indulge your anglophile sensibilities with a daily online read of the still prim and proper *Times* of London.

Off the Record

The Times is a patron as well as a watchdog, co-sponsoring the London Film Festival (with the British Film Institute) and the popular Cheltenham Festival of Literature.

RATING

The news of the world, rendered in the King's English.

81

Times-Picayune
www.nola.com

Overview

Hurricane Katrina—two words that instantly evoke images of devastating destruction and utter despair—will long be considered one of the worst disasters in U.S. history. It also proved to be a momentous event in the history of online news. The *Times-Picayune*, a major daily newspaper in New Orleans, won two Pulitzer Prizes for its coverage of Katrina and its aftermath. In awarding the gold medal for public service (the most prestigious Pulitzer) and the prize for breaking news reporting, the judges called the newspaper's work "courageous" and its coverage "heroic."

The remarkable feat is not that the *Times-Picayune* won two Pulitzers but that it did so largely as a result of its online content. For three days during Katrina's initial onslaught, the newspaper lost the capability to print and turned to the Web as its sole means of informing the public. By continuously updating blogs and posting an electronic edition of the newspaper each night on its affiliated site (NOLA.com, although owned by the same company as the newspaper, functions as a separate entity), the *Times-Picayune* overcame what could have been a devastating blow—failing its readers when needed most. Instead, the Internet rescued the drowning newspaper. And for the first time in history, the Pulitzers not only accepted online content as part of a newspaper's entries, but the venerable institution also applauded it.

As a result of a few days in the late summer of 2005, the *Times-Picayune* (and NOLA.com) now truly knows the value and importance of the Web in fulfilling its mission better than any other news organization in the country.

What You'll Find There

Since its launch in 1998, NOLA.com attracted visitors through the site's Mardi Gras section and numerous Webcams spying on partygoers around town. People now log on for a much different reason. What they'll find is news, mostly from the *Times-Picayune* but some from a local ABC affiliate, either directly or tangentially related to Katrina, along with coverage of topics typically found in a metro daily (i.e., crime stories). Some of its content extends to other parts of the world, but that is certainly not the main attraction.

A news or feature photo from the newspaper dominates the top left of the home page and is accompanied in the right column by a corresponding headline. The home page is divided into two columns—the left side slightly wider than the right. Below the lead photo are several teasers to various online-only content: blog, slideshows, videos, forums, and interactive graphics. A list of headlines/links fills the right column, followed by a box where users can search the current edition of the *Times-Picayune* by selecting a section, scrolling a complete index, or viewing a PDF of a page as it appeared in print. Visitors to the site can also access all of the newspaper's online content (a page of headlines organized into familiar sections: "Front Page," "Sports," "Latest Updates," "Metro," "Editorials & Opinions," "Obituaries," "Business," "Living," and "Special Sections") by clicking the masthead logo just below the navigation menu at the top of the home page or by typing www.nola.com/t-p/ into the browser's address bar.

Users can expect a special hurricane preparedness and resources center on the home page each hurricane season, along with in-depth coverage of the recovery effort. The site's "Katrina Flashback" section, usually teased on the home page, provides access to its award-winning coverage and is worth a look. Although the unforgettable storm forever altered the landscape, it has had little effect on the city's Mardi Gras atmosphere—at least according to NOLA.com, where Bourbocam and Beadcam continue to capture this city's spirit.

Why You Should Visit

Since August 29, 2005, when Katrina ravaged New Orleans and much of the Gulf Coast, the story of her enduring repercussions have gradually slipped from the front pages of national newspapers and faded from the spotlight of major broadcast networks. While New Orleans, along with the rest of the ravaged region, might eventually return to "normal," it remains for now—and probably for many years to come—a one-story city. And no one covers that story from as many angles with as much understanding, depth, detail, and clarity than the writers and editors of the *Times-Picayune*. It's their backyard; it's their home. While reporting on the story, they are also unavoidably part of it, resulting in what some might call crusading or advocacy journalism. The journalism practiced here in the wake of Katrina is unmistakably energetic and passionate.

Keep This in Mind

Scores of news organizations can promote their sites as award-winners; few, if any, news sites can lay claim to saving lives. NOLA.com can. Many stranded citizens used cell phones to text message family and friends about their location; those who received the SOS's posted the information in forums on the site or e-mailed it to NOLA.com, which in turn posted the calls for help on its "NOLA View" blog. According to its editor, rescuers constantly monitored the site, and when a server glitch caused the site to crash momentarily, the editor received a note: "Get this up as soon as you can, people's lives depend on it. We've already saved a number of lives because of it."[1]

Off the Record

In 1837, two journalists founded *The Picayune* with gambling winnings, naming their newspaper for the 6¼-cent Spanish coin that people would have to pay for it.

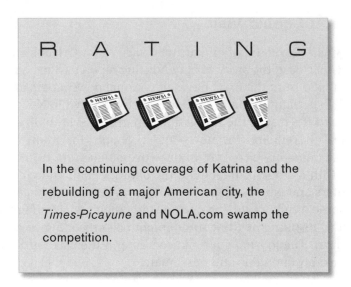

RATING

In the continuing coverage of Katrina and the rebuilding of a major American city, the *Times-Picayune* and NOLA.com swamp the competition.

Endnote

1. Mark Glaser, "NOLA.com blogs and forums help save lives after Katrina," Online Journalism Review, Sept. 13, 2005 (www.ojr.org/ojr/stories/050913glaser).

82

TomPaine.com
www.tompaine.com

Overview

Web surfers can be forgiven for thinking that the Internet was designed for people with short attention spans. Much of the content on the Web—and certainly a good deal of its news and information—seems increasingly bite-sized, condensed for a busy readership with little time to do more than scan the daily headlines.

But once in a while, Web users are reminded that the power of the Internet lies in its ability to expand, not shrink, a person's understanding of the world. Those who'd like a regular reminder of this important notion should bookmark TomPaine.com, a Web site that combines politics, general news, informed opinion, and progressive social action. Although this stew might not be to everyone's liking (especially those who don't share its progressive political agenda), how refreshingly appetizing it is to sit down in front of a computer and be served a lengthy meal of thought, persuasion, and eloquence.

What You'll Find There

The site is clean and clutter-free with a home page that is divided into three parts, all appearing under the slogan "TomPaine.common sense: The best progressive insight and action. All day." The most prominent part of the Web site is, fittingly enough, "Opinion." In this section, readers can click on any one of four to six op-ed pieces culled daily from both national and international sources, such as the U.K. newspaper the *Guardian*, the *New York Times*, the *Washington Post*, and news agencies from around the world, as well as Web sites maintained by think tanks and activist groups. (As the editors explain in the "About Us" section, "TomPaine.com is for people who want to keep in touch with the progressive community but don't have time to surf dozens of Web sites. We do it for you.")

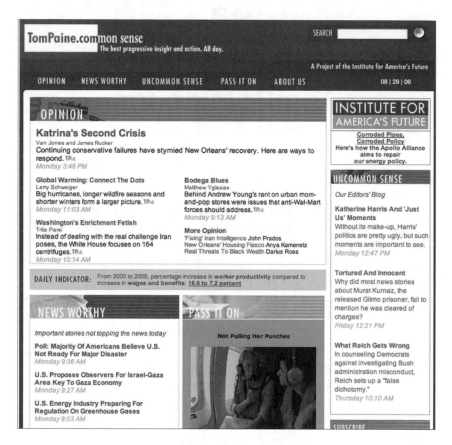

The "Opinion" section is the meat-and-potatoes of TomPaine.com, addressing issues such as energy consumption, freedom of information, and international diplomacy. The editorials are sometimes coordinated to expand upon ads published on the op-ed page of the *New York Times* (and the site maintains an archive of these ads).

Another important section of the Web site is "Newsworthy," a roundup of "important stories *not* topping the news today." Most of these stories are pulled from newspapers, whose sites you'll link to when you click on such headlines as "War on Terror Undermines Human Rights" and "One in 136 Americans Behind Bars."

There's a "Pass It On" link, often featuring a video clip from a documentary or a political ad or an article about some hot-button issue convulsing the nation's collective punditry.

And finally, the "Uncommon Sense" section—perhaps the highlight of the site, where TomPaine.com's editors post "think pieces" about issues of importance to the progressive community, from global warming to gay marriage, from the USA Patriot Act to the minimum wage. These pieces are thoughtful, informed, and written in an accessible style. Not everyone will agree with the editors' spin on all these topics, but the writing is first-rate and the issues are framed with clarity and intelligence.

Why You Should Visit

Whether you agree or disagree with the perspectives on TomPaine.com, there's no quibbling with the importance of the issues the site wrestles with. In an online world demarcated by breathless headlines about celebrity philandering and sports figures earning multimillion-dollar salaries, any Web site that seeks to engage a reader's mind is a welcome respite.

NEW AMERICAN AGENDA

Thursday September 07, 2006

Righteous Opposition To War
An interfaith coalition campaigns to end the war in Iraq. *Thursday 9:00 AM*

Wednesday September 06, 2006

Adapting To Win In 2008
Democratic presidential politics will never look the same after this midterm election. *Wednesday 8:55 AM*

Wednesday August 30, 2006

'Don't Feed The Homeless'
An increasing number of cities are criminalizing homelessness rather than solving it. *Wednesday 9:17 AM*

Tuesday August 29, 2006

Levees Still Broken
Protecting New Orleans—and the nation—means reforming the Army Corps of Engineers now. *Tuesday 10:01 AM*

Thursday August 24, 2006

Mission Not Accomplished
We should take the rebuilding of New Orleans as seriously as we take the crisis in Iraq. *Thursday 9:49 AM*

Between the news stories, op-ed pieces, and the editors' blogs, you'll emerge from your time on this Web site—and it *does* demand your time—with your political IQ (and maybe your blood pressure) raised.

Keep This in Mind

There are at least two major drawbacks to the site. Since it only high-lights the news that *didn't* make the front page, you will have to go somewhere else for the news of the day. And, because it offers no counterbalancing in its Opinion section, readers on the moderate to conservative side of the political spectrum will find lots to chew on but no red meat to satisfy their political appetites.

Off the Record

TomPaine.com is a project of the Institute for America's Future, an organization supported entirely by grants and private donations (hence the refreshing lack of distracting ads on the Web site).

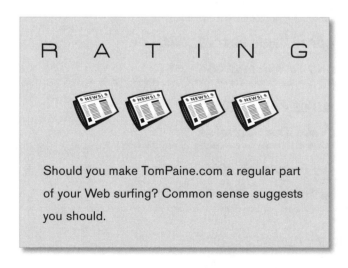

R A T I N G

Should you make TomPaine.com a regular part of your Web surfing? Common sense suggests you should.

83

Topix.net
www.topix.net

Overview

Searching the Web for news about topics of specific interest to you covered by the sources you want to read can quickly become a full-time job. With thousands of news sites—each reporting some beats better than others—newshounds will find themselves skipping meals and surrendering free time just to find the information they crave.

Enter Topix.net.

Founded in 2002, Topix.net scans more than 27,000 sources non-stop to gather the latest stories from newspapers large and small, radio and television stations, magazines, trade journals, government and corporate information sites, and blogs. The site then conveniently sorts its findings into one or more appropriate category, resulting in the more than 360,000 "micro-news" pages—each based on a specific subject or a particular locale—that form what it likes to call "the Internet's largest news site."

What You'll Find There

If it's news, it's here. And here, "news" is by no means limited to the latest lead story on the *New York Times* home page or to the most recent "ALERT" on the Fox News Channel.

Topix.net's "News Front Page" (its home page) is indeed a safe place to start, especially for a site as expansive as this one. The current "Top Story," usually accompanied by a photo and lead paragraph, is teased across the top portion of the page. The "Latest News"—typically top stories culled from mainstream media—fills the left column below the dominant package. Each story includes a headline, a source, and a time stamp. The "More Latest Headlines" link takes you to "Top Stories Page 2." There you will find about 30 additional headlines, the aforementioned information, the story's lead,

and a link for users to post a comment. Below each headline, Topix.net lists the number of sources reporting on the topic. By clicking on that information, you are taken to another page for "full coverage," which consists of links—sometimes as many as 300—to each source's story.

Topix.net provides you with several options for navigating its site. At the bottom of the home page, you can access various sections of the site, where the top story from traditional news categories—"U.S.," "World," "Sports," "Business," "Entertainment," "Health," "Science/ Technology," and even "Blogs"—are packaged in individual boxes. The navigation menu at the top of each page—above the Topix.net banner, where the search tool is located—is another useful tool for exploring the site, listing many of the same sections that appear at the bottom of the home page along with links to "Offbeat" and "Local" stories.

One of the great aspects of the site is the many sources made available to you, from the Associated Press and *USA Today* to your community paper (if it has a Web site). You can set the local page to your community's ZIP code—or to any area you want—by clicking on "Local" in the site menu. (Three story packages from local news sources appear on the home page below the "Latest News" section.) Once that page is set to a certain ZIP code and you want news from another locale, you can click the "Browse All Topix" link at the far right of the menu, where you can choose any city or town, and, in some cases, even neighborhoods, in the country. With more than 30,000 choices, Topix.net exemplifies the notion that all news is local. On the "Browse All Topix" page, you can also scroll through the more than 360,000 topics Topix.net offers.

Why You Should Visit

If you want news on a specific topic but don't want to spend all day searching for it, Topix.net is the perfect site. While some sites might report on national news well but on entertainment poorly, Topix.net provides complete coverage of every topic imaginable. Plus, as an added bonus, you can search its expanded news archive to find stories published within the last year. Remarkably, this incredible service is completely free.

Keep This in Mind

While the site does not traffic in original content, it does deal exclusively with reputable, reliable, and credible news organizations. Remember, Topix.net is a gatherer of news, not a reporter of it. In fact, there are no editors selecting the stories that appear here. Instead, Topix.net employs artificial intelligence. Using this AI, called NewsRank—a technology the site's founders developed—allows the site accomplish to its mission: making it quick and easy for Internet users to obtain complete coverage of the news from a variety of sources. It would be impossible, and certainly untimely, for a human being—or a team of them—to search tens of thousands sources, categorize the resulting stories into subject-specific sections, and then post them in their appropriate area on the sprawling site. NewsRank, however, can do all of that—and do it quickly. Although NewsRank eliminates the need for human editors, who are certainly prone to bias in their selection and placement of stories, technology is not without its faults—evidenced by the occasional story on Topix.net that certainly appears out of place.

Off the Record

Since March 2005, a few of the largest newspaper publishers in the country have owned a stake in Topix.net: The Gannett and Tribune companies have 31.9 percent each and McClatchy has 11.25.[1] While some questioned whether the deal would affect Topix.net's independence, the site still controls the operation[2] and its chief executive said stories from the more than 140 newspaper sites owned by the media corporations would not be given any special priority and its stories no higher placement.[3]

R A T I N G

At Topix.net, there's no source unturned, no newsworthy (or trivial) topic left uncovered.

Endnotes

1. "Topix.net expands news archive," Reuters, Aug. 7, 2006.
2. Katharine Q. Seelye, "Newspaper giants buy Web news monitor," *New York Times*, March 23, 2005.
3. David Kesmodel, et al., "A mixed blessing: News portals like Google News and Topix attract the masses, but irk some editors," Wall Street Journal Online, March 23, 2005.

84

U.S. News & World Report

www.usnews.com

Overview

When the space shuttle *Columbia* exploded upon re-entry on Saturday, February 1, 2003, *Time* and *Newsweek* scrambled to revamp the upcoming week's edition—both cover and inside content. The two magazines, facing deadlines later that night for issues scheduled to hit newsstands Monday, managed to publish relatively comprehensive coverage of the national tragedy. But *U.S. News & World Report*, the third member of the holy trinity of major national newsweeklies, failed to include any mention of the monumental event as it was too far along in the printing process to change strategy.

For *U.S. News & World Report*, that's been an all-too-recurring theme throughout its history. When journalist David Lawrence merged his weekly newspaper *U.S. News* with his magazine *World Report* in 1948, *Time* and *Newsweek* had a 25- and 15-year head start, respectively. And *U.S. News & World Report* has been playing catch-up ever since. In the race for readers, it has consistently finished a distant and disappointing third with paltry circulation numbers in comparison to those of its competitors—partly a result of *U.S. News & World Report*'s resistance to celebrity features and insistence on hard news despite consumer trends.

What You'll Find There

Browsers will find a typical three-column Web page format below the title banner and navigation bar. Playing on its strength, USNews.com prominently positions a "Special Report" for which the publication is best known. Roll the cursor over "Rankings & Guides"—the second choice in the horizontal navigation menu after only the USNews.com "Home" link—and a drop-down menu of options, from best colleges and graduate schools to best hospitals and health plans, appears. In

the far-left column directly below the navigation bar, those links are listed again in a blue-shaded box and under an "America's Best" heading.

For those checking in daily, the site places the "Latest Headlines"— a bulleted list of eight—at the top right of the page. These headlines link to Associated Press stories, where you will also discover related links—stories, videos, photo galleries, and interactive features—lining the right side of the text.

The middle column of the page begins with the site's top stories (under the heading "Today on USNews.com"), one of which is usually that week's print edition cover story. Five sections follow, each including four headlines. Four of these five sections—"Nation & World," "Inside Washington," "Health," and "Money"—also comprise the rest of the navigation bar, along with a final link to the site's columnists. The front pages of these four sections all possess a style nearly identical to the home page and each other. The fifth section, near the bottom of the home page, is titled "Student Center" and features an opinion column from a university newspaper along with other helpful tips for high school and college students.

The second item in the left column of the home page—the print magazine's front cover—lets you access all of the "Current Issue" through a page that lists the headlines/links according to section. The site's original photography, presented as subject-specific essays that each contain about a dozen captivating images, is worth thumbing through.

Washington Whispers >> BY PAUL BEDARD

(Illustration by Joe Ciardiello for *USN&WR*)

New in West Wing: Clock watching
With President Bush's sagging poll numbers and the possibility that Democrats might take back the House in November, White House Chief of Staff Joshua Bolten has developed a special motivational technique to keep West Wing staffers focused on getting things done in the next 2½ years.

Paul Bedard's new blog dishes on President Bush's 9/11 travel plans, Greta Van Susteren's tech fetish and why Speaker Dennis Hastert might get fired.

Pentagon Payback
In the halls of the Pentagon, defense officials are awaiting the arrival of Brig. Gen. Mark Kimmitt, currently U.S. Central Command's deputy director for plans and policy...

Barenaked band courts race fans
You'd think racing fans would be more country than alt rock, but Barenaked Ladies becomes the first band to launch an album at a nascar race this Saturday, when it plays the Chevy Rock & Roll 400 in Richmond, Va.

The official book on Dick Cheney
Vice President Dick Cheney is finally getting the book-length biography treatment—and he's playing along.

All aboard the Bush Express
Chicago had its artsy cows. Washington was flooded with colorful elephants and donkeys. But art trains?

Editorial Cartoon
Scott Stantis cartoon on E-stuff overload

Why You Should Visit

There's a real sense that the content on USNews.com is meant to help readers in very practical ways, especially on its "Health" and "Money" pages. And for those who want to feel like a Washington *insider*, this site is surprisingly effective. Because the site still very much mirrors its weekly print edition, there's no reason to check in hourly or even daily. But the longstanding feature "Washington Whispers"—a collection of snippets about media figures and politicians (that might be able to lay claim to creating the blog form before that word, or the Internet, even existed)—and the top "Out Loud" quotes of the day provide reasons to listen in regularly.

Keep This in Mind

After 22 years as an employee-owned company, *U.S. News & World Report* was bought by Mortimer B. Zuckerman in 1984. (Nine years later, he purchased the *New York Daily News*.) Zuckerman, a billionaire who accumulated much of his wealth through real estate, was ranked 382 on the *Forbes* list of wealthiest people in the world in 2006. But his *U.S. News & World Report*, for which he also writes a regular opinion column (often espousing his pro-Israel stance), has failed to make him much richer, resulting in the downsizing of its editorial staff to far fewer than its competitors—through several rounds of recent layoffs that included the magazine's chief political correspondent. But for those who would rather surf the Web than shop at newsstands, the publication's struggles to generate profits aren't all bad. The monetary concerns have forced the company to pay more attention to its potential online, realizing "the Web for us is a growth business" and consequently investing more than $2 million in 2005 to reinforce its Web site.

Off the Record

In the midst of his first presidential campaign, George W. Bush would chat with Doug Wead, a friend and former aide to his father—conversations Wead secretly recorded. While Bush frequently criticized the media during these taped talks, for both its liberal bias and its "campaign" against him, the soon-to-be president called *U.S. News &*

World Report "halfway decent"—high praise compared to his description of *Time* as "awful."[1]

R A T I N G

U.S. News & World Report's Web site gives you both national news and world reports—but nothing you couldn't get elsewhere.

Endnote

1. David D. Kirkpatrick, "In secretly taped conversations, glimpses of the future president," *New York Times*, Feb. 20, 2005.

85

United Nations (UN)

www.un.org

Overview

The idea is elegant in its simplicity and optimism: one group representing the entire world, a small community standing in for all the
planet's people. The United Nations (UN) has for decades tried to be
that body, diffusing disputes, aiding the Earth's downtrodden, and
implementing policies that would leave the world a better place for
future generations. At least, that's the organization's intent. Not surprisingly, success has been intermittent.

The UN and its constituent agencies put an awful lot of ideas in
play every single day. Any Web site that tried to keep up with all the
policies, speeches, debates, resolutions, and interventions of this
famously busy body would certainly have its hands—and pages—full.

That's the case with UN.org, a site that takes the massive mission of
the UN and translates it into print for the cyber age. The site is as loaded
down as a peacekeeping troop in some distant, unpronounceable land.
And because the UN addresses (ostensibly) the needs of every country
on Earth, there's plenty of ground for the site's gatekeepers to cover. To
its credit, UN.org does a good job of keeping tabs on most of the important and relevant activities of its namesake. It might not be the most
thrilling site you'll encounter as you cruise for information on the
Internet, but it certainly delivers more of the world to your computer
than most other Web sites purporting to "cover the world" but only providing a taste.

What You'll Find There

There's a welcome page that is deceptively clean and almost completely text free. Click on "Welcome" and you'll be directed to another
lightly annotated page that offers the real menu of possibilities, from
"Member States" and "Speeches and Resolutions" to "UN News

Centre." Clicking on any of those icons takes you to thoroughly stuffed Web pages on that specific area. The "News Centre" page is where most of the "breaking news" can be found—though the news that's breaking wouldn't usually lead the evening newscast or front page of the newspaper. The stories listed here deal more with the actions—the dozens of often technical and legal actions taken that day by the UN assembly and its various subcommittees. You'll get summaries of all the actions taken, speeches in support of or against those actions, messages from the secretary general's office related to those actions, and memorandums from ambassadors, staffers, and special assistants providing commentary or context on those actions.

If it all sounds very bureaucratic, you're beginning to catch on. The UN is really just a collection of hundreds of little bureaucracies. But as any cub reporter in any small town can attest, bureaucracies make news, so the site lists the meetings, conferences, actions, and agendas of dozens of its committees and subcommittees.

There is also a great deal of background information and history about the countries that make up this imposing body, as well as information about regional conflicts, political leaders, and pending policies dealing with everything from agriculture and soil conservation to famine relief and refugee rescue.

Why You Should Visit

With increasing frequency in the news cycle of the modern world, the UN has been in the spotlight. As a result of wars, famines, natural disasters, and nuclear-era brinkmanship, the UN is often the forum of last resort to solve these intractable problems. The key figures in the UN—the secretary general and the ambassadors from the nations of the industrialized world—exercise a lot of political sway. When they speak, they *do* make it onto headline news services and front pages around the world.

Keep This in Mind

There's no denying the importance of the events recorded on UN.org, but there's also no denying the eye-glazing quality of much of the content there. The site is top-heavy with speeches from long-winded career diplomats but so is the UN itself, so perhaps it's justifiable. If the abbreviated digests and regular updates of the UN's activities, available on most mainstream news sites, don't satisfy your thirst for thoroughness, fear not. UN.org will drown you in the ocean of geopolitical posturing, watered-down clause after watered-down clause.

Off the Record

Want to start off on the right foot on your way to becoming a career bureaucrat? It's never too early to learn the ways of the UN. That's the

reasoning behind the "CyberSchoolbus" section. This kid-friendly page offers youngsters a chance to learn about "Millennium Development Goals" and "How to Fight World Poverty." Noble aims, to be sure, but they're unlikely to interrupt your stickball game.

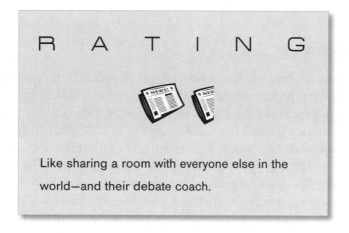

R A T I N G

Like sharing a room with everyone else in the world—and their debate coach.

86

USA Today
www.usatoday.com

Overview

Once upon a time, American newspapers depended solely on words to fill their front pages, which consisted of column after column of small black typeface. While the look of newspapers had already changed since those primitive paginations by September 15, 1982, *USA Today*'s arrival radically altered the visually drab design into a colorful, eye-catching display. But during the course of its evolution as "The Nation's Newspaper"—a self-appointed moniker—*USA Today* limited story lengths to free up editorial space for prominent photos and other dominant graphics, adopting a mantra that would appeal to a country of readers seemingly struggling with attention-deficit disorders. That strategy—one it calls "An economy of words. A wealth of information."—has apparently worked, at least in terms of popularity and commercial success. After only five years, *USA Today* reached a circulation of more than 1.5 million. By 2005, it was read by more than 5 million people a day (and now has average daily circulation of nearly 2.5 million). But the *USA Today* approach, which has unfortunately afflicted many other newspapers, has helped to usher in a dumbed-down era of newspapering—not only in its frequent inability to provide depth and context but also its selection and placement of "news." On any given day, readers are more likely to encounter an above-the-fold feature about *American Idol* than an investigative piece about weapons of mass destruction.

That said, the newspaper's Web site appears much less in love with infotainment and much more concerned with reporting news of weightier consequence.

What You'll Find There

Unlike the mess that usually litters the newspaper's front page, USAToday.com's home page seems surprisingly clutter-free.

Bordering the masthead on the left is a vertical navigation bar where you can access each of its seven color-coded sections—the same that appear in the Monday-through-Friday print edition ("News," "Travel," "Money," "Sports," "Life," "Tech," and "Weather"). Located to the right of the *USA Today* logo are five continuously rotating teasers (headline and photo) to stories within those varying sections.

The latest top news, which USAToday.com often posts quicker than other news organizations, receives prominent placement on the home page. A photo, headline link, and any related stories or multimedia lead the way in the middle of the page directly below the masthead. In the wide right column beneath the flashing teasers, a bold headline and descriptive subhead, which are accompanied by a link to the full story and perhaps even a related blog or other sidebars, draw attention. Filling the rest of the right column under a "Latest Headlines" label, five bolder but smaller headlines link to full stories. While much of what's available in this top block of news on USAToday.com is pulled from the Associated Press wire, the content is a refreshing drink for those whose thirst for news cannot be quenched by sipping from the print edition's infotainment-filled well.

Why You Should Visit

USA Today is, although not in the class of other more serious newspapers, the most popular newspaper in the country, making it a must-read. Luckily, the online version is actually worth reading. USAToday.com uses every tool available online. As a result, it tells more complete, more interesting, and more informative stories. The site also maintains some of the best blogs on the Web, including "Today in the Sky" and "On Deadline," which brings you the latest breaking news before or as it happens with links to numerous sources—from full stories reported by local newspapers or international wire services to complete transcripts and statements—embedded within its frequent briefs and updates. USAToday.com is updated regularly throughout the day, and its range of coverage—breaking news throughout the world or the pop culture of America—makes the site a must-visit.

Keep This in Mind

In late 2005, *USA Today* decided to join its print and Web site newsrooms together—a move undertaken by the *New York Times* earlier

■ News

USA TODAY brings you the latest breaking news and must-read stories.
Read On Deadline blog
Subscribe to this blog's feed XML

What are 16- to 25-year-olds thinking and talking about?
Read Generation Next blog
Subscribe to this blog's feed XML

■ Travel

USA TODAY's Ben Mutzabaugh delivers the latest news and analysis about airlines, airports and air travel.
Read Today in the Sky blog
Subscribe to this blog's feed XML

in the year—with the goal of "conceiving and planning our coverage as one unit" and "to develop a better understanding of the expanding storytelling capabilities." In making the move to one news operation, the Web site's editor-in-chief was promoted to co-executive editor of *USA Today*. Both changes serve as proof that *USA Today*, which is owned by one of the country's largest newspaper chains (Gannett), realizes "the growing importance of the Internet as a vehicle for news delivery" and plans to shift its site into high gear.

Off the Record

During the 2004 presidential election cycle, when news organizations first began dealing with how to handle online campaign ads not governed by the rules of print and broadcast, USAToday.com elected not to run political ads in its political and elections sections. Its smart policy, which garnered the approval of media critics concerned about the juxtaposition of political ads and political news, eliminated any possible confusion among users as to what was a paid ad, what was an endorsement, and what was actual editorial content.

R A T I N G

Unless you find it lying on the floor outside your hotel room door, *USA Today* should be experienced online rather than in print, and you should check in daily and stay a while.

87

Vanity Fair
www.vanityfair.com

Overview

An oasis for the great practitioners of longform journalism in today's desert of depth-deficient publications, *Vanity Fair* is a refreshing and regularly riveting read. Now a thick and colorful monthly magazine, the first issue of a periodical bearing the title *Vanity Fair* was published in England in 1860. Fifty-three years later, Condé Nast paid $3,000 to buy the "musty British social, literary, and political review"[1] that took its name, in part, from William Makepeace Thackeray's 1847 novel (adapted for a popular 2004 film starring Reese Witherspoon). Nast combined it with another of his recently purchased publications to form *Dress and Vanity Fair*. After only four issues, the magazine dropped the first part of the title and relaunched a revamped *Vanity Fair* in 1914. At the age of 22, however, it fell victim to the Depression and was folded into *Vogue*.

Vanity Fair's reincarnation into its current state began in 1983. Nearly 20 years into its second life, the magazine is healthier than ever and in much better shape than most periodicals, thriving on a rich and balanced diet of coverage, from celebrity profiles (allowing for its standard sultry cover photos) to global politics, from arts and culture to intriguing investigative reports. *Vanity Fair*'s table of contents any given month is as extensive and diverse as the oversized menu of a Chinese-food eatery.

Despite the vigor of *Vanity Fair*, its Web site—born in October 2004—is still nursing. And while the online world is running at full speed, VanityFair.com has managed only a few baby steps.

What You'll Find There

VanityFair.com's home page is divided into three main columns and is easy to navigate. The site's top feature is easily found—at the top of

the middle (and widest) column of the page. Running down the left column of the page are "New" and "Recent" headlines, followed by "Video" clips and "Photo" slideshows. Below the site's main feature, you'll find headlines from the "Current Issue" (for a full table of contents, click "The Magazine" link in the navigation bar at the top of the page). Further down the page, you can check out the "Previous Issue" or a "Classic" article like "The Deep Throat Revelation" or "Christopher Hitchens on the Long and Storied History of the Blow Job."

Spanning the top of the home page below the *Vanity Fair* banner is a navigation menu with links to the various sections of the site, including "Entertainment & Culture," "Politics & Power," and "Fame & Scandal." Clicking on any of those links leads to a section-front designed in similar fashion as the home page. Most of the stories on the site are shoveled to it from the print edition. *Vanity Fair* isn't afraid of long-form journalism, and neither is its Web site. But VF.com does post exclusive content, including photo slide shows (Annie Leibovitz is a regular contributor to *Vanity Fair*) and often behind-the-scenes video of those photo shoots.

On the "Entertainment & Culture" page, check out the "Fanfair" section—brief (compared to the usual article length found here) reviews of music, theater, film, books, and more.

Be sure to check out the must-read and thoroughly enjoyable "Proust Questionnaire," a template of interpersonal Q&As with prominent people. VanityFair.com also supplies a fix for Web junkies with its "On the Web," a portal to more than 200 links to Web sites in a variety of categories, including news, politics, blogs, opinion, entertainment, and gossip.

Why You Should Visit

There are many reasons to check out VanityFair.com: namely, Christopher Hitchens, James Wolcott, Buzz Bissinger, Dominick Dunne, Seth Mnookin, Sebastian Junger, Michael Wolff, David Halberstam, William Langewiesche, and Craig Unger. *Vanity Fair*'s roster of writers and contributors is matched by few other publications. While the magazine is still the best way to read them, the potential of *Vanity Fair* on the Internet—where the infinite news hole would certainly lend itself perfectly to its style—is limitless. But if you're not

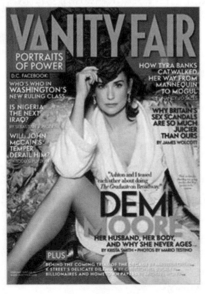

THE MAGAZINE

February 2007

· Todd S. Purdum on John McCain

· James Wolcott on why British sex scandals are so much juicier than ours

· Michael Wolff on whether billionaires can save the newspaper industry

· Frank DiGiacomo on John Mellencamp

· Todd S. Purdum on Washington's new ruling class

· Sebastian Junger on the struggles over oil in Nigeria

· Fanfair: Hot Tracks ... Bruce Handy ... A.M. Homes ... *Vivre*

· Proust Questionnaire: Sidney Poitier

· George Wayne Q&A: Imelda Marcos

· Graydon Carter: Editor's Letter

a regular reader of the print version, then log on. Don't expect breaking news; expect great writing from great writers on the great issues of our day.

Keep This in Mind

Who is Deep Throat? For more than three decades, that question produced only speculative guesses and remained one of the most intriguing mysteries among historians, journalists and politicians. Then on May 31, 2005, the secret source who assisted Bob Woodward and Carl Bernstein (*Washington Post* reporters portrayed by Robert Redford and Dustin Hoffman, respectively, in the 1976 Oscar-winning movie *All the President's Men*) in exposing the details of the Watergate scandal, revealed his identity—to, of all publications, *Vanity Fair*.

But as the news of the magazine's super-scoop aired on every television news station and appeared on scores of Web sites that morning, John D. O'Conner's exclusive exposé—scheduled for publication in the July issue of *Vanity Fair* that was set to hit newsstands in one to two weeks—could not be found anywhere on VanityFair.com. While it eventually posted two bland lines of copy on its home page late in the day, linking to the full story, media observers rightly criticized the unjustifiable delay, which exhibited *Vanity Fair's* inability to both recognize and utilize the immediacy the Internet affords.

"When that story is one that has bewitched, bothered and bewildered the nation for decades, you would think the magazine would want to tout its coup in every way possible," mused Washington Post.com staff writer Robert MacMillan. "In the Internet age, waiting for more than four hours for a sign of life from the original source feels like buying a ticket to the Jurassic-Cretaceous double-feature."

Off the Record

Marie Brenner's five-part, 17,500-word piece in the May 1996 issue of *Vanity Fair*, titled "The Man Who Knew Too Much," served as the basis for the script of *The Insider*—the 1999 film starring Russell Crowe and Al Pacino about the efforts of top tobacco executive Jeffrey Wigand to "blow the whistle" on the deadly practices of his company and other cigarette manufacturers.

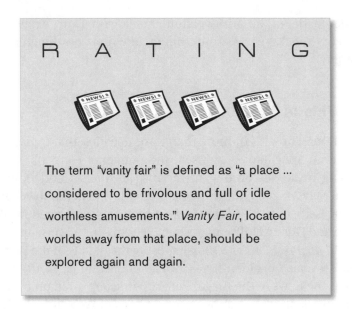

R A T I N G

The term "vanity fair" is defined as "a place ...
considered to be frivolous and full of idle
worthless amusements." *Vanity Fair*, located
worlds away from that place, should be
explored again and again.

Endnote

1. From "V.F.: The early years" by Amy Fine Collins on the "Vintage V.F." page of
VanityFair.com (www.vanityfair.com/magazine/vintage/articles/earlyyear).

88

Village Voice
www.villagevoice.com

Overview

With a few select publications, the mere act of reading in public can be seen as a political statement. Whether such explicit gestures will survive the transition to the digital age (where, after all, the most blatant acts of free speech, from anti-Bush blogging to perusal of pornography, are done in the private, and anonymous, world of cyberspace) is uncertain. But it's hard to believe that reading the *Village Voice* will ever cease to be a tinglingly satisfying act of editorial sedition. The lefty politics and muckraking leitmotif of this celebrated periodical have made it what it is—which can be best summed up by their trite-yet-true advertising slogan from the 1980s: "Some people swear by us ... other people swear AT us."

Founded in 1955 as a counter-culture tabloid, the *Voice* became a national refuge for the hard left during Vietnam, the Reagan years, and the Bush ascendancy. The Web site combines the *Voice*'s trademark bravado with a cyber-slick presentation, ensuring an even wider audience for this once-niche publication.

What You'll Find There

There's much to like about the *Village Voice*'s Web site, but first you have to be willing to suspend your expectations for a balanced presentation of the news of the world. From its award-winning critics to its award-winning cartoonists, the tone of *Voice* is one of shrill contempt for the powers-that-be—local, regional, national, and global. If you're willing to meet the *Voice* on its own terms, however, you'll find some of the best and most provocative writing anywhere on the Web.

The site offers the news of the day in a magazine-style format, with longer-form journalism (features, news analysis, and critical essays) dominating most of the content. VillageVoice.com generally avoids

simply repackaging the headline stories in favor of a more between-the-lines style of reporting. The editorial board of the *Voice* seems to revel in stories that reveal hidden motives, secret sweetheart deals, and clarion calls against legislation that threatens life as we know it.

It's all presented colorfully and clearly, with descriptive headlines that simply beg to be clicked on, from the super-serious ("Expert Tells What Actually Happened With WMD") to the superfluous ("Guys Would Rather Cum on Your Face Than Talk"[1]). The site is easily navigated and contains several icons that group stories together rather smartly, such as "Screens," which covers television and the Internet (a more and more logical pairing) and "Editor's Picks"—a collection of quirky and often insightful features. And there's always a generous helping of Tom Tomorrow, the canniest editorial cartoonist working today.

Why You Should Visit

If there's an alarmist quality to much of what constitutes the *Village Voice*'s front-page news, there's also good reason to take it seriously.

The *Voice* has earned its reputation as an exposer of corruption and a watchdog of everyone from municipal judges on the take to corrupt UN officials. The recipient of three Pulitzer Prizes, the *Voice* has also won the National Press Foundation's Online Journalism Award and the Editor & Publisher EPPY Award for Best Overall U.S. Weekly Newspaper Online.[2] The tone of the writing conveys an urgency missing from many news sites and the *Voice* speaks to that fabled younger readership that has abandoned so many other mainstream news vehicles.

Keep This in Mind

One hardly needs to be reminded that the *Voice*'s politics inform every significant story it publishes—that can be deduced from the headlines themselves (e.g., "The Bush Family Coup—Thirty Years Later, the Son Revisits the Sins of the Father on America"). And while such activist journalism is in retreat these days and ought to be applauded, it's hard to feel that the reader is getting a fair and thorough presentation of any story. The *Voice* sees itself as a left-leaning counterbalance to the conservatizing of American mainstream news, but for readers who don't have the time to peruse other sources of information, the whole story often remains unexplored.

Off the Record

The initial cost of starting up the paper in 1955 was $10,000. By the year 2000, the paper was sold to a group of investors for $170 million.[3]

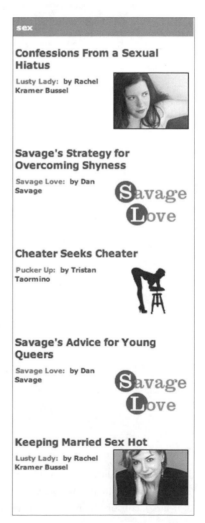

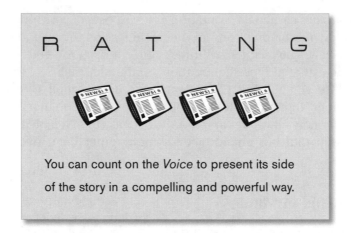

Endnotes

1. www.villagevoice.com, Jan. 4, 2006.
2. From the Wikipedia (wikipedia.org) article on the *Village Voice*.
3. Mark Jacobson, "The voice from beyond the grave," *New York*, Nov. 14, 2005.

89

Voice of America (VOA)

www.voanews.com

Overview

Knowledge is not only power but also a weapon to be used to combat ignorance. The more you know, the better able you are to live your life. At least, that's what most journalists believe. To be unaware of what's happening in the world, to remain ignorant of the forces shaping and shifting your daily existence, is to be sentenced to living in the dark, unable to see your world for what it is.

The idea of news as enlightenment is the idea behind Voice of America (VOA), a service that began shortly after World War II, which aimed to bring the news of the world to a global audience that craved information. Part propaganda tool, public servant, and crusading journalist, the VOA still reaches more than an estimated 100 million people every week through its radio, television, and Internet outlets.

The Web site of VOA—a relatively recent addition to the decades-old news service—extends the mission of this U.S. government-funded entity even further, providing news, features, special reports, and Webcasts to anyone with a computer and a desire to discover what's happening in the world.

Although some critics claim that the service still skews the news to portray the U.S. in a favorable light, a close read of the site reveals that most of the content is no more biased than the rest of the mainstream media, as it draws much of its information from worldwide news agencies such as Associated Press.

What You'll Find There

VOANews.com has a spacious, almost spare, main news page, with the expected lead story—usually a breaking political or foreign policy story—at the top, accompanied by a photo and, just below, a menu of other "Related Stories." The site also features a short roster of "More

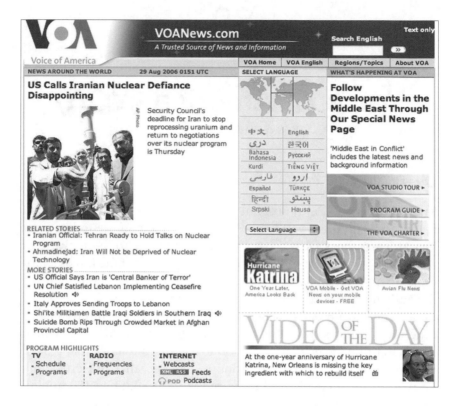

Stories," but that's about it for the main page. The stories are written mostly by VOA News staff, but most contain chunks of reporting from other news agencies.

Sharing space next to the top story is a "Select Language" box, which lets you choose one of 44 languages in which to receive VOA news, audio feeds, and streaming video.

Underneath the VOANews.com banner is a small series of icons. The "Regions/Topics" icon leads you to a much fuller and impressively comprehensive page that allows you to search news by country, continent, or a broad range of topics. Once there, you can also click on the "Special Reports" link, which offers another full and useful page of headlines arranged under "Current Reports" (such as bird flu, the Middle East conflict, and immigration), "Global Issues" (population control, trade talks), "Retrospect" (featuring looks back at such events as the Chernobyl disaster and the Vietnam War), and even "Entertainment" (everything from the World Cup to the Academy Awards).

The main news page also offers schedules and highlights of the VOA's television and radio broadcasts, by country, by show topic, and by time and date.

Why You Should Visit

For news seekers living in countries where the free press is compromised or non-existent, the VOA provides a lifeline. While it lacks the dynamism of its better-funded and more commercial rivals, it compensates with earnestness and reach. And it is something of a vicarious thrill to be reading the exact same news stories on your home computer that are being broadcast into repressive regimes and darkened corners of the globe, helping people understand—perhaps for the first time—the contours of the larger world.

Keep This in Mind

VOA, headquartered in Washington, D.C. and funded by the U.S. government, is supervised by a "Broadcasting Board of Governors." All this bureaucratic oversight and political coziness has bothered some media watchers, who feel that the service is more propaganda than free press. Most of the stories, however, retain the sense of objectivity one expects from a traditional news outlet, though the sharp criticisms of U.S. policy and the unfettered questioning that

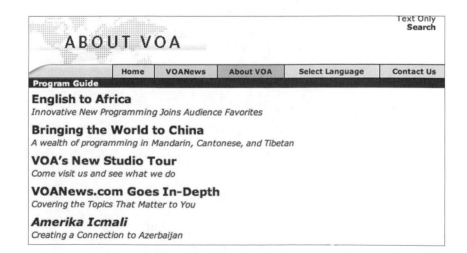

earmark other more "progressive" news Web sites is, admittedly, missing here.

Off the Record

Because of an obscure law known as the "Smith-Mundt Act" of 1948, radio and television broadcasts of Voice of America cannot be aired in the U.S. The law was passed to prevent the U.S. government from using the service as a domestic propaganda outlet and to ensure that the focus of the service remains on broadcasting news to audiences in repressive regimes and in areas where the flow of free information is prohibited.

RATING

Solid, entry-level news for those who are just entering the information stream.

90

Washington Post
www.washingtonpost.com

Overview

American politics has always been—and will always be—fodder for American journalism. What happens in the nation's capital, or as a result of the decisions made by the people working there, is often as newsworthy as it gets. Who better to turn to for that news than the *Washington Post*? Not only because of its prime location when it comes to covering the nation's political scene, but also because of its reputation.

Founded in 1877, the *Washington Post* will long be remembered for its Watergate investigation in the early 1970s that eventually led to President Richard Nixon's resignation. The *Post* remains one of the most important newspapers in the country. It is also one of the largest. But even though many consider the *Post* to be a "national" newspaper, its distribution is limited and largely regional. As a result, the *Post*'s Web site, launched in 1996 and essentially a mirror of its print counterpart, is an indispensable lifeline for a nation of readers far removed but directly affected by the workings of Washington.

What You'll Find There

Much of what one might expect to find from a major daily newspaper's online incarnation is at WashingtonPost.com. At the top of the left column on the home page, a photo (the largest on the page and usually the site) links to a breaking news story. Stacked in the middle column of the first screen are about a half-dozen news headlines—typically ones that might land on the front page of the print edition (a mix of international and national news, along with an occasional lighter news feature)—with a one-sentence digest and, depending on the story, links to related content. About six "More Headlines" are listed (in much smaller text) below the top stories, followed by links to 10 "News Columns and Blogs." In fact, commentary is a mainstay

of WashingtonPost.com, receiving prominent play on the home page in a section labeled "Today in Opinions," where you can read diverse points of view from a variety of thoughtful writers (Howard Kurtz, Tom Shales, Dana Milbank, and Richard Cohen, to name but a few) on wide-ranging topics; a drop-down menu lets you link to that day's editorials and op-eds, dozens of columnists, and more than 30 blogs.

Across the top of the home page is a navigation bar with four main links: "News," "Opinion," "Sports," and "Arts & Living" (links to more specific subsections appear when placing the cursor on any of these). Just below this menu, at the far right of the page, WashingtonPost. com flashes links to a host of multimedia features such as live "Discussions" or transcripts to previous Q&A chats with *Post* writers and various newsmakers. The bottom section of the home page consists mostly of small headings of its many sections—"Business," "Metro," "Technology," "Politics," "Health," "Education," and "Religion"—and three top (but tiny) headlines from each.

Why You Should Visit

Katharine Graham, the newspaper's longtime leader whose memoirs were awarded the Pulitzer in 1998, once said, "A world without newspapers would not be the same kind of world at all." Well, this country would certainly not be the same without the *Washington Post.* Whether it's campaign season or a legislative session, WashingtonPost.com will provide all the context and depth you could want. And while the site varies slightly from its print counterpart, a newspaper with a limited number of pages could never match the multiplicity of voices (including Bob Woodward) offered by WashingtonPost.com—opinions you're not likely to find elsewhere. Be sure to check in regularly with its unique feature called "Think Tank Town," which publishes a column from one of 10 participating organizations—from the American Enterprise Institute to the Center for American Progress—every other weekday, along with providing links to the sites of these influential institutions.

Keep This in Mind

When you think of the *Washington Post*, politics—not sports—naturally come to mind. But the newspaper's sports section is certainly no slouch. Throughout its storied history, the *Post* has been home to some of the great sportswriters of all time, including the late Shirley Povich, who served as writer, editor, and, most notably, columnist

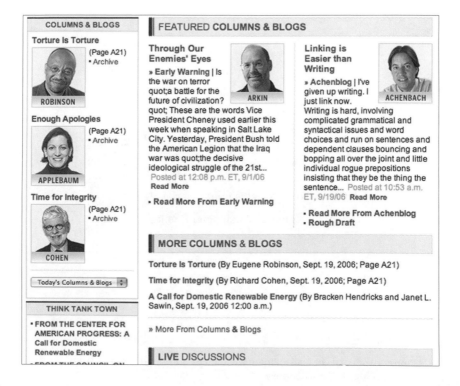

during his 75 years at the *Post* (check out the "Shirley Povich Tribute" at WashingtonPost.com to read a collection of his work). Today, along with in-depth and robust coverage of all the Baltimore/Washington area professional sports teams, the *Post* can boast of featuring commentary from two of the most recognized sports columnists in the country. And while Tony Kornheiser, who landed in the *Monday Night Football* booth in 2006, and Michael Wilbon are better known as ESPN's *Pardon the Interruption* dynamic duo, their primary gig remains sharing their insights—and sarcasm—with *Post* readers.

Off the Record

When Jayson Blair was still a toddler, the *Washington Post* had a scandal of its own to deal with after discovering that Janet Cooke's September 1980 story about an 8-year-old heroin addict headlined "Jimmy's World"[1] was a complete fabrication, resulting in Cooke's forfeiture of the Pulitzer Prize she won for the piece and the *Post*'s embarrassment for publishing it.

If the nation's capital is abuzz, and it always is, expect the same of WashingtonPost.com.

Endnote

1. "Jimmy's World" can be read online at www.uncp.edu/home/canada/work/markport/lit/litjour/spg2002/cooke.htm.

91

Washington Times

www.washingtontimes.com

Overview

The separation between church and state has been the subject of a recent, robust debate in the U.S. But what about the separation between church and journalism?

As odd as that pairing might sound, an avowed religious agenda and a newspaper's journalistic mission do, in fact, collide at a publication with a profile that remains prominent and whose readership is on the rise: the *Washington Times.*

Founded in 1982 by the Rev. Sun Myung Moon, leader of the Unification Church, the paper jostles between proselytizer and public scourge. Though seemingly secular in look—and in most of its content—the paper was founded, in Moon's words, "as an expression of my love for America and to fulfill the Will of God."[1] Such a bald-faced declaration of religious intention has bothered many critics and readers. Yet, by all measures, the paper's roughly 100,000 circulation in the Washington area has been rising slowly over the past couple of years. And it has a Web site—presumably also part of God's plan.

What You'll Find There

The paper's Web site has a pretty efficient and easily navigated collection of news and commentary. Most of the expected kinds of news stories are arrayed across the top half of the page with headlines above the first paragraphs of each of the stories. The writing appears objective and in a traditional news style.

Other news of the day is relegated to the lower half of the page, listed by headlines under the categories "Nation/World," "Business," and "Metropolitan," with dozens of stories to choose from under each heading. There are also links to an abundant "Opinion/Editorial" and "Commentary" section, featuring a half-dozen columns and editorials

Advertise | RSS | Sitemap | Contact Us | Subscription Services | Insider Login | Washington D.C. CLOUDY 80° F

from established (and mostly conservative) columnists and on occasion a Republican congressman.

There's also a search function for stock quotes, breaking business news, a link for "Entertainment and Dining" in the Washington metro area, and a full sports section.

Readers can click their way to a page that lists by headline all the major news stories in that day's edition, or simply click on the reproduced front page of that day's issue. The majority of the stories featured on the Web site are written by *Washington Times* staffers, though there are several stories lifted from the Associated Press wire.

Why You Should Visit

The *Washington Times* is often touted as a corrective to the crusading (and some would charge actively liberal) *Washington Post,* which has almost eight times as many readers. In a town such as Washington where the political spin cycle runs 24 hours a day, it is useful to have a variety of perspectives on what's really happening. But the

Washington Times has earned a reputation of such die-hard right-wingism that few outside its ideological sphere take it seriously.

"It's the Fox News of the print world," said Gene Grabowski, a reporter who resigned from the paper in 1988 in protest of the paper's right-leaning tendencies.[2]

Still, the newspaper has its fans. Conservative Paul Weyrich has lauded the *Washington Times* as an "antidote" to the *Washington Post*, and the paper was reportedly the favorite newspaper of President Ronald Reagan.[3] And most observers of the Washington journalism scene give credit to the *Washington Times* for forcing the *Washington Post* to cover stories that might otherwise fade from their news radar. Stories from the *Washington Times* often get picked up for replay by Web sites including the Drudge Report and Fox News.

Keep This in Mind

Lurking behind every issue of the *Washington Times* is the problematic figure of the Rev. Moon, who has often suggested that the paper's real mission is to promote the work of the almighty. In fact, he sees God's hand in much of what the paper has covered. "I do not have the slightest doubt that God used the *Washington Times* to help bring an end to the most pernicious worldwide dictatorship in history and gave freedom to tens of millions of people!" he once said in reference

to the paper's unremitting support for Reagan's cold war policies, such as the so-called "Star Wars" defense system.[4]

Such proclamations by the publisher may call into question the loyalties of the entire news gathering operation. Is it God's truth they seek to report? Or something a little more in line with standard journalistic protocol?

Off the Record

The *Washington Times* is the flagship publication of Rev. Moon's News World Communications Inc., which also publishes the Unification church's *Insight Magazine* and *The World & I*. And although exact figures are hard to come by, some news industry officials estimate that the *Washington Times* has lost as much as $1 billion since its founding more than 20 years ago.

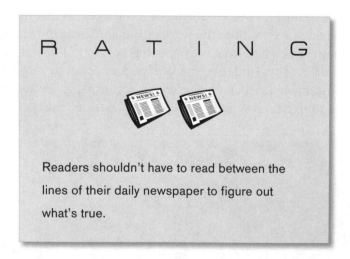

RATING

Readers shouldn't have to read between the lines of their daily newspaper to figure out what's true.

Endnotes

1. From SourceWatch: A Project of the Center for Media and Democracy at source watch.org.
2. From the Southern Poverty Law Center's "Intelligence Report" titled "America's Newspaper?" available at splc.org.
3. From the Wikipedia (wikipedia.org) article on *Washington Times*.
4. From "SourceWatch."

92

Weather Channel

www.weather.com

Overview

Once upon a time, in the infancy of cable television, the idea of a 24-hour-a-day weather report seemed more a novelty than a necessity. Who would want to spend hour after hour watching high pressure isobars and Canadian cold fronts drifting across their screens at all hours of the day and night?

But the Weather Channel is no longer a quaint curiosity as one rapid-fires the remote from MTV to HBO. Because of some high profile—and deadly—storms over the past decades (and especially the devastation wrought by Hurricane Katrina), the weather has become the news.

Throw in record flooding in the Midwest, mudslides in the Pacific Northwest, wildfires in Texas and California, and the ever-growing threat of global warming, and suddenly you have something to be concerned about. What was once a channel for fishermen, pilots, and the amateur sky-watcher has now become an important front in the tempest of television programming.

And the Weather Channel's Web site isn't just for weather geeks; the site is comprehensive and oddly compelling. Though much of the information is not urgent, it's reported in a way that's entertaining and educational.

What You'll Find There

Who knew that weather could be so interesting? OK, so maybe it's not Disney World, but there is a lot of stuff—some useful, some just plain odd—on the Weather Channel's site. There is, of course, the major weather-related news of the day, whether it's heavy snow across the Rocky Mountains or a Nor'easter bearing down on New England. The

397

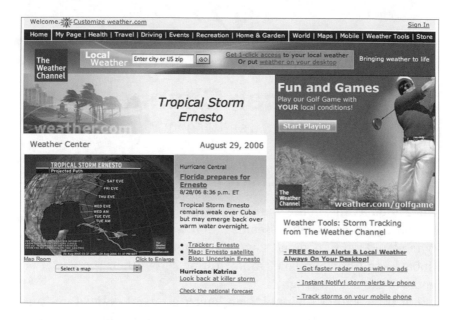

breaking weather stories are illustrated by maps, of course, as well as comprehensive news articles, sidebars, and videos.

The weather map on the top half of the page features links for current temps in the major cities across the U.S. as well as short-term forecasts and reports about such issues as mold and pollen counts, high tides, and lunar phases. Gardening buffs and lawn-care obsessives can get specialized maps showing rainfall patterns and specific regional precipitation estimates.

Other practical features on the site include a personalized driving forecast that lets you chart the weather along any specified route. The site features air quality alerts for those sensitive to allergens or smog, and even a detailed guide to fall foliage.

For those scouts who like to be prepared for any weather event, the site includes features stories on topics such as how to prepare for a hurricane and when the next meteor shower will be visible.

And there's a blog maintained by the experts at the Weather Channel that is so wonkish that it's really a hoot to read. A recent posting from "Tropical Weather Expert Dr. Steve Lyons" answered a question that only a weather geek would think to ask—or answer:

> *Is there anywhere in the world that has two tropical cyclone (hurricane) seasons?*

Some of you may be thinking, "That's silly, everyone knows tropical cyclones occur in the respective summer and fall of the Northern and Southern Hemispheres!" Some of you may be less judgmental, but still skeptical of such a question, right?

But the answer is YES, in the Northern Indian Ocean (Bay of Bengal and Arabian Sea) there are two tropical cyclone seasons! One begins in mid-April and is gone before summer starts; the next begins in late September and is gone by mid-December.

It's the exclamation points that make reading such postings a surreal delight.

Why You Should Visit

You can't escape the weather. Given the potentially destructive impact of some of Mother Nature's recent offerings, it certainly seems sensible to try to stay one step ahead of a coming flood, wildfire, snowstorm, or hurricane.

Plus, reading the Weather Channel site gives you the chance to recoup at least a little of that stuff everybody slept through in high school science class. You don't have to be a meteorologist to be fascinated with things like the aurora borealis (the "northern lights"), the fierce destructiveness of a twister, or the long-term impact of global warming. The site makes it easy to learn about these topics with plenty of maps, charts, videos, and even chat rooms.

Keep This in Mind

The weather is often big news, but that's the only kind of news you'll find on this site. Unless the president is visiting a flood-ravaged farm town or flying over tornado alley, political news might as well not even exist. The Weather Channel keeps its gaze fixed firmly skyward.

Off the Record

For those diehards who simply can't get enough of the weather, online or on screen, there is a book that is a must-read: *The Weather Channel: The Improbable Rise of a Media Phenomenon* by Frank Batten and Jeffrey L. Cruikshank (Harvard Business Press, May 2002).

R A T I N G

Paradise for weather wonks; a handy,
occasional resource for everybody else.

93

WebMD
www.webmd.com

Overview

The idea was to reform the healthcare system in America. James Clark, two years after he created Netscape in 1994, founded a dot-com startup company called Healtheon, which he envisioned would "connect consumers, doctors, health care organizations and insurance companies in a megasite that would make the medical industry more efficient."[1] In 1998, another entrepreneur named Jeffrey Arnold developed WebMD. By late 1999, the two companies merged, hoping to change the state of healthcare through Internet technology while "creating the largest Web site devoted to providing health care information for consumers."[2]

Anyone who has visited a doctor's office in recent years or called the "customer service" hotline for his or her insurance company would likely attest that nothing about the process has been revolutionized. But log on to WebMD.com, and it is clear that the latter (and more realistic) of the two goals has been achieved: offering a wealth of knowledge to patients, consumers, and those with an interest in health and medicine.

What You'll Find There

The WebMD home page can seem a bit crowded at first, but its organization makes sense after you become acquainted with the site's layout. For users who are logging on to the site to look for information on a specific topic, the search tool at the top middle of the page is a useful place to start. Just below the search window, you will find a row of links to various sections, which include "Today's News," "Diseases & Conditions," "A-Z Guides," "Healthy Living," "Health Care Services," "Pregnancy & Family," and "Boards & Blogs." Each link provides a drop-down menu of more specific subsections.

The dominant area of the page is in the left column below this navigation bar, where WebMD rotates graphics teasing four of its top features—usually a combination of health tips ("Midnight Munchies? Tips for getting nighttime snacking under control") and medical information ("What Causes ADHD? New research looks into the family connection"). To the right of this slideshow-style menu, you will find links to several of the site's more practical features: "First Aid & Emergencies: Get quick info on 250+ topics"; "Drug Search," an extensive catalog of prescription and over-the-counter medications that can be searched by name (brand or generic) or by condition; and "Symptom Checker," which helps identify a health problem and then offers some suggestions about what to do about it.

Below the home page's main graphic, a list of the 10 "Latest Headlines" are provided, linking you to staff-written articles about health and medical news ("Fatty Fish Fight Cancer," "Spinach E.coli Outbreak Still Growing," and "Brand Rx Prices Rise Another 6.3%"). From this area of the home page, you can also link to the "Top 12 Health Topics," a ranking of the most popular searches that day as well as "Interactive Checkups," where WebMD provides easy access to more than 100 tools, from an ovulation calculator to step-by-step directions on how to allergy-proof your home.

A-Z Guides

Your ultimate guide to reliable health information on topics from A to Z.

Health Topics A-Z
Browse our comprehensive directory of over 4,000 diseases and conditions.

Drugs A-Z
Find information on your prescriptions, supplements, and over-the-counter medications.

Health Videos A-Z
Watch original health videos on topics that matter to you.

Diseases & Conditions A-Z
Get instant access to information from our quick list of health topics.

Healthy Living A-Z
Improve your personal health and well-being with WebMD Wellness A-Z guides.

Medical Tests A-Z
Get explanations of medical tests and learn how you can prepare for them.

Newsletters A-Z
Stay up-to-date with FREE information delivered to your inbox.

Boards & Blogs A-Z
Connect to expert opinions and others who share your health concerns.

Tools A-Z
Manage your health with quizzes, calculators, self-assessments and guides.

Why You Should Visit

Logging on to this site is definitely better than having to pick up a five-pound medical encyclopedia—and much more user-friendly. Whether you're looking for breaking medical news, information about a specific illness, or tips on how to lead a healthy lifestyle, WebMD is the leading source, most notably through its extensive collection of "A-Z Guides." Whether you're searching for a doctor in your area, trying to better understand how to make make your health insurance work for you, connecting with people who are struggling with or have conquered a similar ailment, or learning how to lose weight, the resources provided by the site are invaluable.

Keep This in Mind

Mark Twain once wrote, "Be careful about reading health books. You may die of a misprint." If he were alive today, Twain might offer a similar warning about searching through the thousands of "health" sites on the Internet. After all, just about anyone can now disseminate "medical" information. Deciphering whether these sites are trustworthy is often more difficult than reading a doctor's handwriting. But you can take solace in WebMD's credibility. The site's content is monitored by an "Independent Medical Review Board" to check for accuracy and timeliness, and even the news and feature articles are reviewed by medical professionals (usually with an MD appended to their names) before they are posted. Along with the byline of the writer, you will see the name of the reviewer below headlines on story pages.

Off the Record

WebMD Health, a publicly traded corporation (NASDAQ: WBMD), also publishes a bimonthly waiting-room magazine, along with several other Web sites, including Medscape (aimed at doctors and healthcare professionals), MedicineNet, eMedicine, eMedicine Health, RxList, and theheart.org.

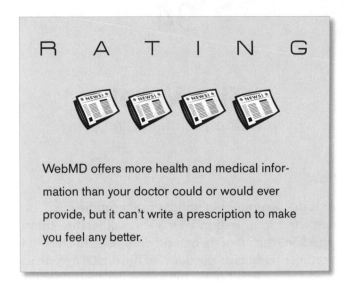

R A T I N G

WebMD offers more health and medical information than your doctor could or would ever provide, but it can't write a prescription to make you feel any better.

Endnotes

1. Karen Southwick, "Diagnosing WebMD: Ultimate dot-com survivor faces new challenges," *CNET News*, May 11, 2004.
2. Ibid.

94

The Week
www.theweekmagazine.com

Overview

The Week is the byproduct of an idiotically simple idea: As the number of news and information Web sites proliferates, there just isn't time to check in with all of them. And despite all the talk of labor saving by Internet prophets at the dawn of the digital age, an awful lot of people find themselves busier than ever. So the dilemma for most working news junkies—or busy people in general—is how to reconcile their need to know with their limitations of time and energy. How great it would be to have a corps of dedicated news researchers sift through the Internet and provide brief reader-friendly digests of the news making headlines around the world.

Welcome to TheWeekMagazine.com, the online version of a publication that claims a distinguished British parentage: "*The Week* has built a fiercely loyal following in the United Kingdom with its succinct summaries of news and opinion, its wit and its hubris," according to the Web site. "Like its British progenitor, this magazine is designed as a briefing for intelligent people who are simply too busy to read everything they'd like."

The online edition of *The Week* not only provides a capsule of the news—complete with varying takes on the major events—but also opinion pieces and editorials that complete the contextualization by offering a variety of perspectives.

What You'll Find There

Although *The Week* is, obviously, a weekly publication (most of the site features content that is posted on Friday and left unchanged until the following Thursday), the site leads with three main sections that are updated daily: "Today's U.S. News and Opinion," "Today's International News and Opinion," and "Today's Business News and

The Week of 8/29/2006

THE WEEK

Search The Week [SUBMIT]

The Best of the U.S. and International Media

U.S. News & Opinion
Main Stories
Controversy of the Week
Talking Points
Briefing

International
World At A Glance
How They See Us
Best Columns

Arts & Leisure
Books
The List
Art
Film
Music

Obituaries
Links
FAQ

From the Editors
A Look Back at *The Week*
Archive

Service Center
Subscribe
Gifts/Passalong Offers
Newsletter Signup
Customer Service

About Us
The Opinion Awards
Advertising Information
Press Room
Contact Us

Good Week For
Faith-based initiatives, after Madonna approached the nuclear industry with a plan to clean up nuclear waste by washing it in a "magical" Kabbalah fluid.

Bad Week For
Spontaneity, after the city of Las Vegas announced that

The Best of Today's News & Opinion

Today's U.S. News and Opinion
The domestic editor is on vacation.

Today's International News and Opinion
The international editor is on holiday.

Today's Business News and Opinion
Google challenges Microsoft with a new package of business software. Kinder Morgan agrees to be sold for $22 billion. And are news junkies headed for the poorhouse?

In the Magazine...

MAIN STORIES
The Truce in Lebanon Holds, for Now
The political and military fallout continues.

Iran's Nuclear Defiance
The international community mulls over a strategy for Irani nuclear disarmament.

Archive

Controversy of the Week

Talking Points
Vacations: An endangered tradition.

THE WEEK

Are we safer?

Subscribe Now

advertisement

To protect your online freedom,

symantec.

THE WEEK
NEWSLETTER
Start your weekend out Right!
[SIGN UP NOW!]

THE WEEK
Subscribe Now

Opinion." Each of these section headings leads you to a main story or two, accompanied by a brief paragraph and linked to a news site that is usually allied to a major media outlet. Most of the sites linked to the Web page tend to be publications that break the most news: the *Washington Post*, the *New York Times,* Al Jazeera, etc. (They also tend to be publications that conservative commentators often label as "the liberal media," though a closer look at the site reveals a commitment to balance and links to conservative publications and commentators as well as to those that are more "progressive" in tone.)

The rest of the site consists largely of the following: "Main Stories," which provides a prepared digest of the biggest stories in the news, packaged in four to six lengthy paragraphs, complete with annotations listing the different takes by the major media outlets; "Controversy of the Week" focusing on a hot-button issue and discussing how various news outlets and commentators have begun spinning the story; "Talking Points," which addresses some trend, ranging from online gambling to the growing gap between the haves and have-nots, sifting it through the sieve of newspapers, magazines, and online publications; and "Briefings," an in-depth look at some recent news event that is complex and continues to vex readers—and editors (this section includes stories such as stem cell research and the search for more humane methods of execution).

There's a similar section aimed at synthesizing "International News" and an interesting peek into the larger world's media and its impression of U.S. policy called "How They See Us."

Brief digests are available under the heading "Arts and Leisure" that offer an overview of critical opinion about books, movies, music, and the art world. There are other Web sites with more extensive information about the world of entertainment, but the summaries are comprehensive, well-wrought, and useful for the busy person who wants to know which works of popular art are creating some buzz.

All of these digests and summaries are prepared by the staff of *The Week*, except for those few stories that direct you to another Web site's report.

Why You Should Visit

This Web site is ideal for that demographic that considers itself overworked, overstressed, and under-informed. Rather than spending a half-hour watching the nightly news or feverishly pressing the AM pre-set buttons as you crawl through your daily commute, you can check in with TheWeekMagazine.com to ensure you have some grasp of what's going on with a minimal amount of time and effort.

Keep This in Mind

The world moves fast—and given all that happens in a daily news cycle, TheWeekMagazine.com is simply not poised to keep up with it all. At the risk of pointing out the obvious, a digest of the news is not the news itself. If you want depth and context, you'll need to find a more thorough and comprehensive traditional news source.

Off the Record

The online version of *The Week* does not have all the content of the printed magazine, but even the printed edition prides itself on its breeziness, promising readers they can go "Cover to Cover in Under 90 Minutes."

RATING

If you had to skim this review because you didn't have the time to read the whole thing, TheWeekMagazine.com is a Web site for you.

95

Weekly Standard
www.weeklystandard.com

Overview

Some publications pride themselves on the access their reporters have to newsmakers. But in the case of the *Weekly Standard*, it's the other way around: It's the newsmakers who boast of having access to it. Vice President Dick Cheney's office reportedly receives a special delivery of 30 copies of each issue,[1] and the publication exerts an immense influence among conservative thinkers who form the core of the "Neo-Con" movement in American politics.

Such a level of influence is all the more surprising given the journal's youthful tenure—it's barely 10 years old. Founded in the mid-1990s, the publication has brashly positioned itself as the voice of reason for those who espouse a conservative philosophy, and it furthers this objective by publishing nervy, no-holds-barred commentary that goes for the jugular. Its executive editor Fred Barnes and, especially, editor William Kristol have made themselves indispensable to bookers of political talk shows on the mainstream networks as well as cable.

The *Weekly Standard* maintains a Web site that is doubly influential: There is a *Weekly Standard* Web site that contains much of the content of the print publication and a "Daily Standard" Web site comprised of Web specials and commentary on the daily news embedded within the journal's Web site.

Although there's no information about how often the vice president logs on, it's likely that many neo-cons who have come to worship at the altar of the *Weekly Standard* visit with religious regularity.

What You'll Find There

The site offers a straightforward listing of articles and essays drawn from the weekly publication, but it also teases readers with a number

of articles that are available only to subscribers of the print publication. There is still a healthy amount of free content, including each week's cover story—often written by Kristol himself. The rest of the print-derived site contains a menu of stories and op-ed pieces about—what else?—politics and the current culture clash between liberals and conservatives, and increasingly, among conservatives themselves. The *Weekly Standard* never shies away from a good fight—even if it's a family feud (it was the first conservative publication to call for the resignation of Secretary of Defense Donald Rumsfeld). There is a smattering of arts coverage—mostly about books, and mostly about political books.

And then there's the "Daily Standard," a separate listing of stories within the site that offers a more up-to-date look at the major news of the day. Almost all of the pieces in both the daily and weekly sections of the Web site are opinion-laced essays rather than traditional news stories. Normally, a site so top-heavy with pre-set opinions could risk being rather grating—to say nothing of monotonous (think of talk radio). But the site does feature the work of some gifted writers such as P. J. O'Rourke, David Frum, and John Podhoretz.

The site also offers a "Postings" section—which is just a blog under another name—and, for subscribers, a special "Features" section. One laudable quality of all the content on the Web site is the length. WeeklyStandard.com has a refreshing disdain for short, cute stories.

Why You Should Visit

Web surfers can have access to the same information that the country's decision makers are perusing. Many media observers and political pundits have claimed that the publication is the most influential political periodical in the history of American politics. If so, that's a good reason to check it out yourself.

Keep This in Mind

The writers and editors of WeeklyStandard.com are advocates, not journalists. They've declared war on anything that fails to embrace and advance their cause—a new conservative-ruling hierarchy. While the passion is admirable—and makes for some intensely satisfying reading—there's no masking the absence of contrary viewpoints.

Off the Record

The *Weekly Standard* is owned by Rupert Murdoch's News Corp., which also owns Fox News. Many of the most visible editors and writers for

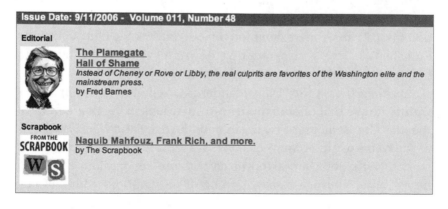

Issue Date: 9/11/2006 - Volume 011, Number 48

Editorial

The Plamegate
Hall of Shame
Instead of Cheney or Rove or Libby, the real culprits are favorites of the Washington elite and the mainstream press.
by Fred Barnes

Scrapbook

FROM THE SCRAPBOOK
Naguib Mahfouz, Frank Rich, and more.
by The Scrapbook

the publication have become regular guests—or even hosts (Brit Hume and Fred Barnes)—on the conservative news network.

RATING

Unless you subscribe to the brand of conservatism endorsed by WeeklyStandard.com, there's not much to keep you coming back.

Endnote

1. *Vanity Fair* first reported this anecdote, which has been widely circulated. See David Carr, "White House listens when weekly speaks," *New York Times*, March 11, 2003.

96

WhiteHouse.gov
www.whitehouse.gov

Overview

Behind the words "the White House" lurk two very different connotations: one benign, another a bit more divisive. One could, obviously, be referring to the building itself—that iconic mansion with the world's most-famous street address. A national symbol since 1800, the White House is home to a history like no other—that of the American presidency. But it's much more than a monument to the political past. "The White House" is often used when referring to the current president's administration.

At the official White House Web site, launched in October 1994 by Bill Clinton's staff and now under the control of the current administration, you will find information about both—historical and political —in a breadth as expansive as the six-story, 132-room landmark itself.

What You'll Find There

The home page of WhiteHouse.gov features predictable content, fashioned to look much like a traditional news site: a half-dozen headlines—each joined by a thumbnail photo, brief summary, and related links—running down the middle of the page, nearly all of which begin "President Bush Discusses ..." or "President Bush Meets with ..." (a clear indicator of the type of news presented here). Bordering the main column to the left are barely readable links to "Issues," from the federal budget and national security to the "Renewal in Iraq" and "Social Security." Farther down this menu, you will find links to press briefings, the president's weekly radio address and radio interviews of White House staff and cabinet members, and transcripts, along with video and/or audio of presidential speeches and press conferences. The most dominant visual element of the

home page is at the top of the right column, where a photo and extensive caption tease a slideshow of a recent presidential trip.

If you are more history buff than policy wonk or political junkie, it's worthwhile to click on the "History & Tours" link in the navigation menu in the title banner. Visitors to this section of the site will discover many options for exploring the White House and its history. Prominently featured are rather banal video tours of various offices and rooms within the White House and West Wing, hosted by the president, his staff, even his spouse. Thankfully, the multimedia experience doesn't end there. From 360-degree panoramic views to videos narrated by the White House curator and trivia-laced articles about the White House's many rooms, furnishings, and art to "Now and Then" historical photo essays (although several Democratic presidents seem not to have liked their picture taken), you can find various ways to get lost in the White House site. There are also short bios of all 43 presidents, links to the sites of the White House Historical Association, every federal office and agency, and presidential libraries, and an entire section of the site designed for kids—featuring the wildly popular Barney cam, which offers video from the perspective of the president's dog.

Why You Should Visit

In these post-9/11 days, the White House is more inaccessible than ever before. Visiting this virtual address might just be the closest you can get to 1600 Pennsylvania Avenue anytime soon. So if you want to keep tabs on what the leader of the free world is doing, which you should, it won't hurt to visit the White House site—provided that you remember you're only getting one side of multifaceted issues. While you're there, check to see who the guest of the semi-regular online

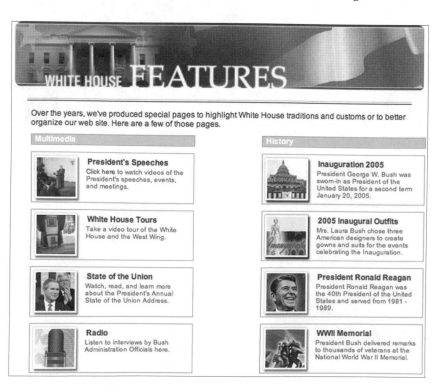

discussion "Ask the White House" is. You might just want to submit a question for that week's featured administration official to address. (Softballs are preferred.)

Keep This in Mind

The White House Web site created a disturbance in the blogosphere in the last days of December 2005 when an Associated Press inquiry discovered that it uses a Web bug "to anonymously keep track of who's visiting and when"[1] and that the National Security Agency (NSA) site was "placing files on visitors' computers that can track their Web surfing activity despite strict federal rules banning most files of that type."[2] The NSA admitted a "mistake"; the White House vowed to investigate its use of such technologies. A few days later, the White House said the site records only the number of visitors and not personal information; therefore, they say, the site was in compliance with federal rules for government Web sites.[3] The storm already at full strength, many bloggers remained skeptical, bolstered by the fact that the White House—though it claimed to do so without violating set guidelines—didn't deny using the technologies.

And another thing worth remembering: Web sites can change frequently; WhiteHouse.gov is guaranteed to change by January 2008 and every four to eight years after that.

Off the Record

During the week America began its invasion of Iraq on March 20, 2003, nearly 40 percent of the 198,000 average daily unique visits to the official White House Web site came from outside the U.S.

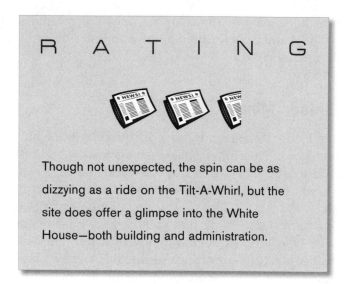

R A T I N G

Though not unexpected, the spin can be as dizzying as a ride on the Tilt-A-Whirl, but the site does offer a glimpse into the White House—both building and administration.

Endnotes

1. "WhiteHouse.gov uses cookies, bugs," Associated Press, Dec. 29, 2005.
2. "Spy agency removes illegal tracking files," *New York Times*, Dec. 29, 2005.
3. "White House: Counting site visitors OK with federal rules," Associated Press, Dec. 21, 2005.

97

WhiteHouse.org
www.whitehouse.org

Overview

If you happen to stumble across this Web site because you're planning to visit Washington, D.C., or if you're thinking of sending a letter to the president and want his e-mail address, or if you just want a virtual tour of our nation's most famous residence, you're in for something of a shock. WhiteHouse.org is a satirical site—an acid-tongued spin on President George W. Bush and his administration. When you realize your mistake, you may be tempted to exit the page and head to the *real* White House Web site (www.whitehouse.gov). But if you flee, you'll be missing one of the best examples of biting, incisive satire on the Web.

As with all effective satire, WhiteHouse.org is impolite, perhaps even a touch vulgar. Fans of the Republican administration will likely be put off by the harsh tenor of much of the site's "news" articles. But if you believe that the purpose of the popular press is to comfort the afflicted and afflict the comfortable (the creed of many professional journalists), you'll realize how firmly this site is rooted in the American tradition of muckraking.

What You'll Find There

Because the site's purpose is to slay sacred cows, be prepared for some butchery. The commander-in-chief is taken to task for pretty much all his alleged shortcomings: his policies, his insensitivity to minorities, his lack of intellectual depth, and his uncertain oratory. Take, for example, this excerpt from a mock transcript of a Bush speech on immigration: "Immigration is important. Without it, Don Corleone would never had come to America and then there never would have been any *Godfather* movies. And without Jews, there would never have been Chinese food."

The site features mock Q&A interviews with everyone from Jerry Falwell to Mary Cheney, the vice president's daughter. Here's how her interview is prefaced: "Mary Cheney is the daughter (technically) of Vice President Dick Cheney and Second Lady Lynne Cheney. A legacy graduate of Colorado College, Mary woke up one morning and, sometime after her second cup of coffee, decided to be a lesbian."

Sure, it's rude, and occasionally beyond the pale, but most of the articles focus on the big questions of our time: war (there are "Quagmire: Accomplished!" bumper stickers available on the site); the role of religion in government ("The Presidential Prayer Team: Meet the Elite Force of Spiritual Warriors Who Wield More Destructive Power Than the Entire US Military"); and even the Geneva Convention ("America's Kinder, Gentler Guidelines for Torturing Maybe-Terrorist Trash").

The site also features downloadable posters—"Prove Your Love of Country! Smother Your Town With Officious White House Propaganda!"—as well as a fully-stocked gift shop with bumper stickers, T-shirts, and coffee mugs.

Why You Should Visit

Many media-watchers have lamented the loss of a robust, muckraking press. Some see the White House press corps and the administration in a cozy and comfortable relationship that deprives the public of a real watchdog. The existence of sites such as WhiteHouse.org testifies to the democratic compulsion to discover, criticize, and correct.

Satire has always been a potent weapon in the war against ruling-class elitism and political hubris. Any site that has the gumption to run stories such as "President Bush Responds to Bill Clinton's Communist Plot to Deny America's Youth the Freedom to be Diabetes-Ravaged Lardasses" deserves at least some credit for calling out our leaders for their petty, political posturing and their self-aggrandizing behavior.

Keep This in Mind

Those who are currently in power are the logical targets of society's satirists, so you won't find many barbs directed at the political left. This creates a sense of imbalance on the site. Although figures such as Hillary Clinton and Katie Couric do merit the occasional mention, the lion's share of snarling comes at the expense of Bush, Cheney, and the religious right. As this site makes no pretense whatsoever to be a legitimate news site or to keep things "fair and balanced," it deserves

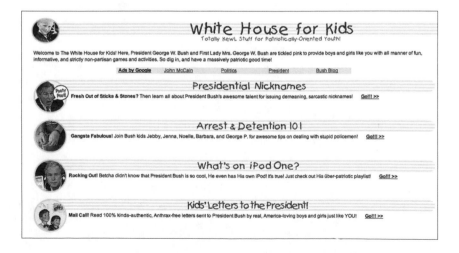

to be judged for what it is: a soapbox for the cynical and increasingly marginalized independent thinker.

Off the Record

Since satire ought to cut though the political chicanery of every administration, you are urged to consult any of the satirical sites that shish kabob Bill and Hillary Clinton. The best place to start is www.politicalhumor.about.com/od/billclintonsatire, a menu of sites aimed at lambasting the U.S. president affectionately known as "Bubba."

RATING

When you stop laughing at WhiteHouse.org, you'll be left with plenty to think about.

98

Wired News
www.wired.com

Overview

Throughout history, invention has played an integral role in the progress, and perhaps at times the regression, of humankind. Technological innovation, though, has never before occurred at such breakneck speed—so much so that new computers can seem outdated shortly after setup. Technology is constantly changing, and often revolutionizing, the way we work, play, and communicate. But with the seemingly daily arrival of new gadgets, updated software, and groundbreaking ideas, how do we keep pace?

Because the technology sector impacts every aspect of life from national security to medicine to video games, it is big business—and big news, spawning a cottage publishing industry to cover all the rapid developments. Since its inception in March 1993, *Wired*—described recently as a magazine "that is equal parts technology culture trend-spotter and glossy product catalog"[1]—has remained one of the most popular sources for people who want to stay connected. Critically, the San Francisco-based monthly magazine has been praised (winning National Magazine Awards for general excellence in 1994, 1995, 1997, and 2005 and for design in 1996) and panned (mostly for its unconventional, difficult-to-read layouts).

Only a few months after its inaugural issue, *Wired* magazine became, not surprisingly, one of the first to launch a Web site. But Wired News, its Internet incarnation formally known as HotWired, has experienced as rocky a past as the Web itself, although both the print and online editions have outlasted the dot-com bust of the late-1990s. In 1998, however, the two split when Condé Nast purchased the magazine and Lycos bought the site, which remained responsible for posting the publication's content. *Wired* and Wired.com were reunited in July 2006 when Condé Nast paid $25 million to acquire

the online property. Analysts predict the deal will yield "a better site in the end."

What You'll Find There

Riveting is not a word that comes to mind when describing the design of Wired.com, but its content isn't exactly dull. These characterizations become evident soon after logging on to the Wired News home page, where you will encounter a list of three dozen stories presented in simple fashion. Stories are listed one after the other with no obvious order of priority in a single column that runs down the left two-thirds of the page—each teased with headlines/links and a summary blurb. Most also include a thumbnail photo to the left of the headline and a tiny icon indicating the type of story.

Clicking on any of the menu options that span the top of the home page—"Technology," "Culture," "Politics," "Columns," "Blogs," "The Outside World," and "Wired Mag"—opens the section's front page. These pages look identical to the home page (several stories appear on both, but another navigation bar becomes available, directly below the main menu, for users to open specific subsections).

Most of Wired.com's content is connected to the impact of, or effect on, technology. Even "The Outside World" section, located in both the main menu and right column of the home page, remains in the realm of technology—only the news found here comes exclusively from an "outside" source, the Associated Press. If you enjoy particular *Wired* writers, the site provides easy access to their previous stories with a link—"Also by this reporter"—next to the byline. If you want to read the magazine, you can do so here with access to content of the current edition and to a complete archive of past issues.

Why You Should Visit

There are not many news sites where you'll find the juxtaposition of headlines like "Lifelong Effects of Cybersex," "Bomb Threats Posed by Pants, Belts," and "Giant Robot Imprisons Parked Cars." You will at Wired.com. This often-odd but pleasurable combination of news—proof of technology's influence over nearly every facet of life—transforms what would otherwise be complicated subject matter into a fun read. While the MIT tech-geek set will probably cut the cord on Wired News after only a short stay, novices stand to benefit from

---

⊘ ALL BLOGS   Photos/Summaries: On | Off

Autopia
Wired News blogger John Gartner examines high tech on wheels, from GPS and stereos to new methods of cutting dependence on fossil fuels.

Beyond the Beyond
From Wired Magazine's Bruce Sterling.

Bodyhack
Wired News senior editor Kristen Philipkoski dishes on med-tech and biotech.

Cult of Mac
Leander Kahney's unique take on Apple Computer and the fans who've made it a cultural phenomenon.

occasionally plugging into this *Wired* outlet, provided they remember it merely supplies news about technology, not a model of how to use it.

Keep This in Mind

Michelle Delio and Philip Chien are certainly not as notorious as Jayson Blair and Stephen Glass, but these Wired News contributors had their own ethical lapses.

The work of Delio, who authored more than 700 pieces for Wired News from 2000 to 2005, came under scrutiny when another publication retracted two of her stories because of its "inability to confirm a source" and another then edited out anonymous quotes. After reviewing fewer than one-third of her articles in May 2005, Wired News discovered two dozen stories with sources that could not be confirmed. Rather than retracting any, the site marked the articles to highlight unidentifiable sources. It also adjusted policy: "Wired News will now require freelance reporters to submit contact information for all named sources."

Chien, however, subverted that new requirement a year and three months later, creating and submitting fake contact information for supposed sources. Wired News discovered the transgression in the draft stage of one article, prompting an investigation of the freelance space reporter, which led to the retraction of three of Chien's five articles published in July 2006.

Off the Record

Wired helped pioneer the now-standard practice—for most publications, from community newspapers to national magazines—of printing the e-mail addresses of its writers with their articles or columns.

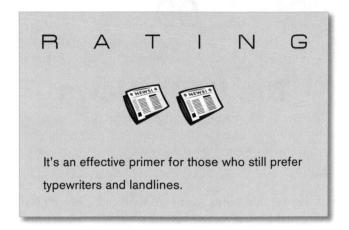

RATING

It's an effective primer for those who still prefer typewriters and landlines.

Endnote

1. "*Wired* pays Lycos $25 mln to recover Wired.com site," Reuters, July 12, 2006.

99

The Write News

www.writenews.com

Overview

Not only is the domain name of the Write News clever, it is also apropos and accurate, explicitly encapsulating what people will encounter after typing www.writenews.com into their browser's address bar.

The media world is evolving at an unprecedented pace, and the Write News aims to keep you up to speed. Launched in September 1997, the Write News is part of the Writers Write Lifestyle Network, an entity comprised of widely and wildly diverse sites, from its flagship site for writers to a host of others for nearly everyone—health freaks and science geeks, book lovers and bloggers, video game addicts and shopaholics, and even automobile enthusiasts.

A Web-only source, the Write News concentrates its coverage exclusively on "the latest in the publishing and writing worlds." While its target audience is clearly media and publishing professionals, WriteNews.com, which strives to avoid insider lingo, is certainly accessible to a much wider audience.

What You'll Find There

The Write News is essentially a blog. There's no original reporting here; rather, the site consists of news briefs culled from other credible sources, all of which are always clearly credited. But that method proves useful, turning hard-to-find, easy-to-miss media news into the center of attention (much of the content prominently featured on the Write News is buried within the sites of the original sources).

At the top of the page, three links—"Book Blog," "Media Cynic," and "Industry Blogs"—are featured. News briefs, which can range in topic from the launch of a new magazine to the sale of a newspaper chain to the anticipated look of news sites in 10 years, are posted in a

wide column in the middle of the page, with the most recent posting first and oldest last. Other than the occasional magazine cover or company logo that accompanies the text, there are no noteworthy graphical elements to the Web page. The postings, which are at times infrequent, include a link to the original source's article and typically excerpts it (set off from the rest of the copy by using a smaller font) quite liberally. The dated postings are separated by advertorials, which can clutter the page.

Links to other areas of the site and the Writers Write network border the main postings of the Write News in vertical columns along the left and right sides of the page. Twenty of the Writers Write blogs, which as previously mentioned vary vastly in topic, are accessible from the Write News home page. WriteJobs.com—a job-posting site for journalism, media, and publishing jobs—is also available, but it is sometimes as blank as an unused notebook.

While WriteNews.com can keep you up-to-date on the most important happenings in the media sphere and is not a bad place to familiarize yourself with the volatile atmosphere of the industry, it is not the site to turn to for depth or context—or thrilling multimedia experience. It's simply an introductory course.

Why You Should Visit

The subject of mass media is one worth studying—even if you are not directly involved in the industry. Plus, after browsing WriteNews.com, you can click your way through a throng of other Writers Write blogs and find a topic that appeals to your own personal and professional pursuits. And for those aspiring writers, WriteNews.com offers information and inspiration that can help you establish a career in media.

Keep This in Mind

The Write News is only one component of an expansive resource. And while it is geared toward media professionals, there are several reasons the lay population should log on to the site. Topping that list is the "News Resources" page—a compilation of links to domestic (categorized by state) and international newspaper Web sites, college newspaper sites, and "specialized" sites. The portal provides you with an opportunity to open the doors to thousands of Internet news sources you might have previously neglected to visit or not known of prior to finding its link in this practical portion of the Write News.

Off the Record

In February 2001, the Write News launched a new section on its site called "The Editorial Dead Zone" to keep tabs on the elimination of editorial jobs, the closings of media companies, and the fates of publications and Web sites. "Recent Passings" is the staple of this feature, using blog-like entries to update users on the latest industry fatalities. "The Dead List," which simply lists the name of the publication, Web site, or company (along with the date of its death), is frighteningly longer than the list of those who managed to escape the grasp of the Grim Reaper to become "The UnDead."

R.I.P. The Editorial Dead Zone™

Recent Passings I Archives I Search
The Dead List I The UnDead I Report a Passing

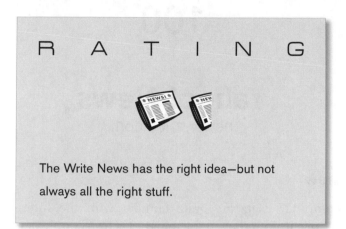

R   A   T   I   N   G

The Write News has the right idea—but not
always all the right stuff.

100

Yahoo! News

news.yahoo.com

Overview

Most computer users are quite familiar with the Internet giant Yahoo!. Since its founding in the mid-1990s by a couple of enterprising computer jocks, Yahoo! has established itself as a popular Internet portal, a Web directory, and an e-mail and text-messaging service. With annual revenues of more than $5 billion and a roster of 10,000 employees,[1] Yahoo! is clearly one of the biggest names in this first phase of the information age.

So it's not terribly surprising that Yahoo! also provides a news Web site that emulates the features of many of its better-known journalistic rivals. It's also not surprising that the best aspects of this otherwise commonplace Web site come from a forward-looking embrace of technology.

Since you're probably already bookmarking one or more of the Yahoo! brands, adding news.yahoo.com is an easy way to keep up with what's going on in the world. Although the site has its flaws, a daily read of news.yahoo.com will give you enough information to join the conversation about the day's events.

What You'll Find There

Most of the news on the site comes directly from the Associated Press along with other mainstream news operations such as CNN, Reuters, and *USA Today*. The first thing you'll find when you sign on is a "Top Story" and accompanying photo, followed by a roster of four or five of the day's main stories and a link to a video news or feature piece provided by CNN or ABC News.

The stories are solid, but there's no new reporting by Yahoo! (with one exception, discussed later), so you're really just getting reprints of stories already posted by other news sites. Yahoo! News also tends to

be dominated by stories about the White House and national politics. There's an institutional bias toward the kind of easily reported news that comes from press briefings at the White House, Pentagon, State Department, and Congress.

The site is clean and can be navigated easily. At the bottom of the page are small icons that link you to many of Yahoo!'s news providers.

On the second page is a menu of the most popular stories—usually light, entertainment-related features—and links for more stories from the World, U.S. News, and even an opinion and comics section, which again take you to other news services' Web pages. (Clicking on "The World" takes you to various pages that let you get specific news for particular countries or regions, from Australia and Asia to the Middle East and Russia.)

So it's all fairly useful and well reported, if a bit bland in its *a la carte* approach. But what makes Yahoo! News a site worth checking regularly has nothing to do with its borrowed news postings from other more established journalistic agencies. Yahoo! has a secret weapon, and his name is Kevin Sites.

Why You Should Visit

Yahoo!'s only real contribution to original content on its news site is the work of Kevin Sites, who serves as Yahoo!'s "first news correspondent." Sites is an award-winning independent reporter whose work in war zones around the world has made him one of the most prominent globetrotting journalists reporting today. Yahoo! was smart to sign him up, and readers can reap the benefit of this alliance by checking in regularly with Sites on his page, which is linked to news.yahoo.com. Sites' first-hand accounts of life on the street—and in the middle of the shooting—in the Middle East, South America, and Africa are significant contributions to our understanding of modern conflict and the human face of warfare and oppression.

Though he works alone in the field—what Yahoo! calls the "Hot Zone"—Sites has the assistance of a production team in the U.S., which disseminates his reports. As the site explains, "As a solo journalist, Sites carries a backpack of portable digital technology to shoot, write, edit and transmit multimedia reports." Significantly, Sites' page notes that though he works in the new era of "backpack journalism,"

he abides by the ethical code of the Society of Professional Journalists—as close as a reporter can come to being licensed as a legitimate journalist.

Keep This in Mind

Other than Sites' work, there's little groundbreaking news here. Though most news sites would deny they have a political bias, they usually *do* have a personality, a feel for the news they cover and the way they cover it. Yahoo! News is flavorless, a bland amalgam of once-told news from a miasma of mainstream news sites.

Off the Record

There are different versions of how the name Yahoo! was chosen. One suggests it's an acronym for "Yet Another Hierarchical Officious Oracle," while another story suggests the name came from Jonathan Swift's *Gulliver's Travels*, where it's used to describe brutish, primitive humanoid creatures.[2]

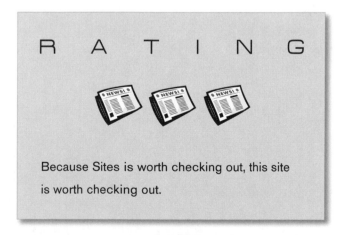

R A T I N G

Because Sites is worth checking out, this site is worth checking out.

Endnotes

1. From the most recent company report available at www.wrightreports.ecnext.com.
2. "Yahoo!: A History" at www.bbc.co.uk/dna/h2g2/A805970.

Afterword

As the 100 reviews that comprise this book have made clear, news and information providers are wrestling with the emergent means of delivering content. While it could once be assumed that all news consumers would get their information from static, largely uncontested formats (the daily newspaper or the evening network news), today's digital landscape has created the opportunity for readers, viewers, or listeners to plug in—quite literally—to thousands of sources.

What we've learned, however, is that merely having a Web presence or the ability to transmit news through any of the new and impressive-seeming technologies does not guarantee the credibility of a source or the quality of information. Still, one can't deny the value and satisfaction that comes from scrolling through an updated, well-designed, and user-friendly Web site. The Internet can do some things better than the traditional rolled-up newspaper lying on your doorstep every morning. Most importantly, writers and editors aren't constrained by the physical limitations of the product. Some stories just need more space—and the Internet provides unlimited space for today's storytellers to really explore an issue. And no one, except technophobes or die-hard traditionalists, would deny the value of tools like streaming video, hyperlinks, and online archives—all at the touch of a computer key.

We hope this guide has helped point you toward some useful, perhaps even illuminating, news and information Web sites. We've discovered some pleasant surprises in our review of the diverse, eclectic, and informed offerings on the World Wide Web. Given the speed, however, with which the Web is changing, it's likely that many of the sites we've discussed will change in ways impossible to predict today. We will continue to monitor the sites referenced in this book and will post our thoughts on those changes at our Web site (www.The ReportersWell.com). We invite you to visit the site, and while you're there, we encourage you to share your comments and questions with us. (For more information, see "About the Web Site" on page ix.)

Sharing news and information has always been a potent means of creating communities, and it is our hope that *Consider the Source* helps to expand and strengthen the ties among people who care about what's happening in the world.

Appendix: Ranked Sites

British Broadcasting Corporation (BBC) News (news.bbc.co.uk)
Christian Science Monitor (www.csmonitor.com)
Columbia Broadcasting Service (CBS) News (www.cbsnews.com)
Guardian Unlimited (www.guardian.co.uk)
National Public Radio (NPR) (www.npr.org)

American Broadcasting Company (ABC) News (abcnews.go.com)
Cable-Satellite Public Affairs Network (C-SPAN) (www.cspan.org)
ESPN (espn.go.com)
First Amendment Center (www.firstamendmentcenter.org)
MSNBC (www.msnbc.com)
National Geographic (www.nationalgeographic.com)
New York Times (www.nytimes.com)
Sydney Morning Herald (www.smh.com.au)
The Times of London (www.timesonline.co.uk)
USA Today (www.usatoday.com)
Washington Post (www.washingtonpost.com)

allAfrica (www.allafrica.com)
American Association of Retired Persons (AARP) (www.aarp.org)
Asia Times Online (www.atimes.com)

Bloomberg (www.bloomberg.com)
Cable News Network (CNN) (www.cnn.com)
The Center for Public Integrity (www.publicintegrity.org)
CNET (www.cnet.com)
MichaelMoore.com (www.michaelmoore.com)
Mother Jones (www.motherjones.com)
National Aeronautics and Space Administration (NASA)
    (www.nasa.gov)
Poynter Institute (www.poynter.org)
The Progressive (www.progressive.org)
Public Broadcasting Service (PBS) (www.pbs.org)
Slate (www.slate.com)
The Smoking Gun (www.thesmokinggun.com)
TomPaine.com (www.tompaine.com)
Topix.net (www.topix.net)
Vanity Fair (www.vanityfair.com)
Village Voice (www.villagevoice.com)
WebMD (www.webmd.com)

Al Jazeera (www.aljazeera.net)
Amnesty International (www.amnesty.org)
Federal Bureau of Investigation (FBI) (www.fbi.gov)
Library of Congress (www.loc.gov)
Miami Herald (www.miamiherald.com)
National Review (www.nationalreview.com)
New Yorker (www.newyorker.com)
The Onion (www.theonion.com)
Times-Picayune (www.nola.com)

AlterNet (www.alternet.org)
Associated Press (www.ap.org)
Canadian Broadcasting Corporation (CBC) (www.cbc.ca)
Central Intelligence Agency (CIA) (www.cia.gov)

Chicago Tribune (www.chicagotribune.com)
Congressional Quarterly (www.cq.com)
Consumer Reports (www.consumerreports.org)
Foreign Affairs (www.foreignaffairs.org)
Los Angeles Times (www.latimes.com)
MTV (www.mtv.com)
The Nation (www.thenation.com)
New York Daily News (www.nydailynews.com)
New York Post (www.nypost.com)
Reuters (www.reuters.com)
Rotten Tomatoes (www.rottentomatoes.com)
Salon (www.salon.com)
The Week (www.theweekmagazine.com)
Weekly Standard (www.weeklystandard.com)
WhiteHouse.org (www.whitehouse.org)
Yahoo! News (news.yahoo.com)

American Civil Liberties Union (ACLU) (www.aclu.org)
Forbes (www.forbes.com)
Google News (news.google.com)
Jerusalem Post (www.jpost.com)
National Association for the Advancement of Colored People
   (NAACP) (www.naacp.org)
National Rifle Association (NRA) (www.nra.org)
Rolling Stone (www.rollingstone.com)
San Francisco Chronicle (www.sfgate.com)
Sports Illustrated (sportsillustrated.cnn.com)
Time (www.time.com)
Weather Channel (www.weather.com)
WhiteHouse.gov (www.whitehouse.gov)

Democratic National Committee (DNC) (www.democrats.org)
Drudge Report (www.drudgereport.com)

Entertainment Weekly (www.ew.com)
Globe and Mail (www.theglobeandmail.com)
Irish Times (www.ireland.com)
Newsweek (www.newsweek.com)
Prevention (www.prevention.com)
U.S. News & World Report (www.usnews.com)
Voice of America (VOA) (www.voanews.com)
Washington Times (www.washingtontimes.com)
Wired News (www.wired.com)

MoveOn.org (www.moveon.org)
OhmyNews (english.ohmynews.com)
Republican National Committee (www.gop.com)
Times of India (timesofindia.indiatimes.com)
United Nations (UN) (www.un.org)
The Write News (www.writenews.com)

Agence France-Presse (AFP) (www.afp.com)
Hispanic News (hispanic.cc)
National Enquirer (www.nationalenquirer.com)
People (www.people.com)

Fox News (www.foxnews.com)
Rush Limbaugh (www.rushlimbaugh.com)

About the Authors

Darren Miller has worked as a reporter and editor for newspapers in New Jersey and North Carolina and is the recipient of several journalism awards. A resident of Western North Carolina, Miller lives with his wife Heather.

Jim Broderick, a former reporter and copy editor, currently teaches journalism at New Jersey City University in Jersey City, NJ. He is author of two previous books. Broderick lives in Glen Ridge, NJ, with his wife Miri and his daughters Olivia and Maddy.

Miller and Broderick are currently working on a book about conspiracy theories and the World Wide Web and can be reached through their Web site, TheReportersWell.com.

Index